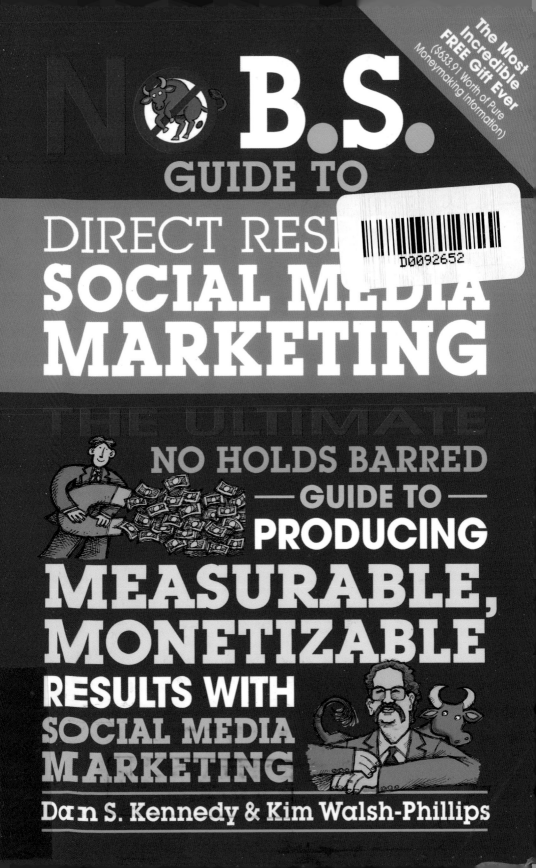

NO B.S.

GUIDE TO

DIRECT RESPONSE

SOCIAL MEDIA
MARKETING

THE ULTIMATE

NO HOLDS BARRED
— GUIDE TO —
PRODUCING

MEASURABLE,
MONETIZABLE
RESULTS WITH
SOCIAL MEDIA
MARKETING

Dan S. Kennedy & Kim Walsh-Phillips

It's one thing to use social media to try to gain followers and get your name out there; it's a totally different game to use proven direct response marketing principles to drive more leads and profits. This book delivers the keys to selling directly to cold traffic on social media, increasing your lead flow and opt-ins, to creating celebrity status online. Whatever measurable result you're after with social media, there are step-by-step strategies and simple, effective techniques in this book that will speed up the time it takes for you to get there and save you from frustration.

—JOE POLISH, FOUNDER OF GENIUS NETWORK, WWW.GENIUSNETWORK.COM

This is the best book in the market today to drive sales to your business through social media marketing. It shows you how much more money you could be making every day.

—BRIAN TRACY, AUTHOR OF *THE PSYCHOLOGY OF SELLING,* WWW.BRIANTRACY.COM

Forget about highlighting text or dog-earing pages . . . I actually ripped several pages right out of the book and taped them on my office wall for easy reference. I was just thumbing through at first and found a Facebook tactic that I used on my own group page and got massive engagement within the hour. Crazy! This is absolutely the best social media marketing book available.

—KEVIN KRUSE, *NEW YORK TIMES* BESTSELLING AUTHOR AND FOUNDER OF THE KRUSE GROUP, WWW.KEVINKRUSE.COM

Doubters Beware! Grizzled, head-in-the-sand marketers take note. Those who believe "clicks" are marketing, awaken! Yes, you must measure effectiveness of your campaigns. Yes, you want a highly leveraged ROI. And, yes, most firms have not yet figured out how to monetize internet-based marketing. That was me. But it doesn't have to be you. Each chapter reveals solutions to help you implement a profitable social media marketing strategy.

—LARRY V. PARMAN, FORMER SECRETARY OF COMMERCE FOR THE STATE OF OKLAHOMA, AUTHOR OF *ABOVE THE FRAY: LEADING YOURSELF, YOUR BUSINESS AND OTHERS DURING TURBULENT TIMES,* WWW.CEOMAESTRO.COM

As the CEO of a company that lives and breathes automation, I can say with certainty that the everyday entrepreneur should get their hands on *No B.S. Guide to Direct Response Social Media Marketing*. Kim does a great job laying out the tools, templates, and resources you need to create high social media ROI. Dan's commentary focuses on creating, tracking, and monitoring those social media posts which align with his focus on direct-response marketing. All in all, if you are looking to grow your business using social media make this book your guide.

—CLATE MASK, CEO AND CO-FOUNDER OF INFUSIONSOFT,
WWW.INFUSIONSOFT.COM

If you want to understand how to move people to action with social media, dig into this book.

—MICHAEL A. STELZNER, FOUNDER OF SOCIAL MEDIA EXAMINER, WWW.
SOCIALMEDIAEXAMINER.COM

This book puts the "direct" in "direct response" with clear, candid, practical advice for anyone trying to rise above the avalanche of social media outreach. Their emphasis on results—meaning revenue, not awareness—is honest and a refreshing reminder how to allocate our time and resources most efficiently.

—NELL MINNOW, AUTHOR, COLUMNIST, MOVIE CRITIC FOR BELIEFNET, AND
FOUNDER OF MINIVER PRESS, WWW.MOVIEMOM.COM

Social media can be a gigantic waste of time and energy or a seriously smart investment for your business. If you want to know the ROI-based way of doing it right read this book.

—YANIK SILVER, FOUNDER MAVERICK1000 AND AUTHOR OF *MAVERICK STARTUP*,
WWW.YANIKSILVER.COM

FINALLY, a book that cuts through the social media BS and teaches the real secrets for turning leads into new and repeat business. If you're ready to super-charge your business with social media, then read and absorb the strategies from Kim Walsh-Phillips and Dan Kennedy. It will change your business.

—JAMES MALINCHAK, FEATURED ON ABC's *SECRET MILLIONAIRE*, FOUNDER OF "BIG MONEY SPEAKER® COACH BOOT CAMP," WWW.BIGMONEYSPEAKER.COM

A lot has been written about leveraging social media and we have been conditioned to believe it's easy, and it just happens. I haven't found a book that clearly tells you how to leverage social media to generate leads—until now. Dan and Kim show you how to get a strong ROI, increased sales, and explain why you shouldn't worry about metrics that don't matter: "likes" and "comments."

—DAVID H. MATTSON, CEO AND PRESIDENT OF SANDLER TRAINING, WWW.SANDLER.COM

This book is so valuable that I've handed it to my staff to implement its techniques. Kim and Dan lay out exact methods with case studies on how they got the results, which are so often held close to the chest of marketers. They teach you how to convert cold leads to paying customers, and the exact metrics of options and lifetime value of a customer.

—DR. JEREMY WEISZ, FOUNDER OF INSPIREDINSIDER, WWW.INSPIREDINSIDER.COM

I'm usually a speed reader who can finish a book in a couple hours, but this book is so helpful that I savored it and read it slowly. I freakin' love how Dan puts down social media because he's voicing the issues that kept me from buying ads there. And I learned a lot from seeing how Kim's process can lead to the measurable results that Dan demands.

—ANDREW WARNER, FOUNDER OF MIXERGY.COM, WWW.MIXERGY.COM

Social media marketing takes paramount importance in any business that seeks to grow. This book is loaded with ideas and strategies to help you grow an extraordinary enterprise.

—DR. NIDO R. QUBEIN, PRESIDENT OF HIGH POINT UNIVERSITY,
WWW.HIGHPOINT.EDU

If you are an entrepreneur or marketer, I highly recommend you get this book. After reading, and more importantly, applying direct-response marketing principles to your social media presence, you will be ahead of 99% of the marketers out there.

—SCOTT DUFFY, FOUNDER AND CEO OF CONTENT.MARKET,
WWW.CONTENT.MARKET/

Walsh-Phillips and Kennedy deliver everything you need to accelerate your business' growth online without any extraneous fluff. In hard-hitting bullets, two masters arm you with actionable tactics you will benefit from immediately. I'm personally starting to implement their strategies and will be advising my clients to do the same.

—KAIHAN KRIPPENDORFF, CEO OF OUTTHINKER LLC, AUTHOR OF
OUTTHINK THE COMPETITION, WWW.OUTTHINKER.COM

If you want to grow your company with social media, you must read this book. I've read and reviewed a lot of business books. There's so much fluff out there. Not this book. Dan and Kim go into detail with specific business building strategies for a return on your time and money.

—CLAYTON MORRIS, CO-HOST OF FOX & FRIENDS, FOUNDER OF READQUICK APP,
WWW.READQUICKAPP.COM

Every time you communicate, you are either adding value or taking up space. *No B.S. Guide to Direct Response Social Media Marketing* teaches marketers how to cater messages for their audience. Dan and Kim's combination of direct marketing principles and social media know-how make it easy for business owners to target their audience and stand out from competitors.

—Sally Hogshead, *New York Times* bestselling author and creator of the Fascination Advantage® Assessment, www.howtofascinate.com

If you want success and a life of purpose, you can't let fear and doubt bring you down. Read this book to empower you to own the social media space and let your light shine to those who desperately need to hear your message.

—Marshawn Evans Daniels, attorney, author, and speaker, Miss America and NBC's *The Apprentice* finalist, www.Marshawn.com

A lot of time and money is wasted on social media marketing. Many so-called "experts" expound theories and strategies that simply don't work. In direct contrast, this book details how to take Dan Kennedy-style direct response marketing and apply it to social media to ensure real results. If you are going to use social media marketing for your business, arm yourself with this book by Kennedy and Walsh-Phillips.

—Rich Schefren, founder of Strategic Profits, www.strategicprofits.com

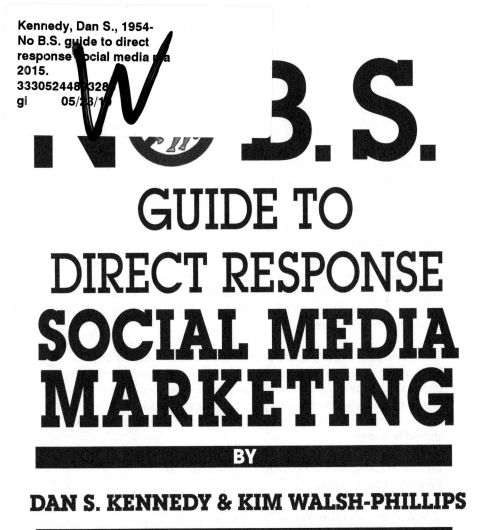

N🛇 B.S.

GUIDE TO
DIRECT RESPONSE
SOCIAL MEDIA
MARKETING

BY

DAN S. KENNEDY & KIM WALSH-PHILLIPS

WITH

SHAUN BUCK, ARI GALPER, KELLY LEMAY,
GRAIG PRESTI, AND PARTHIV SHAH

Ep
Entrepreneur
PRESS®

Publisher: Entrepreneur Press
Cover Design: Andrew Welyczko
Production and Composition: Eliot House Productions

Library of Congress Cataloging-in-Publication Data
Kennedy, Dan S., 1954–
    No B.S. guide to direct response social media marketing/by Dan S. Kennedy and Kim Walsh-Phillips.
        pages cm
    ISBN-13: 978-1-59918-577-4 (alk. paper)
    ISBN-10: 1-59918-577-6 (alk. paper)
    1. Direct marketing. 2. Internet marketing. 3. Social media. I. Walsh-Phillips, Kim, author. II. Title.
HF5415.126.K463 2015
658.8′72—dc23   2015022192

Printed in the United States of America

20 19 18 17   10 9 8 7 6 5 4

Contents

Introduction

Why Would I Write a Book About Social Media and More Importantly, Why Should You Read It?

by Dan Kennedy

Everyone's talking about it, but nobody knows what they're talking about.

As pervasive as this nonsense is, the buzz is becoming quantifiable, and more businesses are feeling pressure to join the social media bandwagon. But what are consumers' purchases really telling us about social media's influence? And what mistakes can you hope to avoid without falling victim to the buzz?

An unbiased, independent poll conducted by Gallup in May and June of 2014 revealed that 63% of consumers are not influenced by social media regarding their buying choices, and only 5% claim social media has significant impact on their buying decisions.

I have no love affair with social media. In broadest context, I consider it a "cancer of narcissism" destructive to society, a way for people to feel important with zero reason or merit, thus removing essential motivation for a creative and constructive work. It brings other ills, too, with which I won't bore you.

As a marketing and sales media, I lean toward Tupperware CEO Rick Goings' characterization of it as "anti-social media." I see enormous waste of time and money by people creating small and unscalable traffic but also, in some cases, huge traffic to YouTube videos, Facebook sites, etc., with little monetary results.

But with all that said, I hold stock in a tobacco company, so I am not above making money on things I would not personally consume, and even consider a plague on society.

I also know smart people who manage to consistently use social media for real lead generation, and produce directly creditable sales results.

So despite being a giraffe on a tricycle about all this, I'm in it. The reason I tell you this is to make the point: There are times in your life you are going to feel like, maybe actually be, and certainly be looked at like a giraffe on a tricycle.

Sometimes you volunteer for this—like my early days in speaking. "Awkward" doesn't even come close. Sometimes it is pushed upon you. My corporate and personal bankruptcies all those moons ago. "Humiliating," "depressing," and "frightening" are inadequate adjectives.

When asked how he arrived at his brilliant discoveries, Einstein said, "I grope."

Much has been said and written about trying to abbreviate the qualities and characteristics and behavior of top achievers, mostly in futility. There are no correct simple answers to anything, but if you had a gun against my pet—The Million Dollar Dog's cute little head—and demanded the ultimate abbreviation, I'd say, resilience.

Which includes a lot of groping. With the new, with the difficult, with problems.

For at least as long as I choose to keep working at my trade, I must agree to some groping and coping. It's all okay. It is never what you bungle that need define you or your success.

Robert Downey Jr. is today a hugely successful and extremely rich actor. Only a handful of years ago, he was in and out of rehab, unbankable, uninsurable, and written off for dead by most in Hollywood.

Two real estate crashes ago, Donald Trump was fundamentally bankrupt, bedeviled by multiple creditors (including Chinese bankers), publicly embarrassed, and written off as dead by much of the media—the same media that genuflects today. Such stories are THE true stories of the rich, and most of the rich and famous.

The fact of the matter is, I decided it was important to co-author a book about direct response social media marketing because no matter what I say, you are most likely still going to move forward with it. And in fact, some of the time, I recommend that you do.

I do have clients getting direct, profitable results, and I do see legitimate marketing being done in this venue. If you venture into social media, handle it with care. Do not be peer-pressured to follow how others are using it. I'd say 99% of them are doing it wrong.

The Wolf of Wall Street is a bad movie, ridiculously long and pretentious, and beyond vulgar—yet it is worth watching if you focus on the warning that fakers and fraudsters exchanging mysticism and nonsense for money will circle around you like vultures around road kill. What you see from a distance, what you see glorified in business media, is often not what it purports to be. Men with briefcases steal more than men with guns.

One of your best defenses is to stay grounded about profit.

Not gross revenue. Real profit, as the only proof of sound strategy or (as an investor) of capable management. I actually sat in a corporate boardroom and listened as a board member urged the small company's leaders to copycat a Facebook strategy, using a big name company (in a different, unrelated industry) as the shining example to emulate—despite there being no evidence of any kind of profit derived from its grandiose exercise.

Incredibly, the others took him seriously. They should have burned him at the stake.

This is not to say that online or social media can't be made to disgorge profit. Chris Cardell, a client of mine, described his uses of this media to earn great profits. My co-author Kim Walsh-Phillips is also creating real, measurable, and profitable results from social media for clients I know personally—and people I know can count.

This is why I wrote this book with her. She uses direct response marketing principles to drive real results and profit for her clients.

This must be your standard—money math—and no other.

Unfortunately, most businesses proceed without caution and make a lot of mistakes in the process. Proceed with extreme diligence to ensure you are not in the majority. Once again, that isn't the wise place to be.

Data Speaks Louder Than Beliefs

by Kim Walsh-Phillips

My darn shoes kept coming off. He was walking quickly and I couldn't keep up, especially because my shoes kept sliding off.

They were supposed to be my power shoes, but instead they were decreasing my power by the second.

My husband had bought me a pair of Christian Louboutin shoes for my birthday as a momentous celebration of the success I had earned. I am a shoe nut, and Louboutins are the pinnacle of footwear. (And yes, I have the pinnacle of husbands.)

I was wearing these "Power Shoes" for what was to be one of the most important meetings of my life. Dan Kennedy had introduced me as a potential social media marketing provider to Charlie Lathrop, Chairman of GKIC Insider's Circle, the organization Dan had founded. Charlie and I were walking to a quiet meeting spot in the midst of one of GKIC's biggest events to talk about the possibility of working together.

When my shoes came off the third time, I thought, "Screw it," and I took them off. I am only 4'11", and Charlie has to be at least 6'3". There I was, walking beside him through the hotel venue barefoot with fancy shoes in hand. I was already shaken with nerves before the shoe issue so I was a bit of a wreck as our conversation began. (At least on the inside. By that point, I had been in enough hairy business situations to keep my fear hidden.)

As we started talking about the possibilities of what social media could do for his organization, I relaxed. I was in my element. I had been a member of GKIC for two years and had followed its social media path closely. I knew what it was doing and what it could do better.

I detailed strategies I would start with, like targeting unconverted membership leads and creating "Look Alike" audiences with the same characteristics as its best members. We talked about its main lead magnet, and I suggested strategies to break it apart into bonuses we could test on different audiences. We discussed celebrating its members' success stories on the GKIC newsfeed and leveraging social platforms to access its members' circles of influence.

Thankfully, Charlie liked what he heard and suggested that GKIC's staff leadership continue the dialog. Their leaders asked great questions about my past experience—what I thought I could do for them and what I wanted in return.

Admittedly, they were quite skeptical. These were brilliant marketers who live and breathe GKIC's marketing strategies. However, they had yet to come across social media marketing that could show results worth supporting. Eventually, they agreed to work with me and my firm, but under a big cloud of doubt.

When I was awarded the contract, I too had mixed feelings. I was ecstatic to work with an organization I so admired and had learned from… but holy incredible pressure, Batman!

I would be doing direct response social media marketing for an organization founded by the Alpha Male of No B.S. Direct Response. Not only they, but all of their members' eyes would be on everything my firm did. And Dan Kennedy himself would be watching. We better bring our A game. (Is there any other way?)

We started slowly, with only a few hundred dollars in advertising, but as results scaled, so did the social media marketing spend. The more members our social media marketing brought in, the stronger our relationship has become. We brought GKIC measurable results, and we have earned the position as one of its largest vendor contracts.

For GKIC, the first 180 days of an individual's membership is worth about $600. Through Facebook marketing, new members are now being brought in for under $200 each at the high end and only a few dollars at the low end.

One of the most successful campaigns takes cold traffic and turns it into warm traffic, then pushes it through a sales funnel, which converts at 50 to 60%.

A snapshot of how it works:

FIGURE I.1: Send Cold Traffic to a Blog Article

1. Cold traffic is sent to a blog article (see Figure I.1). Cost-per-click is $0.29 each with a click-through rate of 2.247% for one of the cold traffic audience segments.

2. Next, an offer is sent to those who visit the blog within two days of their visit (see Figure I.2 on page xxii). This ad has a 2.156% click-through rate. In one ad from this subfunnel, 100 people ordered the lead magnet at a cost of $6.36 per conversion and a conversion rate of 45%. This meant GKIC obtained 45 members for $14.13 each—from cold traffic, including the blog click. Holy Batman, indeed!

FIGURE I.2: Follow Up with an Offer within Two Days

Admittedly, this is one of its better funnels. Some are closer to that $200 mark and a few have been duds. But overall, even including my firm's fees and GKIC's shipping costs, it is still getting a 3 to 1 ROI.

Don't get me wrong. GKIC is no longer a doubter! But these results don't fall out of the sky. My company isn't doing daily optimization of this account. We're performing hourly optimization and adjusting ads and campaigns accordingly. We monitor Facebook's changing algorithms 24 hours a day, and test and measure everything.

The more you spend on marketing, regardless of the channel, the more you need to monitor results. With social media, you must be nimble and always, always, always test.

Ninety-nine percent of companies are doing social media wrong. Throughout the rest of this book, Dan and I will detail what the minority are doing. We will share stories and tactics of the small percentage of social media marketers who are driving real results.

Whether or not you plan to do this work yourself or hire out, take a cue from the leadership team at GKIC. Arm yourself with best practices and keep a doubter's watch over the results. Only let profit change your mind and nothing else.

After all, social media marketing still carries the same rules as all other marketing—results rule. Period.

#NoBSsm Tweetable Takeaways

Note: Throughout the book, you will find a synopsis of key points. Use them to post on your social media networks and be sure to use the hashtag #NoBSsm. We will be monitoring this hashtag and will jump in to reply, continue the conversation, and give out prizes. Go ahead and post one from the list below now.

- One of your best defenses is to stay grounded about profit. #NoBSsm

- Let profit be the true measurement of results. #NoBSsm

- Arm yourself with best practices and keep a doubter's watch over the results. #NoBSsm

- Social media marketing still carries the same rules as all other marketing—results rule. Period. #NoBSsm

---

CHAPTER 1

In Search of Something Better

How to Find Profit in an Unprofitable World

by Dan Kennedy

To be candid, this book struggles.

Some media readily lends itself to direct-response advertising and marketing. Some doesn't. Social media, for the most part, doesn't. It is like trying to use Jell-O as cement.

Marrying social media (which has its own profound culture, cultural norms, and participants' expectations) with direct-response (which has clear and, by definition, *direct* purpose) is like an arranged or forced marriage between strangers distrustful of each other and from different ethnic, religious, or socio-economic backgrounds. To reach back, it is reminiscent of Lonesome George Goebel's line about feeling like a pair of scuffed brown shoes worn with a formal tuxedo. It is, frankly, a poor match.

Still, it is also now *necessary*.

If I bowed to my own preferences, I'd advise you to ignore all of it. But even if I did, you won't, and I'd be a tree falling in a distant, deserted forest.

If you are going to be drawn into the ever-expanding morass of social media (and it is extremely unlikely you won't be), then you need to insist it repay all the attention, time, and money you invest in it. I doubt you'll stay a stubborn opt-out as I am personally. You obviously bought this book because you're already in and getting deeper.

With two exceptions, all my private clients (as of this writing) are in. Most are managing—with some difficulty—to make it pay. That's the thing. You cannot afford to just let it *play*. It must *pay*.

You can't afford to buy into nonsensical "new metrics" promulgated by the promoters of social media or by users ignorant of, or by virtue of employment by big, dumb companies, divorced from real economics. If you feel you must have presence, if you must participate, you must make it pay. In real dollars, not imaginary, hopeful metrics. *Money*.

We are all in the money business. Not the likes, friends, views, tweets, retweets, and viral videos business. The Money Business.

Most fail miserably at The Money Business. Only 1% get rich, and only another 4% achieve significant financial independence from owning and operating businesses of their own. 95% come up way, way short. One reason for all this failure is naïve, fantastical, delusional thinking and false optimism vs. *accurate* thinking. Weak-minded, thus overly influenced by peers, staff, a vocal minority of customers, popular fads, and each new, bright, shiny object vs. *tough-minded* thinking focused on direct profit from every investment. To that end, incidentally, I urge getting and reading my scariest, toughest, bluntest book, *No B.S. Guide to Ruthless Management of People and Profits (2nd Edition)*. You don't want to fail at The Money Business.

Social media as a direct-response marketing tool has another problem. A growing hazard. Its chief owners at Google, Facebook, and others don't like it. They dislike harsh, factual measurement of return on investment. They are openly, busily striving to attract more and more big, dumb corporate advertisers with big buckets of Wall Street money and a love of brand and image and brag-rights through numbers divorced from direct sales. They are in hot pursuit of advertisers who do not insist on direct return on investment. They have outright said as much, and I have been reporting on this evolution in my newsletters, notably *The No B.S. Marketing Letter* (GKIC.com).

Trouble for you is, these big, brand advertisers are kings, queens, princes, and princesses moving into the social media castle. They view you as part of a rat infestation, and the castle landlord is very sympathetic to their wishes.

Trying to do marketing that actually works in this environment grows more difficult by the day. In fact, Facebook is regularly throwing advertisers right out the back door of the castle. To get back in, they are required to redo their sites and behavior in ways that neuter effectiveness. Do not underestimate this problem.

Still, it now seems *necessary* to engage in this struggle—as sanely and smartly as possible. It is for that reason that I agreed to act as "chairman" of this book, and that I chose Kim Walsh-Phillips to be its "CEO." In a field rife with fools and charlatans, I and my clients have found her to be a rare truth-teller—someone who views this media collection accurately and not through rose-tinted glasses under the influence of Ecstasy, and someone who does understand direct-response. She is a trustworthy guide through a dangerous jungle.

My Two Instructions

My message about all social media and about this book is a simple one: Be careful and be demanding. Brook no bullshit.

Consider Twitter's own CFO, Anthony Noto, who infamously erred in sending a private message out into the public arena. As he painfully discovered, once such an error—of mechanics or of impulse—is made, it can be forwarded to the universe—fast—and it can't be stopped.

The news is chock-full of executives, celebrities, and athletes being wounded, and, in a few cases, ruined by an ill-advised tweet or Facebook post. Or, for that matter, hacked email. Even the private is no longer reliably private. Sony Pictures execs found this out. These same mistakes made even more commonly by small-business owners and entrepreneurs never make the TV news or get reported in *The Wall Street Journal*, but they foster mayhem just the same. This is also an environment where every complainant and every looney bird has a megaphone. The more you are present and active, the more you expose yourself to their type of social media terrorism: negative reviews, outright attacks, and bothersome complaints to the Facebooks of the world. This must be closely monitored and managed. It's a price of playing in this sandbox. It carries an actual price tag.

Be careful, too, not to treat any or all of this as a replacement for any other media or for a sensible multimedia business strategy. The worst number in business is *one*. Don't count Facebook, Twitter, LinkedIn, etc., as three, five, or 50. Social media is One. If you are overly dependent on any One, you are overly vulnerable. At enormous risk.

My client Chris Cardell in the UK is extremely clever about using Facebook profitably. At the time I wrote this, he was merrily minting money with it. But you couldn't take direct mail away from him at gunpoint. He also uses pay-per-click and email, online video sales letters, radio, TV, and newspapers. He won't be caught being lazy about this. And if Facebook boots him from the castle, he'll survive quite well. More than enough will still be coming for tea 'n crumpets.

A different client, after months of tussling with Facebook, getting booted and then getting back in, finally walked away. It has upped its advertising in newspapers nationwide, and is happy about the results.

I can't tell you what your decisions should be. However, this book can certainly help you make the best possible choice. What I can tell you with ironclad certainty is that overdependence puts you in peril. *The only* secure strategy is a multimedia marketing strategy and a multichannel sales strategy.

If you are a success with social media, fine. This book can be a huge help. But if more than 20% of your leads, customers, or revenue comes from social media or more than 20% of your relationship with customers relies on it, you are a fool who is cruisin' for a bruisin'.

Next, be demanding. In a poll reported in *USA Today*, 61% of small-business owners could not document or prove any direct return on their investments in social media activity, yet 50% said they were increasing time and money commitments—and only 7% said they were cutting back on it. Incredible. The CEO of a social media agency insisted those latter business owners were wrong. He claimed they do get returns from social media activity—*they just don't know what they are when they see them*. If you like being told you are an idiot, you'd love this guy. I sleep pretty soundly, but I know if I've had sex during the night, and nobody's going to tell me I am having a lot of sex but just not smart enough to know it.

After one of retail's big days, Black Friday, another *USA Today* article reported an increase in social media campaigns by retailers like Walmart, Sears, and Amazon of 40%, yet IBM Smarter Commerce (which tracks sales of the top 500 retail sites) reported a decrease in online sales that day. Then an expert said, "While it may be hard to track how all this drives sales, most retailers agree that having people talking about their brand or store is better than not." If that is consensus-thinking, the consensus is made up of morons who've lost a grip on the business they're in. You are not in the business of being talked about. You are in the business of selling things. You are not in the buzz business. You are in The Money Business. Refuse to be dissuaded from that simple, straightforward fact.

The Marketing Success Triangle Has NOT Changed

RIGHT Markets Get RIGHT Message By RIGHT Media.

Simply broadcasting a message to millions by social media accomplishes little, for most businesses. Companies like GoPro (the camera company) and Red Bull are great examples of brand-builders using viral videos and social media to rise from obscurity to fame in the marketplace. But your business is probably not kin to theirs. You have to be very careful—again that advice: Be careful—to model and emulate businesses with much in common with your own. Capital and human resources, for example. If you are funding your business's growth from its profits or money borrowed by mortgaging your home and your grandma's wheelchair, you are in an entirely different place than a company into which hundreds of millions of dollars of venture capital and Wall Street money flows.

Further, viral explosions are not all they're cracked up to be, as Greg Levitt of 33Across.com, a social media sharing platform, admits. From his firm's research:

- Consumers are most likely to share articles, news, and content related to science, but only 9% of person-to-person recipients click on the shared links regarding these topics.

- Timely news and political items are less widely shared at 2%, but the click rates are 86% and 77%, respectively.
- Business-related: only a 4% share, and a 24% click on the shared links.
- Health: 3% share, 15% click.
- Celebrity and entertainment: 2% share, but 40% click.
- Consumer reviews of products, businesses: 1% share, 4% click.
- Personal finance: 1% share, 11% click.

(The above stats were based on 500 publishers of online content.)

Levitt explains the wide disparity between share and click rates as "ego sharing": senders sharing content they believe boosts their perceived intelligence, informed status, etc., regardless of whether they think recipients will find it interesting or not. The overall average is 3% sharing of content, 24% of recipients clicking on shared links.

To me, this says there are only two useful plays: First, work with a tightly targeted list of thought-leader, market-leader, and influential recipients to deliver content of high interest and value that enhances their status if shared—to hit or beat the 3% bar, but so that the 24% of those recipients shared with are ideal for you; or second, you need a massive volume outreach, so the 3% matters.

The stats about forwarding/sharing of "reviews" about products and businesses suggest that angst over this—and time and money spent on it—may be overdone.

Ironically, and in the face of what I have pointed out above, you can make a case that it is important to include social media as part of your integrated marketing plan. But approach it strategically, with the same direct response and sound business principles that you would in any other media channel. Social media is no different than any other media.

The Stuff of Bank Deposits Has NOT Changed

You can't go to the bank and deposit likes, views, retweets, viral explosions, social media conversations, or brand recognition. Bankers are extremely narrow-minded. They won't even accept vegetables grown in your backyard garden or bitcoin. They want real money.

You must insist on exactly the same thing, from all media. Contrary to popular belief, no media is different. No media gets a pass because it is different. Don't be fooled. Be open-minded, creative, and opportunistic. But always keep a watchful eye on the bottom line.

Opportunism and skepticism are not mutually exclusive. They can and should work in concert, like partners, like Walt Disney The Visionary and Roy Disney The Money Watcher worked in tandem. Approach social media this way, and you'll avoid being burnt.

From *In Desperate Need* to *In-Demand*

by Kim Walsh-Phillips

I have a sign in my office that defines my modus operandi since becoming a Dan Kennedy convert:

> *In God we trust, all others bring data.*
> —William Edwards Deming

Like so many, my introduction to Dan was through his *No B.S. Guide to DIRECT Marketing for NON-Direct Marketing Businesses*. That was the starting point of a series of life-changing events that led to the unlikely combination of a legendary contrarian marketer (who is not a fan of social media or women with hyphenated last names) writing a book with a female marketing maven who uses both social media and a hyphen on an hourly basis.

It started like this . . .

I was thinking to myself, "She looks so beautiful."

My daughter was only a couple of weeks old and was perfect. Blue eyes that sparkled. Ten toes. Ten fingers that loved to wrap around my pinky. Her skin smelled like heaven, and she was beautiful.

But . . . she cried. A lot.

Pretty much anytime she was awake and wasn't nursing, she cried. She needed me all of the time to comfort her and bring her solace. I was needed by this little person.

She was sleeping peacefully at this moment and content. Swaddled up in her pink blanket in her pack-and-play, she looked so peaceful. She looked so beautiful.

And now it was my time to cry.

Warm stinging tears ran down my face as I faced a harsh reality. If I didn't go back to work in the next week or so, my company would go bankrupt. I had enough cash to cover one more payroll and that was it.

My baby needed me. My staff needed me.

The thing was, up to this point, my business was built on a lot of hard work: 18-hour days/7 days a week sometimes. That was the only way I kept the business afloat. For ten years, our survival was dependent on me running around all day—networking and volunteering for groups like the Chamber and Rotary Club (also known as "working for free"). I would then spend all night doing client work and weekends getting caught up.

The work we did back then was the traditional marketing agency kind—awareness-based public relations and marketing. We did a lot of branding work for our clients without much thought on how that would result in sales. The truth is, we didn't know any better.

We were successful in creating beautiful designs and logos and in getting our clients' faces in the paper, but nothing we did was measurable. While we were often told how much our clients loved us, we were the "fluff" of the budget. I spent so much time selling new accounts only to lose them at contract renewal time.

I would staff up for the work we got and then be left covering a big payroll when clients ended their contracts. I kept this house of cards together with cheap imitation Elmer's Glue® and it worked—but barely.

When I took time off to take care of my new baby, it all fell apart. I never wanted to be in that position again. Not just for me now, but for my innocent and perfect daughter.

I am a woman of faith, and so I did the only thing I thought could help . . .

I prayed. I prayed that the struggles I faced for the last ten years would end. I prayed that I would stop killing myself working around the clock just to be poor. (Let me tell you, there are much better ways to be broke than working your fanny off.) I prayed for dramatic change.

It was then that my dear friend Jon Toy gave me a book. It was Dan Kennedy's *No B.S. Direct Marketing*. In a few days I had devoured it and started putting it into action. A few changes caused dramatic results.

Later, I will go into more of what I needed to change in order for those dramatic results to happen. It is important to me that you know that no matter where you are in the journey, you can change the outcome. Starting today.

And you have a good head start.

How is my outcome different now? In every way possible.

When we started offering direct response social media services, our monthly fee to manage Facebook was $375. Our clients' minimum monthly budget is now $5,000. Being ROI focused is very profitable.

I control my own schedule now, starting early in the morning before my kids wake up and stopping around 5 P.M. to spend the rest of the night with them. I usually have two or three children's activities to attend during a workday and have arranged my schedule to be there for my children at every milestone, celebration, and heartbreak.

My big indulgence (besides shoes) is travel, and with the changes I have made to the business, we are able to vacation for ten days, three times per year. Plus I take off most summer Fridays.

And during these times, my business still grows!

The real difference is that now I wake up excited every day for what's in store. I am so thankful for this journey. The gifts I have bring value to those I work with, and I find great pleasure in doing so.

And so should you.

You have value that should be shared with the world. You just first need to reach those who need you and convince them to respond to your ad.

Don't get me wrong. Dan's cautions are valid. You should only approach social media with caution and only if it makes sense for your business. This book's goal is to give you the power of knowledge. I want you to approach your decisions on social media with both eyes open, fully informed about what you see.

I am thankful for this opportunity to share strategies with you and hope you will find at least one idea that makes a difference in your business.

Back when I was totally broke, working around the clock, I couldn't have worked any harder—well, without fear of being hospitalized. My real change came when I discovered how to work smarter and not harder.

So now I ask you to do the same thing.

I want you to say to yourself right now:

"If it's not going to get me results, I am not going to do it."

C'mon, I know it's hokey, but say it out loud right now as a commitment to yourself and your future growth. You have value and deserve to be paid for it.

"If it's not going to get me results, I am not going to do it." You in?

If you are in, go ahead and post this on your social media profiles right now:

If it's not going to get me results, I am not going to do it. #IAmIn

In the next chapter, I have a story about what is possible and real with direct response social media marketing. If you do it right, it attracts new qualified leads and sales even while you are asleep.

Let's rock this.

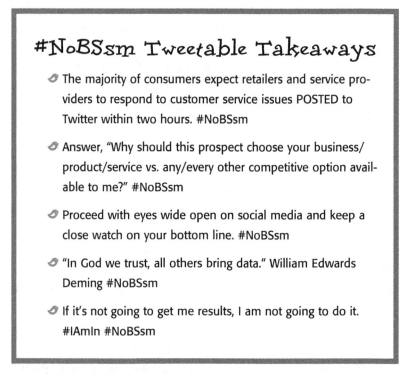

#NoBSsm Tweetable Takeaways

- The majority of consumers expect retailers and service providers to respond to customer service issues POSTED to Twitter within two hours. #NoBSsm

- Answer, "Why should this prospect choose your business/product/service vs. any/every other competitive option available to me?" #NoBSsm

- Proceed with eyes wide open on social media and keep a close watch on your bottom line. #NoBSsm

- "In God we trust, all others bring data." William Edwards Deming #NoBSsm

- If it's not going to get me results, I am not going to do it. #IAmIn #NoBSsm

CHAPTER 2

Social Media Is Not
Marketing

Media is Not Marketing

by Dan Kennedy

In the 2012 Olympics, U.S. swimmer Michael Phelps became the most decorated Olympian of all time (beating gymnast Larisa Latynina's prior record of 18 medals). Phelps earned his 19th Olympic medal in the men's 4 × 200-meter freestyle relay. His current medal count of 22 is made up of 18 gold, two silver, and two bronze.

Although he had a great Olympics, it could have easily not gone his way.

In fact, prior to the Olympics Phelps fell short of many people's expectations, including his own. His problems began after the 2008 Olympics when he got lazy. He stopped doing the things that brought him success in the first place, like going to the pool to train every day. Until 2011, when he was bested by his teammate Ryan Lochte in the 200-meter individual medley at the world championships.

That's when Phelps got back to the basics, doing the things he needed to do to win again.

The funny thing with swimmers is that no matter how long they've been swimming, they do the same thing day in, day out to prepare for their races.

Take U.S. swimmer Dara Torres, who at the age of 41, became the oldest Olympic swimming medalist in history when she won two Olympic silver medals in 2008. Despite having swam her whole life, she never forgot the basics. She did the same workouts as every other sprint swimmer on her team such as kicking and drills. She kept the foundational pieces in place as circumstances around her changed.

Unfortunately, this is not how so many business owners behave when it comes to social media. They have forgotten the practices that apply to any media that brought them success in the first place.

Contrary to Popular Belief . . .

The internet is not as special as most people think, and media is not marketing. The same disciplined business and marketing practices must be kept in place to drive real results. Very few will do this, so very few will ever see results through social media marketing, or any marketing for that matter.

Social media has a lot of the same dangers that email marketing does. It is free and can be distributed quickly with a very low barrier to entry. Not much thought or strategy needs to be put into place in order to launch messaging or paid ads.

Why So Many Businesses Are Failing

Just because it is social media doesn't mean it shouldn't use all of the same principles as direct response marketing.

It's been 40 years or more since I replaced old-fashioned prospecting grunt work for a 100% measurable way to attract a predictable, reliable stream of ideal clients.

Success at getting qualified clients, customers, or patients has a lot more to do with understanding the real secrets of direct response marketing and a lot less to do with chasing prospects through tweets and status updates.

I've been entirely DR (direct response) since 1975, and pioneered a few things of my own; although the fundamentals and the principles of this do not change, it is still really about applying tested and proven mail-order methodology to nonmail-order businesses.

The overwhelming majority of commerce of all kinds is driven by direct response.

Everyone from the credit card industry to the apparel industry, from the information business to the local service business is using direct response. The fundamental principle of my approach to marketing is this: Let's make sure we're talking to highly interested, highly motivated, very appropriate prospects for what it is that we have to offer people, who will have a high level of interest the minute we show up.

Do a decent job of selling to them, instead of trying to reduce everything to 146-character tweets, videos no longer that 3.8 minutes, and no sales letters with words more than two syllables, so that everybody can pay attention.

Why You Are the Same

Everybody believes their business is different. That this doesn't apply to them. That no one else is doing this in their industry.

Just because they aren't using the written word to sell, it must be acceptable because they are making sales. Maybe it's "acceptable." But using better sales copy gives you a competitive edge. Especially when you possess this number-one skill and they *don't*.

Darin Garmin was making sales in real estate, but he wasn't happy with the process and was becoming increasingly frustrated doing a lot of work only to lose the sale to a competitor.

No one was using sales letters to sell apartment buildings until Darin decided to do it. Not only did he succeed at selling apartment buildings with sales letters, he also got the people HE predetermined were good candidates to respond. Plus, when he did some research, he found he had moved into a position where his office handled 70% of all apartment building transactions. That was NOT the case before he started using sales letters.

It does not matter whether your clients are the CEO or the broom pusher or which media channels you use, everybody buys the same way. They all go through the same process. They all go through the same emotional journey.

The Basics of Effective Marketing

There are just a few plain and simple direct marketing rules to follow, and by committing to them you'll reap the long-term benefits you desire and develop a long-lasting business foundation.

These basics are skipped by most businesses using Facebook, Twitter, and LinkedIn as their primary sources of communications. Realize you have choices, and you can make your marketing dollars work harder for you by offering people more than one reason and more than one means of responding to you.

However many channels you market in, there are basic rules you need to understand in order to succeed. These foundational concepts must be fully comprehended, practiced, managed, and enforced.

1. There Will Always Be an Offer

There is a popular saying out there that "content is king." I would disagree. The sale is the king. Without it, you have no market share and no kingdom to rule over. Your social media marketing needs to have an offer, telling your ideal prospects exactly what to do and why they want to do it right now. It should be irresistible and time sensitive and give them some type of transformative value if they take action.

Ideally, yours is a Godfather's Offer: an offer that the appropriate prospect or customer for you can't refuse.

2. There Will Be a Reason to Respond Right Now

The hidden cost and failure in all advertising and marketing is in the almost-persuaded. They were tempted to respond. They nearly responded. They got right up to the edge of response, but then set it aside to do later or to mull over or to check out more the next time they were at their computers. When they get to that edge, we must reach across and pull them past it. There must be a good reason for them not to stop short or delay or ponder. There must be urgency.

3. There Will Be Clear Instructions

Most people do a reasonably good job of following directions. For the most part, they stop on red and go on green, stand in the lines they're told to stand in, fill out the forms they're given to fill out, and applaud when the Applause sign comes on. Most people are well conditioned from infancy, in every environment, to do as they are told.

Most marketers' failures and disappointments result from giving confusing directions—or no directions at all. Confused or uncertain consumers do nothing. And people rarely buy anything of consequence without being asked. Sharing content alone will not bring measurable results from your social media. You must walk your prospect through the steps you want them to take in order to make the sale.

4. There Will Be Tracking and Measurement

If you want real profits from your marketing, you are no longer going to permit any advertising, marketing, or selling investments to be made without direct and accurate tracking, measurement, and accountability. You will be given all sorts of arguments against such a harsh position by media salespeople, by online media champions talking a "new" language of "new metrics" by staff and by peers. You will hear terms like "engagement" and "reach" and "virality" with no data to back up the results. You will smile and politely say, "Rubbish." Each dollar sent out to forage must come back with more and/or must meet predetermined objectives. There will be no freeloaders; there will be no slackers.

5. There Will Be Follow-Up

Often, I find business owners with more holes in their bucket than they've got bucket! People read your ad, get your letter, see your sign, find you online, call or visit your place of business, ask your receptionist or staff questions, and that's it. There's no capture of the prospect's name, physical address, email address, and no offer to immediately send an information package, free report, coupons. This is criminal waste.

I've been poor, so I abhor and detest and condemn waste. Just how much waste are you permitting to slop around in your business? Probably a lot. When you invest in advertising and marketing, you don't just pay for the customers you get. You pay a price for every call, every walk-in. Every one. Doing nothing with one is like flushing money down the toilet.

To be simplistic, if you invest $1,000 in an ad campaign and get 50 phone calls, you bought each call for $20. If you're going to waste one, take a nice, crisp $20 bill, go into the bathroom, tear the bill into pieces, let the pieces flutter into the toilet, and flush. Stand there and watch it go away. If you're going to do nothing with 30 of those 50 calls, stand there and do it 30 times. Feel it.

You probably won't like how it feels. Good.

Remember that feeling every time you fail—and it is failure—to thoroughly follow up on a lead or customer.

6. RESULTS RULE

Results Rule. Period. Consider the simple agreement: You want your car hand-washed and waxed outside, vacuumed inside, for which you will pay your neighbor's teen $20. If he does not wash or wax or vacuum the car but wants the $20 anyway, what possible "story" could he offer in place of the result of a clean car that would satisfy you? I would hope none. You didn't offer to pay for a story. You offered to pay for a clean car. The same is true with advertising and marketing investments in social media. Do not let anyone confuse, bamboozle, or convince you otherwise. Further, no opinions count—not even yours.

Only results matter.

Breakthrough Moments

by Kim Walsh-Phillips

If you are going to reach your destination, you have to take your first step. Of course, it does help if you have great shoes.

When I first read Dan's *No B.S. Guide to DIRECT Marketing for NON-Direct Marketing Businesses*, I was hooked. I felt like I did as a kid when I was finally able to ride a bike beyond my driveway by myself. The possibilities were endless.

I couldn't wait to try the strategies I learned from him to see what improvements I could make for my company and financial well being.

What I Needed to Change First

1. *Positioning.* I had to change my position to in-demand instead of "in desperate need." I needed to stop competing in a crowded marketplace of local "full service" marketing agencies that could do everything for everyone. I had to stop being a commodity. Commodities compete on price, and the cheapest one wins. That is what working really hard for free looked like, and I couldn't survive that way any longer.

   I had to become THE expert in my industry so that when prospects came my way, I was the only firm they were going to talk to. It needed to become more of a privilege for them to meet with me vs. the other way around. It wasn't all smoke and mirrors though. I AM the industry expert when it comes to direct response social media marketing with a high ROI. There is no other person with the same expertise as me.

2. *Pricing.* Being the cheapest wasn't paying the bills, and that needed to change. I slowly started to increase new-client pricing. Admittedly it wasn't until two years later that I finally raised prices with some of my long-term accounts. A lot left, but some stayed even though their monthly services fee was triple what it was when they started. This gave us fewer clients but more profit. Those clients that stayed were still profiting from our work (now that we could measure results!), and everyone was happy. Our minimum monthly fee to work with private clients is now Ten Times what it was when I started this process. Being fluff-free is very profitable.

3. *Target market*. Local brick-and-mortar businesses in my community couldn't afford to pay what we needed to earn in order to survive or for the level of service they really needed to get tangible results. My target market had to grow beyond the five-mile radius of my office to a national and international stage in order to reach those who understood direct response marketing and were hungry to expand to the digital marketplace. Thankfully, we knew the media channel that could reach a larger audience.

4. *Media*. First, I needed to use media. Up to this point, my marketing centered around my hand reaching out to someone else's as I shook it. I owned a marketing company, yet grew my business by prospecting personally. In fact, it was all person-to-person, and I needed to scale quickly. I had to grow my list to include those I was targeting and to go beyond those I knew. I started in a channel I was most familiar with, LinkedIn, and then moved on to Facebook, Twitter, and Google+. My results were astonishing. But more on that later.

Of course, I had no money, so I couldn't start by buying media. I also had limited time balancing the baby and my business. So I started simple.

I began by writing a weekly email that I also posted on my blog. I then distributed links to the blog through my social media channels. I focused my messaging on marketing equaling results and shared that anything else was pointless. I tried to be a little controversial to stand out in a crowded marketplace. Dan's advice of "trying to be everything to everyone results in being nothing to anybody" stuck in my head. I had to focus on working with those who wanted results beyond just awareness. I had to focus on those who wanted measurement of results, and accountability for their marketing, and a high ROI. Those who just wanted "branding" were no longer my target market.

THE RESULTS

The amazing thing was that my social media and blog strategy started to work. My strategies were producing results. I began to get prospect inquiries from businesses I had not met at a networking event. They were coming to me because I was THE social media expert on getting a high Return On Investment. I used these same strategies in my clients' businesses and they were working there as well. At contract renewal time, our contracts weren't being cut. In fact, clients were increasing our budgets.

I landed some large accounts and cash flow improved, and I started to be able to choose my clients, instead of taking anyone with a pulse and a checkbook. I admit, saying "No, thank you" to someone who proves to be difficult during the sales process has become one of my greatest joys. I love having the ability to prevent future pain for my team (and myself for that matter) from someone who will obviously be a tyrant. (In case you were wondering, tyrants do not make great clients.)

During this time, I also got more involved in the organization Dan Kennedy started, the GKIC Insider's Circle. I attended a few events, joined its Diamond Level of Membership (at first it was just to get access to the VIP Networking Event because I knew no one to start), and devoured as much as I could of the people surrounding Dan. Unfortunately, I learned that Dan doesn't have an affinity for women with hyphenated last names and also despised social media. Both were because he had never received much ROI from either.

But I persisted.

I would test all the direct response strategies I learned in the channel I knew best: social media. I would try out these strategies first with my own business and then use what worked best to benefit our clients. Through this process, I grew my email list from 1,200 names (all of which I had received by going to a networking event, getting a card, and then entering it manually into my database) to more than 21,000 in just over one year using Facebook as our primary lead source.

I also grew our revenue over 327%. We went from a company struggling to make payroll to a seven-figure business. I woke up every day with gratitude and kept up the strategies I was learning—and they kept paying off.

My Lucky Broken iPad

About a year into this large company shift, I was driving home one night after picking up my iPad from a repair shop. My then 1-year-old had shattered its glass doing what 1-year-olds do. That happened to be one lucky iPad because as I drove home that night I listened to the last month's audio program I received for being a Diamond member of GKIC. On that CD, I discovered I could apply for "Diamond Marketer of the Year." The prize was a Mastermind Weekend with Dan at Disney World.

The day I learned of this potentially life-changing opportunity also happened to be the last day of the contest. Never being one to shy away from a challenge of time, I raced home, helped my husband put the girls to bed, and with him cheering me alongside (thankfully I am blessed to have a supportive husband [who also happens to be very cute, I might add]), I set to work.

I opened up an e-fax account (did I mention Dan doesn't use email?), wrote my application, sent it in, and waited.

Waiting is my least favorite!

But getting faxes from Dan is my most favorite.

The day I received a fax from him about being chosen as a finalist, I did an extended happy dance. Being a finalist meant that I was able to compete in a live phone-in program where I would share with others what I discovered through my time with GKIC and Dan that had changed my business and life. I would speak about the strategies I learned and the practices I put in place because of them. Independent judges would choose the winner, and Dan would announce the results live on the call.

I was born for this challenge! I went into the contest believing that even if I didn't win, this was my chance to share my gratitude with Dan for all I had learned through him that had changed my life.

I spent a lot of time preparing for the competition. Thankfully over the course of the year of being involved with GKIC, I became friends with some brilliant and kind entrepreneurs. I consulted dear friends who had competed as finalists in the past. They offered some poignant insights.

I prepared by writing out a script, buying the domain www. ILiveOnPlanetDan.com to post all of my examples, and spent some time praying before the call.

I was soooooooooo nervous. I sat alone in the most quiet space of my office building—our nursery. I provide childcare for our staff members' children along with my girls, but on this day, none of them were in. So there I sat among jumpers and dolls and pastels bearing these young folks' names, waiting.

Finally It Was My Turn

My hands shook. My voice trembled. My heart beat so fast I thought Dan could hear it. But I kept reading my script. And reading. And reading. Dan, who had a reputation for being a curmudgeon, was supportive throughout and encouraged me to keep going.

I finished my presentation and took a deep breath. Breathing was something I didn't do much of back then.

I had to wait to listen to the other callers. That was torture. Don't get me wrong, they all had great stories, but waiting is my least favorite. It seemed like forever until they were done.

Then it was time for a decision. The judges had chosen their favorite, and Dan was going to announce it after a few housekeeping items.

And the Winner Was

Not me. Dang!

Dan was kind to share that I was the other person he was debating on, but the judges felt strongly about awarding the contestant who was a manufacturer who successfully put GKIC practices in place.

But wait, all was not lost!

In an act of delight and surprise, Dan announced that for the first time ever he was going to allow all of the finalists to come to the Mastermind. We would have to pay our way to come, but if we did that, once we were there, we could participate in all activities for the weekend. We just needed to fax him and let him know if we were in.

I couldn't send in my acceptance fast enough.

Two months later, I had my chance to present at the Winner's Weekend Mastermind at Disney and get to know Dan better. After that event, we started to talk about how we might be able to work together on some projects, including a presentation to his most elite Mastermind, the Titanium Group. From there, he introduced me to GKIC's Chairman of the Board and from there, I was able to secure GKIC as a client. To this day, we still run Facebook member acquisition for GKIC (for more on that, take another look at Chapter 1).

And now, of course, our partnership has produced the book you are reading. Two years into working together, Dan Kennedy is writing a book with the woman with the hyphenated last name about social media. Me.

WORK SMARTER. NOT HARDER.

Amen.

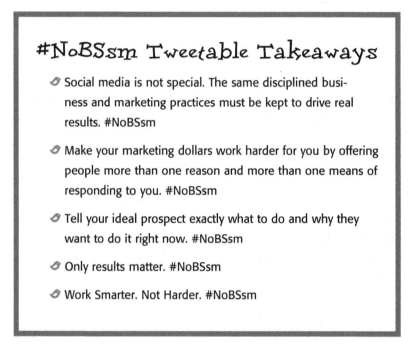

#NoBSsm Tweetable Takeaways

- Social media is not special. The same disciplined business and marketing practices must be kept to drive real results. #NoBSsm

- Make your marketing dollars work harder for you by offering people more than one reason and more than one means of responding to you. #NoBSsm

- Tell your ideal prospect exactly what to do and why they want to do it right now. #NoBSsm

- Only results matter. #NoBSsm

- Work Smarter. Not Harder. #NoBSsm

CHAPTER 3

All About that *Base*, Direct Response

Six Direct Response Marketing Principles That Have to be Applied to Social Media Marketing or You Might As Well Set Your Money on Fire (As Most Companies Do)

by Kim Walsh-Phillips

Some marketing facts according to the Chief Marketing Officer Worldwide Council:

- 28% of marketers have reduced their advertising budget to fund more digital marketing (February 2015)
- Worldwide social network ad spending reached $16.10 billion in 2014, a 45.3% increase from 2013 that pushed social's share of overall digital ad investment to 11.5%. Combined social network ad dollars from North America,

Western Europe, and Asia-Pacific represented 93.7% of global expenditure (January 2015)

- Marketers spent $4.4 billion on mobile advertising in the U.S. in 2012. That figure doubled to $8.5 billion in 2013; and that figure is projected to quadruple to $31.1 billion by 2017. Search advertising represents about half of the total (November 2014)
- U.S. marketers spend an average of 2.5% of their total company revenue on digital marketing activities, according to a new report by Gartner Inc.

Social Media Examiner conducted its annual survey of 3,000 companies on their use and results from social media marketing and the outcomes are horrifying, yet not surprising.

While 86% of marketers indicate that social media is important for their business, 89% said "increased exposure" was their number-one benefit, and only 37% of marketers think that their Facebook efforts are effective. Over 75% of them don't know how to measure their results.

Seriously.

And, this is even worse when you realize that Social Media Examiner is all about social media. Those who engage in such a survey are going to be among the more savvy digital marketers.

How This Way of Thinking Is Dead Wrong

But here's the thing, anyone who either doesn't know if their marketing is working and/or thinks the focus should be awareness building and not revenue generation could make some small but significant tweaks to their efforts and drive huge results.

I have gone back to Dan's collection of teachings time and time again while testing direct response principles on social media. Many direct response marketers think social media is complete fluff—and for a lot companies, it is. That's because most marketers do not apply ANY direct marketing tactics to their strategic approach (if they are even strategic at all).

My company, Elite Digital Group, spends thousands of dollars each day and millions each year in social media advertisements and uses direct response marketing principles to achieve financially rewarding results for our clients, and frankly, for us too, which does make us giddy as well—we are all known to do a daily happy dance or two.

Before we dive into the nitty gritty of marketing tactics in the pages that follow, let's cover a few of Dan's key business principles as applied to social media.

1. Have a Plan to Sell from the Very Beginning

In social media, you never want to come across as the used car salesman pouncing on his next kill, but you do need to ensure you give your prospects a consistent opportunity to connect and do business with you. If you don't, you will not realize a return of your marketing dollars and staff resources spent online. (GM is king of this. They did nothing to give an effective call to action and then declared social media advertising to be a waste of time and money. It is back on now, by the way.)

2. Types of Offers

Lead generation. An incentive for your recipient to provide contact information. This is done through offering something of inherent value that is so good your recipient would pay for it, except they won't have to because you will be giving it away for free. This can include any incentive such as a report, white paper, gift certificate, or ticket to a live event.

Sale. It IS possible to sell directly to cold traffic on social media. We do it every day for many of our clients using Twitter, LinkedIn, and Facebook, but there are a few key things to remember. There should be something special about your offer, such as it is being sold online first, or offered at a special price, or at least it is positioned as though it is something special.

If in contrast you sell the same thing at the same price on social media as you do everywhere else, then you are most likely not going to realize great results. Social media is a cocktail party, not a shopping mall, and the only way to get people to pay attention to something being sold is to make sure it is a really good deal. Do that, and EVERYONE pays attention and wants in first.

One example is financial expert Pamela Yellen, who offers a free chapter of her book, *The Bank On Yourself Revolution: Fire Your Banker, Bypass Wall Street, and Take Control of Your Own Financial Future* (see Figure 3.1).

FIGURE 3.1: Bank on Yourself Ad

The ad sends traffic to a landing page for opt-in (see Figure 3.2).

FIGURE 3.2: Bank on Yourself Landing Page

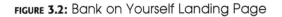

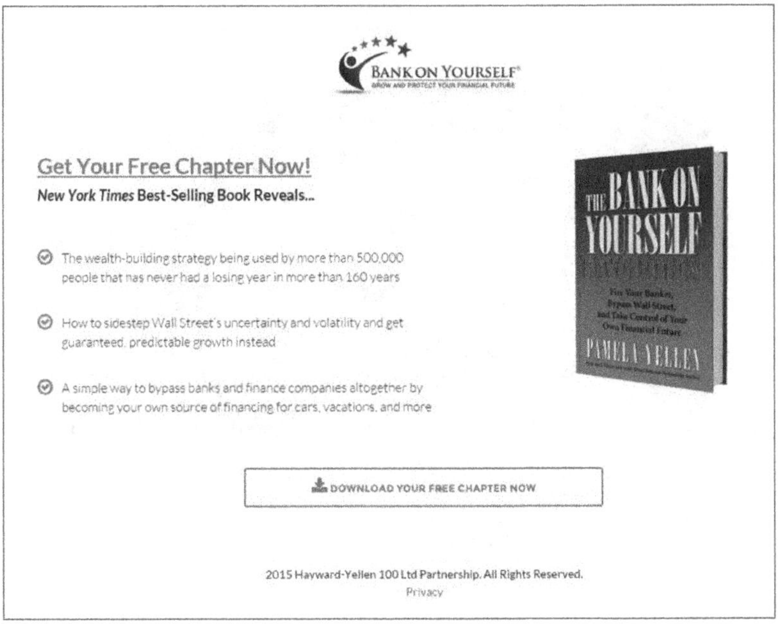

They are then put into a nurture sequence that encourages prospects to talk to a financial planner. This campaign drives leads for $18 each.

Another business that expertly produces amazing ads and results is All-States Medical Supply.

All-States Medical Supply wants to increase sales of its diabetic testing supplies. It offers a free Diabetes Meter with the first supply purchase (see Figures 3.3 on page 32 and 3.4 on page 33).

Results: Average cost per customer: $2.66.

GKIC has always had an exponential amount of growth and memberships by marketing ads in the same way: As you refer to Figure 3.5 on page 34, you will see GKIC Insider's Circle Roadmap to Success as an entry point to membership.

FIGURE 3.3: All States Medical Supply Ad

The prospects are then taken through a series of micro-commitments to add on a full bonus package. On the third page of the funnel, they are asked to add a complimentary subscription. 50 to 60% say yes.

2. Don't Make Delaying a Desirable Option

While automation is possible in social media, setting up your offers and just letting them run forever is not effective in the least. Your offers should be fresh, new, and ever-changing with clear deadlines. Offer weekly perks to purchase, opt-in, comment, or share. Always give a deadline and incentive for taking action now.

FIGURE 3.4: All States Medical Supply Landing Page

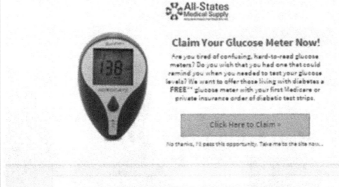

FIGURE 3.5: Roadmap to Success

3. Give Very Clear Instructions on What You Want Them to Do Right Now

Want your audience to click over to your website? Tell them to do it, clearly (see Figure 3.6 on page 35).

In posts, put your link on its own line. Refer to Figure 3.7 on page 36 for an expertly constructed example.

4. There Will be TRACKING and MEASUREMENT

How will you ever know the ROI on your social media marketing unless you track it? We have a lot of fun at my company, but we are a serious bunch when it comes to tracking.

FIGURE 3.6: Awareness Campaigns—Voting Ad

Kim Walsh-Phillips
Written by Kim Phillips [?] · May 14 at 8:23am ·

Hi there...I have a favor to ask.

Could you please spare a minute and click here to vote? "Awareness Campaigns are Stupid" was nominated for a Small Business Book Award.

As, always...you are the cinnamon sugar on my french toast and I am so thankful to you.

Click here to vote now

n "Awareness Campaigns are Stupid and Other Secrets to Stop Being an Advertising Victim and Start Monetizing Your Marketing" Kim Walsh-Phillips does a great job of explaining why business owners must...

VOTE NOW

Like · Comment · Share

 Jason Plotkin and 20 others like this.

 2 shares

Write a comment...

Cate Helmuth Bought it..read it..and voted for it!
Like · Reply · 6 hrs

Kim Walsh-Phillips Thank you Cate Helmuth!
Like · Commented on by Kim Phillips [?] · 2 secs

Write a reply...

FIGURE 3.7: Happy Hour Hangout Post

Use tracking options available in each social media network profile and advertising platform. They all have conversion tracking, analytics, and insights. USE THEM. On your end, you should also track unique forms, landing pages, and URLs. All of this is hard or easy depending on your back-end program. Not all adapt well to intense measurement. This is why most of our private clients use Infusionsoft and why we got certified as one of its partners.

Branding Should Be a Byproduct of Effective Direct Response Marketing, Not the Other Way Around

In social media, all of your posts, promotions, photos, and posturing should have a goal of sales, not branding. This may seem in conflict with the strategic approach to present valuable content 85% of the time and only sell 15% of the time, but the opposite is true. ALL of your content should be developed with a goal of selling 15% of the time, meaning your posts should be cultivating interest and need in whatever pain your product will relieve when you make your pitch. In addition, this means money should only be spent on driving leads and sales, not on post engagement or building "likes." Your page will not end up with 1 million engaged posting fans. Your goal should be ROI instead of popularity.

RESULTS RULE. Period.

There is an endless supply of conjecture by social media "experts." Be very cautious whenever you hear a universal truth about any type of social media marketing. My team places thousands of advertising dollars each day for clients across industries, geography, and products, and what we have found is that NOTHING can be deemed a universal truth, not even within the same industry. The only thing you should use to determine your spend and marketing direction are the results of your ads and posts. This is why EVERYTHING needs to be tracked and checked EVERY DAY. Yup, EVERY DAY. Our client reporting tells them exactly what they spent for ads, for our fee, and how many qualified leads or customers resulted, so they always get an exact ROI on their spend. We then use this data to make their ad campaign more effective. Any other information is fluff and should be ignored.

Are there more direct response marketing truths that should be applied? Absolutely, and that is why you'll need the rest of this book.

The Importance of Creating
Your Unique Selling Proposition

by Dan Kennedy

I was reading an extensive survey about measuring the impact of advertising slogans. Among the slogans and advertising tag lines for 22 of the biggest U.S. advertisers, only six were recognized by more than 10% of the consumers surveyed.

In other words, not even 1 out of 10 consumers could correctly identify 90% of the slogans, 16 of the 22 advertisers had slogans no one knew, although each spending more than $100 million a year advertising theirs!

Three of these much advertised slogans scored 0% recognition. 0%!

Take the test, to see if you can name any of the big, dumb companies that match these slogans:

1. We're with You
2. That Was Easy
3. The Stuff of Life

Only Walmart's "Always Low Prices" was recognized by 64% of the consumers tested. (And by the way, if you can't have the lowest prices, you might as well be the highest. Not much cache in "Almost Always Almost Lowest Prices Most Days".)

Those faring poorly, like number one above, argued that it had only been advertising its slogan for YEARS!!!! Quote, "It takes time to build brand identity." The spokesman for #3 justified its disaster as "only a transitional slogan," stating the company was moving toward yet another new brand-focused identity, whatever the beejeezus that is. Translation: New slogan being thunk up.

The real laughter is that the copy of this article was from *USA Today's* website, and at its end, two companies paid to advertise their services, doing, yep, "corporate branding."

Is a Slogan a Brand? Isn't a Slogan Just Like a USP?

No, a slogan is not a brand, and these results are not exactly an indictment of all brand-building approaches.

For example, the kind of "personal branding" I teach encompasses more than a slogan, and is usually more targeted to a market.

However, it's easy to have that go awry and wind up with branding that looks good but does nothing. There's a tightrope to walk there, and it's easy to fall off. Most ad agency types do.

A slogan is definitely NOT a USP, although it can represent, telegraph, or at least be congruent with a USP in your small-business marketing.

Actually, Walmart's is the only slogan in all the ones tested via this survey that enunciates a USP. It is, not coincidentally, the only effective slogan. The others not only fail the Dan Kennedy USP Question #1 (Why should I, your prospect, choose to do business with you vs. any and every other option?), they are also so generic they could be used by anybody.

For example, "That Was Easy" could certainly work for Boston Market—how easy it is to put a "home cooked" dinner on the family table—or for DiTech—how easy it is to get a home loan.

Warning: If anybody and everybody can use your USP, it ain't one.

If any and every Tom, Dick, and Mary can use your slogan, why on earth would you want it?

In each of these cases, the minute the ad agency charlatans revealed these slogans in the corporate clients' boardrooms, the CEOs should have stood up, pulled out a gun, shot one of them somewhere it would really hurt and bleed a lot but not kill him, and yelled, "Next."

This is the kind of chronic stupidity I encountered when working with big, dumb companies like Weight Watchers and Mass Mutual. (Incidentally, Weight Watchers could use any of the above three dead bang loser slogans. Mass could use two of them. And probably would.)

Every company behind these losers had a spokesperson ready with an excuse. Nobody said, truthfully, "We're idiots."

I have the reputation of being anti-brand.

Actually I'm not "anti-brand" at all and, as you can observe, have diligently turned myself into a personality brand. (Go ahead, Google "Dan Kennedy" and see what turns up. Be sure you've packed a lunch. You'll be there a while.) I also have "NO B.S." as a brand extending over books, newsletters, products, and "RENEGADE MILLIONAIRE" to a lesser extent.

I do counsel AGAINST investing directly into brand-building, especially with large-company-style "image" advertising that cannot be accurately and ruthlessly held accountable.

A few principles and tips about your brand identity:

1. By all means, work at creating name-brand identity and recognition for yourself and your small business, but do it where it counts, with a carefully selected target, niche, or subculture market small enough that you can have impact with whatever resources you have, defined narrowly enough you can create compelling messages for it. A giant market is only useful to someone with a giant wallet. You do not want to waste your life peeing into the ocean. (For example, I have aimed myself at "entrepreneurs" pretty successfully, but "corporate America" has been sacrificed. Stephen Covey may have 10,000 copies of one of his books bought by American Airlines or Citibank. I most assuredly will not.) Whatever your business, nationally or locally, there is a PRIME market, and a PRIME audience. Build brand identity with them.

2. A brand or brand identity is, essentially, a recognized symbol that represents and calls to mind WHAT you

and your business is about. I maintain it should also be designed to resonate with a very specific WHO your business is for. Many marketers are reasonably clear about their WHAT but woefully unclear about their WHO, thus their WHAT is often wrong.

3. By all means, work at creating name-brand identity and recognition for yourself and your business, but do it as a by-product and bonus of solid, accountable, profitable direct response advertising and marketing. Avoid buying it outright, such as with image advertising. Refer to the "Direct Marketing DIET" on pages 20 and 21 of my *No B.S. DIRECT Marketing for NON-Direct Marketing Businesses* book.

4. Do not confuse "brand identity" with logos and slogans. Logos, slogans, color schemes, and other imagery are simply devices used to convey or support brand identity, just as typefaces are a means of conveying words. Brand identity is about ideas, first, and representations of ideas second.

5. If you do develop brand identity, develop a "customer culture" with it, so your brand is theirs. Think Starbucks or Disney. The customers are part of something, not just people being sold to. But, whatever you do, don't blindly copy big companies' advertising practices. Very, very, very carefully learn from the very few smart ones, like Disney. But remember they are playing in a different league with different rules and different means of keeping score. As an example, you may keep score by profit while they must keep score by stock price (which rarely, formulaically reflects profit). And they have more resources than you do.

6. For most small businesses, personal branding is far superior to corporate/business branding. People prefer dealing

with people, rather than with nameless, faceless, soulless institutions. Put yourself out there!

7. Most basic, starting-point summary: Begin with WHO is your business for? + WHAT do you want to be known for, by WHO?, then HOW can you represent, symbolize, and summarize that in a memorable way.

(For more on Direct Response Branding, pick up my *No B.S. Guide to Brand-Building by Direct Response: The Ultimate No Holds Barred Plan to Creating and Profiting from a Powerful Brand Without Buying It* (Entrepreneur Press, 2014). I wrote it with two very successful business owners building a multimillion dollar fitness empire, Forrest Walden and Jim Cavale. They use social media for lead generation, but that is only one of many things they do.)

"Don't be in too much of a hurry to promote until you get good. Otherwise, you just speed up the rate at which the world finds out you're no good," said public speaker Cavett Robert.

In reality, the principles behind the USP have been talked to death. You can call it the Purple Cow, your market position, your winning difference, or just the answer to Why Should Anyone Read Your Blog, connect with you on LinkedIn, "Like" you on Facebook, follow you on Twitter, or click on your ad?

The *reason* the USP has been talked to death is that this core idea is essential to effective marketing. Even though defining your USP is one of the best places to start when you're building a solid marketing plan, it also seems to be one of the easiest places for people to get lost.

USP can be defined this way:

When you set out to attract a new, prospective customer to your business for the first time, there is one, paramount question you must answer:

"Why should I choose your business/product/service vs. any/every other competitive option available to me?"

It simply means "justify your reason to exist."

You must know the facts, features, benefits, and promises that your business makes—inside-out, upside-down, backwards, forwards, and sideways. Because if you can't clearly articulate what makes your business unique, how can you expect anyone else to care?

You *will* need to crow about your business if you expect it to expand, but it's pivotal that you trumpet the right things.

The right USP coupled with the right offer, especially at the right time and place, is important for any business. For a business fighting for attention with millions of other blogs all over the world, it's essential.

It is essential you can answer the following questions:

- What is unique about my product?
- What is unique about my delivery?
- What is unique about my service?
- What industry norms does my company bend or break?
- What is unique about my personality?
- What is my story?
- Who or what are my "enemies"?
- What is unique about my best customers?

Your very first priority as you embark on social media marketing is to get laser focused on what sets you apart. What makes you unique in your industry?

If you cannot come up with very clear answers to these questions, you're going to need to make some changes to your business. Period. This is crucial. This is foundational.

Take a long, hard look at your answers and then ask yourself, "How can I incorporate this uniqueness into my marketing? How can I exploit it? How can I use it in every marketing piece I produce?" Then do it. Take action. Implement. Today.

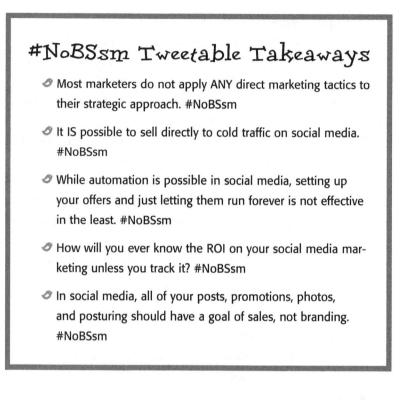

#NoBSsm Tweetable Takeaways

- Most marketers do not apply ANY direct marketing tactics to their strategic approach. #NoBSsm

- It IS possible to sell directly to cold traffic on social media. #NoBSsm

- While automation is possible in social media, setting up your offers and just letting them run forever is not effective in the least. #NoBSsm

- How will you ever know the ROI on your social media marketing unless you track it? #NoBSsm

- In social media, all of your posts, promotions, photos, and posturing should have a goal of sales, not branding. #NoBSsm

CHAPTER 4

It's Not All About You.
Or Is It?

The Most Powerful Marketing Tactic (per Google)

by Dan Kennedy

An age-old copywriting secret is to "enter the conversation already happening in your prospect's mind." One of the easiest ways to do this is to look at what everyone is talking about.

According to *USA Today*, Google reported the top three trending searches for 2014 were for Robin Williams following his passing, Kim Kardashian's wedding to Kanye West, and Jared Leto.

Yahoo! reported the top obsessions for 2013 included Miley Cyrus "twerking," *Duck Dynasty*, the casting of *Fifty Shades of Grey*, and *The Walking Dead*.

The popularity of these searches indicates what is on your prospect's mind. Obviously they are celebrity-related. People love celebrities. They're obsessed with them.

A single celebrity death will often trump media coverage over anything else, even if the reality of other news is far more staggering.

People are fascinated by celebrities, and that trend isn't going to change. It's only growing. And, inexplicably, people confuse celebrity with credibility.

This is good news for smart marketers.

Every year billions of dollars are spent on celebrity endorsements. People will buy whatever celebrities eat, drink, wear, and drive. They want to know what celebrities do, where they shop, live, and do business. Tap into celebrity and you have access to the most powerful marketing force available.

It's easier to do than you think.

If you do business on a local level, it's relatively easy and inexpensive to become a local celebrity. If you do business nationally but in a niche market, it's also relatively inexpensive.

Make yourself famous by writing articles and books, giving lectures, and being active in industry and community affairs. Feature yourself in your advertising, videos and webinars, and social media networks. Get interviewed on radio and TV, and post the files on your website.

It's worth noting that, these days, the lines between PR, public relations, and paid, commercial advertising as a means of creating celebrity status are blurred.

When entertainment TV reporter Leeza Gibbons interviewed and profiled motivational speaker Tony Robbins in an infomercial was that as good as being on the TV show, *Entertainment Tonight*? Yes. In some respects it was even better—because this suggests strategy.

If you could get three-time NFL Super Bowl Champion Emmitt Smith to appear in one of your ads, do you think it would get more attention than an ad without a celebrity?

Using advertorials in newspapers and magazines, paid radio and/or TV time, self-published books, and social media networks, you can do the same thing you once only accomplished through publicity and public relations. Not to mention you can exert complete control over the process, unlike live interviews where you are at the host's mercy.

Whether you hire celebrity endorsers or transform yourself into a celebrity, you want to create a connection between your product and service. Celebrity is undeniably one of the most powerful tools in your marketing toolbox.

This draws attention, enhances the buying decision, and increases the loyalty of your consumers. Plus it increases credibility.

One of the smartest moves you can make is to capitalize on the growing trend of celebrity fascination. Build your own celebrity or connect with others to form an association between them and your business.

How to Create Celebrity Status Through Facebook

by Kim Walsh-Phillips

When *Jon and Kate Plus 8* broke apart as a show and a marriage, Kate Gosselin was *completely* reworked as a brand. (I only watched about 12 minutes of the show before I was filled with anxiety and boredom at the same time, but I am apparently in the minority.)

She dressed hipper and more flatteringly, got long locks, and appeared less "bossy" in TV appearances. Her handlers gave her a new look and a new personality.

She landed spots on *Dancing with the Stars* and *Celebrity Apprentice* and still has her TLC show, *Kate Plus 8*.

Jon Gosselin did not receive a makeover. Not in personality, work ethic, public relations skills, or appearance.

According to *US Weekly*, "Jon Gosselin, 37, had been evicted from his home in rural Pennsylvania after he was unable to maintain payments to rent the property." The former reality star was employed by a credit card company, which "lasted a few months." Seems as though Kate's rebranding was worth it, at least publicly.

Kate's branding focused on a return on investment of continued income. (And to be fair, she didn't pay for most of it. It was part of a TLC special.) Investing in branding makes sense, when it is tied directly to measurable results.

A few iterations ago, my firm, Elite Digital Group, did a lot of work in the Palm Beach/Miami Luxury and Celebrity Market. From launching the Nat King Cole Generation Hope Foundation to planning the event and PR for the restaurant opening of *Top Chef* contestant Stephen Asprinio to running events for *Dine* magazine, where celebrities and pseudo-celebrities would sometimes drop by, there was a whole lot of glam, but little else. I worked with people who valued being "seen" over being "heard." (See Figure 4.1 on page 49.)

And even before Facebook existed, before everyone had a camera on their phone, people were making sure to get their photos taken with the celebrities as much as possible. Just being near these famous people somehow made them more famous.

It's how a lot of organizations sell VIP ticket events today. They offer the chance to have your photo taken with the celebrity.

Let's fast-forward to today and focus on you. Theres something better than rubbing shoulders with a celebrity: Being a celebrity yourself.

No longer do you need to get on the front page of *The New York Times* to launch your book, product, service, or company.

FIGURE 4.1: Stephen Asprinio—Bravo's *Top Chef* Contestant at His Restaurant Opening in West Palm Beach, Florida

No longer do you need to get a spot on the *Today Show* or win a big award to dominate your market.

Note to The New York Times: *If you want to put this book on your cover, I'll take it.*

Now, with simple brand positioning, you can turn yourself into the authority and expert in your market. This allows you to increase your attraction to your perfect prospect, decrease the time needed to close a sale, and increase the amount of money you receive from each customer.

Turn Yourself into a Celebrity Using Facebook to Increase Your Sales

1. DETERMINE YOUR UNIQUE SELLING PROPOSITION

What makes you different from your competitors, and how can you leverage that in your marketing?

My distinction is that I am not just a social media expert, but a direct response social media marketer focused on monetizing all strategies and measuring results. I have brought in millions of dollars in sales for my clients through Facebook and keep growing my firm based on the results we bring them. I share this fact often, and I am the only marketer who can claim this.

2. GET A PROFESSIONAL HEADSHOT

This is the place to amp up your game and go beyond the selfie-iPhone photo. Celebrities have good photos, and so should you. To find an affordable one in your area, check out a site like www. Thumbtack.com. You can post the job there, and photographers will apply to take your photo, giving an estimate upfront. You can usually get a good headshot for less than $100 using this service. (See more on your headshot later in the "LinkedIn" chapter, Chapter 8.)

3. CREATE YOUR COVER PHOTO.

Using free templates at www.canva.com, create your cover photo using your professional headshot and an offer with your Unique Selling Proposition. I switch mine if I am holding an event or promotion, or just working on building my email list. (See Figure 4.2.)

FIGURE 4.2: Kim's Cover Photo

4. FEATURE YOUR CONTENT IN YOUR POSTS

If you are sharing other people's content more than 10% of the time, stop. Your social media pages are your media. Use them for positioning your message.

This is your opportunity to shine and set yourself up as an expert in your industry, so feature your content, and develop your own images and posts.

If you don't know where to start, begin by listing out 25 questions your prospects tend to ask when you meet with them, and start by answering those. That will give you almost a full month of posts.

Or use a site like Quora.com. There you can identify the most popular questions people are asking in your industry. Make a list and start your posts by answering those.

5. HAVE GOOD PEOPLE

Pull in your "team" to help (after all, celebrities have people, don't they?). There are great resources on sites like www. HireMyMom.com, www.Elance.com, and www.textbroker. com to get your posts written, images designed, and schedule your posts for you.

Ready to walk the red carpet to prospecting success?

Then make sure all of your networks reflect your brand.

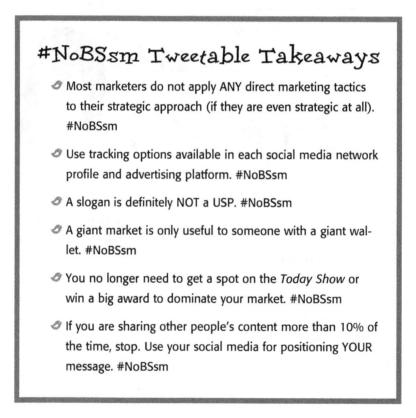

#NoBSsm Tweetable Takeaways

- Most marketers do not apply ANY direct marketing tactics to their strategic approach (if they are even strategic at all). #NoBSsm

- Use tracking options available in each social media network profile and advertising platform. #NoBSsm

- A slogan is definitely NOT a USP. #NoBSsm

- A giant market is only useful to someone with a giant wallet. #NoBSsm

- You no longer need to get a spot on the *Today Show* or win a big award to dominate your market. #NoBSsm

- If you are sharing other people's content more than 10% of the time, stop. Use your social media for positioning YOUR message. #NoBSsm

CHAPTER 5

What Is Your Niche?

Niche Marketing
by Dan Kennedy

There are riches in niches for your small-business marketing.

The first official international convention of The Almagamated Order of Real Bearded Santas was held in Branson, Missouri, attended by over 300 professional Santas with real beards (a niche within the Santa niche!), plus some Mrs. Santas and a few nebbishy elves horning in on the fun.

I was at a National Speakers Association Convention in the late '70s not much bigger than this. Now NSA has 5,000+ members and is the trade association of that industry.

And, with local chapters around the world, and more getting going, GKIC is an international association of a size to be reckoned with.

EACH of these associations and all others (there are thousands) represent a lucrative niche market for somebody.

After he failed to gain the support of his employer, James Perez-Foster, a former partner at Bainbridge Advisors, left his job to focus on the Hispanic market. He saw an underserved market with a lot of potential and wanted to focus on this target market.

He started Solera National Bank, which is dedicated to serving Colorado's growing population of Hispanic and minority-owned businesses. According to an article in *Forbes*, Perez-Foster says, "Banks are sitting on the precipice of an enormous wave of minority-owned, small to mid-sized businesses with upwards of $75 billion in annual capital demands to fuel and scale business growth, and the U.S. Hispanic and women-owned small businesses are the fastest growing small-business segments in the U.S. economy." For the most part, Hispanic business owners—just like any household, Hispanic or otherwise, with at least $100,000 in income—have two key goals: "Retiring with financial dignity and affording to send their children to college," he says.

According to a study done by ShareThis, U.S. Latinos are

- five times more likely to share content vs. nonHispanics,
- twice as likely to click on shared content vs. nonHipsanics,
- twice as likely to **purchase the products** they share vs. nonHispanics, and
- have four times the brand loyalty of nonHispanics.

The point: In EVERY market/business there are specialty opportunities. Find yours.

When Choosing an Audience: Better to Pick a Small Haystack and More Needles than a Big Haystack with Hardly any Needles

We all know the "needle in the haystack" metaphor. The idea here is it's better to choose a small, well-defined niche and have a ton of followers in that small niche than pick a large niche where your message won't be heard.

How To Use This in Your Own Business

If you already have chosen a niche (whether large or small), you can carve out an even smaller niche for yourself through specialization.

You can do this simply by redefining what it is you do and finding a smaller group of people who are seeking those specialty services. Experts within their space are constantly redefining themselves to serve a smaller, more defined niche—"a smaller haystack."

To define this special space and create that unique niche, you just need to ask yourself a few simple questions:

1. *Who?* Who is the specific buyer or person you are trying to reach? Get to know them, define them, and understand their behaviors.
2. *Why?* Why is this important? Why are you doing this?
3. *Needs/Benefits?* What need are you fulfilling? What does that customer want from you and what problem will be solved?

And finally, target a very specific niche market to start with. Finding and selecting a specialized target market is a safer and better bet than targeting the masses when starting out.

Look at it this way. If you want to sell your product or service to the general public, you need a substantial marketing budget because you'll need to run ads in major publications, do massive direct-mail campaigns, and spend larger amounts on internet advertising.

Why not hitch your wagon to a smaller niche market so you can *really* start to make hay?

Be a Magnet to Your Target Customers

by Kim Walsh-Phillips

Kari Voutilainen only sold 50 of his products in 2014. And he was satisfied with that.

Voutilainen is a Finnish watchmaker who specialized in a Vingt-8 wristwatch, a platinum G.M.T. (Greenwich Mean Time) model with hand-fabricated movement. The watches go for about $86,000 each.

Voutilainen doesn't try to create products for everyone. He has a niche that he focuses on diligently. His V-8R watch won the Men's Watch Prize in the esteemed Grand Prix d'Horlogerie competition.

When asked if he was going to limit production if the market decreases, he said, "Even if there is a 10% decrease in interest, that means only five buyers for me. I can go out and find five more people to buy these watches."

50 products, $4.3 million in revenue.

Not bad.

Set Yourself Up for Success

Knowing who you are is important. I used to present my company as a "full-service marketing agency." But really, what does that even mean?

For me, it meant a lot of angst.

With no focus or niche, we attracted every type of local small business that needed help. They usually had no marketing funnel set up, no list to work with, and no budget. We attracted a LOT of businesses like this.

These small businesses were awful at paying, so even when my contracts were close to covering expenses, we couldn't pay our bills. The most important time each day was 3 P.M. because that was when a deposit had to reach the bank to count for that day. Our mail carrier had to arrive before 3 P.M. and there needed to be a check in there so we could get in before 3 P.M., or something would fall apart. Our internet might be shut down. A vendor paramount to a marketing firm, like a printer, might cut us off (rightfully so) or worse, I would risk not being able to make payroll.

Some days the mail carrier came before 3 P.M. And some days she didn't. As I think back on it, she usually didn't. We had a very slow mail carrier in those years who would use my office building to hide out and take an extended break BEFORE delivering the mail. I tried using my Italian death stare, but even that didn't work.

Being all things to everyone means never being able to choose your customers or business growth. You have no control over the future of your company if you try to attract everyone.

Narrow your focus.

Targeting your audience to as small a group as possible allows you to offer content that is valuable to that group so you can build a strong relationship and increase your chances of brand conversion.

It is much better to have 500 raving fans than 10,000 tepid followers. You want to attract and engage exactly the type of person who will pay you what you are worth. Remember . . .

SOMEONE ALREADY HAS THE MONEY THAT WILL BE YOUR NEXT SALE

Your job is to figure out who and why they will give it to you.

- Look at the top 10% of your customers by revenue or, better yet, by profit.
- Make a list of these customers and look for trends.
- Run the "whose vacation do you want to go on?" test. Think about all of your customers and if they invited you on vacation with them or to a conference they were going to and

there were going to be thousands of people just like him or her there, whose conference would you want to go to?

I come from the belief that as long as you are going to work really hard at growing your business, you might as well enjoy it. Whoever you picture can be your niche. As long as you are profitable with this target market and enjoy working with them, then you have found your niche.

And you can create the business you really want.

Unlike most financial planners, Pamela Yellen makes Wall Street the "enemy" in her marketing. She knows her market is made up of independent thinkers who want to control their own future. She does well with Christian Conservatives who are married, educated, and financially well off.

She doesn't hide her political views or thoughts on investing. She shares intentionally, and those who follow her know that.

Once You Determine the "Who," You Are Just Getting Started

Before you start to deliver you message in any medium, you must know who your market is.

It is imperative that you develop your perfect prospect "avatar." This is everything about your key perfect customers who you want to flood into your business.

Things to focus on when creating your avatar: sex, age, profession, marital status, sexual orientation, location, native language, education, income, technological expertise, and family composition. Equally important to discover are their media-buying habits, interests, frustrations, and other favorite brand pages. All of this research goes into the strategy behind our current clients' work.

And sometimes you can find golden nuggets. Facebook gives you the ability to discover a lot of this information through its Ads Manager.

We uploaded the membership list of one of our clients, a major marketing organization, and here is some of the data Facebook Insights told us:

1. Its customers are married and college educated, with many having attended graduate school. All rank higher than the average Facebook user (see Figure 5.1).

FIGURE 5.1: Relationship Status vs. Education Level

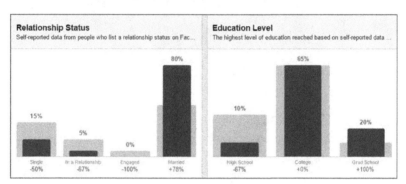

2. Most use desktop and mobile, but a quarter use desktop only. This is signifigantly higher than the average Facebook user and a positive when trying to market online—because this company's ideal prospects are more likely to be looking at their messaging on a larger screen. Only 5% are mobile-only users, which is 86% less than the average Facebook user (see Figure 5.2 on page 60).

3. They spend less money online than the average Facebook user (see Figure 5.3 on page 60). Only 45% ranks medium to high in online spending. Most would assume you should ignore those who don't spend online. These metrics say something different entirely.

4. Its buyers are more likely to make business purchases and to take on subscription services (see Figure 5.4 on page 61).

FIGURE 5.2: Device Users

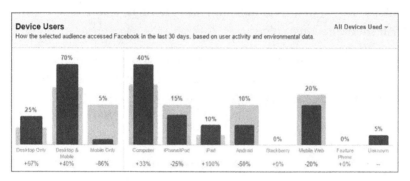

FIGURE 5.3: Online Purchases

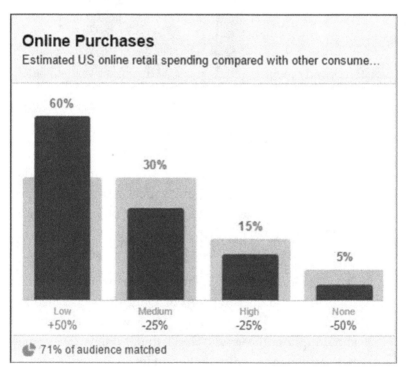

5. They own their home (see Figure 5.5 on page 61).

FIGURE 5.4: Purchase Behavior

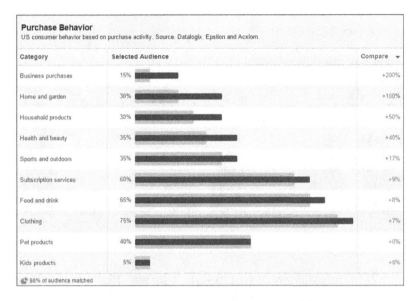

FIGURE 5.5: Home Ownership

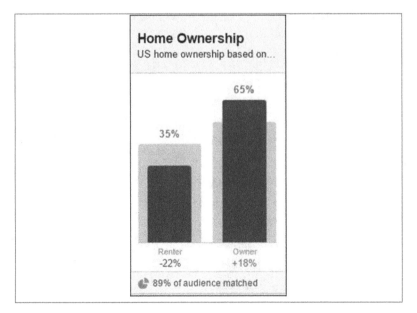

6. They primarily put everything on a credit card, with 20% having a travel credit card and 30% a premium credit card (see Figure 5.6).

FIGURE 5.6: Spending Methods

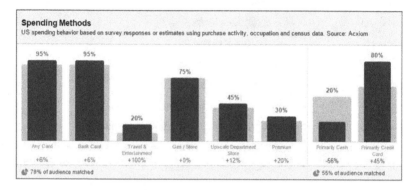

7. In looking at their Lifestyle Cluster, 15% of them are "Summit Estate Families" (see Figure 5.7).

FIGURE 5.7: Lifestyle

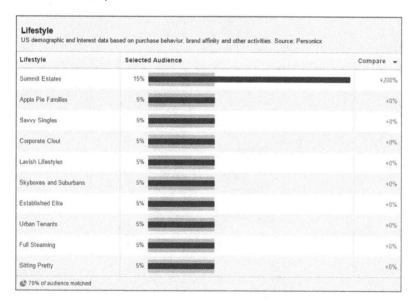

"Summit Estate" families are enjoying the good life—luxury travel, entertainment, and consumption of every kind are within easy reach.

The above information is drawn from Acxiom, the data mining company behind segmentation software "Perspectives." Just think about the Established Elite. They mostly come from segments defined as Active Lifestyle, Corporate Connections, Top Professionals, and Active. How much more effective can your messaging be with this information? You can speak directly to your best target customers to attract more of them and ignore everyone else. Not only will this bring you more ideal customers, but it will save you money as there is no reason to focus on the masses.

The key thing is that this is an analysis of its customers' data, not its list of people who simply opted in and never bought anything. If you take a look at those stats, the picture is much different.

For a website traffic breakdown, see Figure 5.8.

FIGURE 5.8: Website Traffic Breakdown

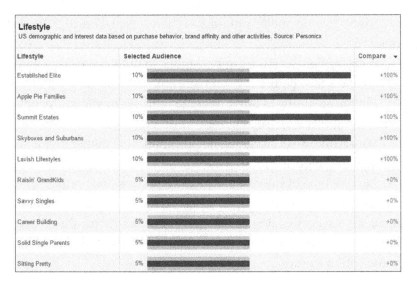

Several profiles rank higher than average (see Figure 5.9).

FIGURE 5.9: Profile Ranking—Online Purchases

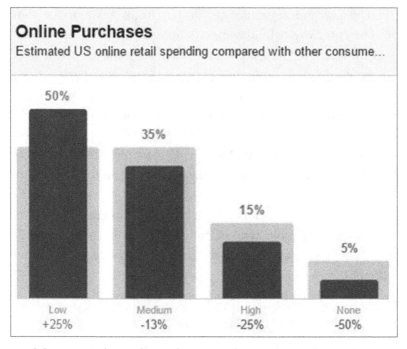

More people make online purchases (see Figure 5.10 on page 65).

Subscription services are no higher than average compared to their fans (see Figure 5.11 on page 65).

Online spending is fairly average with slightly fewer people purchasing this way (see Figure 5.12 on page 66).

Subscription services are not dramatically higher than the average (see Figure 5.13 on page 66).

No one type of interest and demographic stands out.

Clearly, when creating a "Look Alike" audience, it should focus on its best customers to get more like them, those who typically do not spend money online but do spend money on subscription services.

FIGURE 5.10: Purchase Behavior—Online Purchases

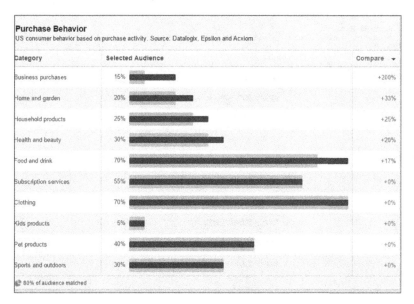

FIGURE 5.11: Online Purchases—Fans

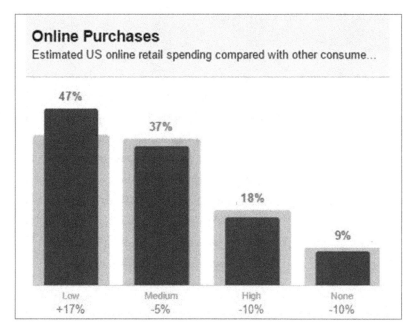

FIGURE 5.12: Purchase Behavior—Online Spending

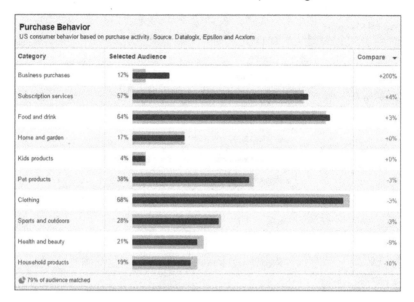

FIGURE 5.13: Subscription Services

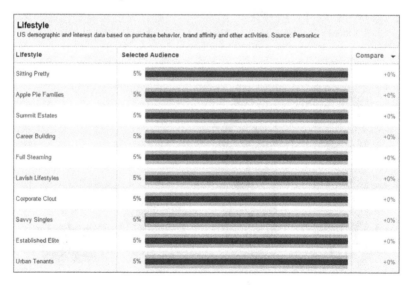

If we had looked at our client's overall traffic and not its customers, our marketing focus would have been a lot different. By comparing what was different among the markets we could pinpoint characteristics of its most profitable prospect.

So how does this strategy all play out? We pinpointed the characteristics of the company's members that were different than others and targeted those with our ads. Looking at those demographics, we saw that business travel ranked high. So we started to target a look-alike of its membership list plus American Airlines. These have produced subscriptions from cold traffic at a return 300% of the ad cost. These golden nuggets are where your real ROI comes in to play because your competitors will not target these hidden demographics. They will stay within the obvious competitors.

(For a how-to on how to use Facebook to access your customer demographic information, visit www.NoBSSocialMediaBook.com.)

Get More of Your Best Customers
by Kim Walsh-Phillips

Focusing on a certain few means creating raving fans who will pay you top dollar to meet their needs.

So how do you get started with diving deep into your best target market?

Look at your sales numbers, and choose from your top 10% of profitable customers. Get to know them better and focus your attention on getting more sales from them and attracting more people like them. Do not be enticed by the new trend, fad, or what pop culture is telling you. Focus on what is currently bringing you the most profit.

Unfortunately, so many businesses get this wrong.

Last year the Las Vegas big boy casinos lost over $1 billion, and several on the Atlantic City strip closed. How could this be?

Their attendance was up, their hotel stays were up, their nightclub business was up, restaurant and bar sales were up. How could their sales be down by $1 billion???

It is because they didn't focus on their most profitable customers. It was their belief that new customers should be pursued. This attracted a lot more customers who were NOT PROFITABLE. These new Vegas, Atlantic City, and Reno fans sleep all day, party all night, and do not gamble. They don't shop nor do they utilize the services and amenities of the buildings. They cannot come close to supporting the 55,000+-square-foot buildings that the nightclubs are housed in, even with their $250 per-night bar tabs.

The casinos became married to the idea that their money should be invested in attracting new younger, hipper, sexier customers, and they achieved that. What they failed to do was to invest in their current very profitable customers who were actually making them money.

Whether or not you support the philosophies of the casinos or Vegas as a whole, there is a lot to be learned from their catastrophic business failure. They were caught up in Shiny Object Syndrome (SOS) and the need to go after something new when their most profitable market was already right in front of them. If they had focused on getting to know their best customers better in order to serve them better, they would be in a far different situation now.

Judging from their Facebook marketing, this unprofitable way of thinking hasn't changed. They feature images of food, pools, nightclubs, and parties.

Vegas's submission to Shiny Object Syndrome now has casinos needing to send out an SOS of a monumentally different variety.

Survey Your Best Customers

by Kim Walsh-Phillips

When you know who your best customers are, your next step is to get to know them better.

Guessing is good.

Like when I am trying to help my kids pass the time in line to board the carousel at the mall, playing the "I spy" game (my youngest always guesses "pink" no matter what we are looking for). Or when I am putting a few dollars down on the roulette wheel when a speaking engagement takes me to Vegas. (I am not their target market, by the way. I much prefer a nightclub to a gambling table.)

Guessing is not good when it comes to marketing, especially when the answers are available to you.

When it comes to marketing, guessing is similar to baking a bad cake. There's a recipe with all of the measurements and measuring cups next to you, but instead you just toss ingredients in a bowl. Sure there is a chance you'll get it right, but it would have been better if you'd followed the recipe. And there's a pretty good chance you'll just screw up the whole thing.

Research is good. But it isn't sexy. So most businesses skip it.

But research can be exciting. Seriously.

You can actually get leads while you are researching your target market. By sending out a simple one-question audience survey, you can gain amazing results that can influence your marketing and generate revenue.

Sample One-Question Surveys

- "What's the number-one question you have about (xyz industry)?"
- "If you could change one thing about (xyz industry), what would it be?"

- "If you had a magic wand, what's the one thing you would like to be different about (xyz industry or their pain or frustration)?"

The answers to these questions can provide you with the following results.

- *Factual data about the likes, habits, hobbies, and needs of your target market.* Effective marketing is based on facts, not guesses. Determining the needs of your target market through research will give you the greatest chance of success.
- *A report you can use to get publicity.* Once your survey is complete, release your findings to the media as a "State of the Industry" report. Done well, this will not only give you fantastic media coverage, but also establish you as "the expert" in your field to the media, making you the go-to choice for future stories.
- *Provides a plethora of effective copy you can use in your marketing.* When you ask your target market what they want to know more about in your industry, their answers come in their own words. This gives you the *exact copy* to use in your marketing and content development. This will not only resonate better with your audience, but will help your Search Engine Optimization—since you will write copy the way your audience will search for it. Also use this copy as subject lines in your emails, headlines in your social media ads, and the opening lines of your email campaigns.
- *Hands you qualified leads (The money question!).* Within the answers of your target market, you can find new customers, upsell opportunities from current customers, and identify referral sources and other business opportunities.

The last time we ran this question, we found a treasure trove of responses, including speaking engagement offers, prospect interview requests, and referral opportunities.

A few tips on a seamless execution:

- Use the free resource SurveyMonkey to draft your question.
- Offer a prize to one lucky respondent or an incentive to each person, like an ebook, free report, or video.
- Distribute the survey through email, your blog, and/or social media channels.
- Give a deadline of only a week to take the survey.
- Review the results.

For a step-by-step how-to on the tech side of things, visit www. NoBSSocialMediaBook.com *for a video tutorial.*

We recently did a rather comprehensive survey about the social media marketing behaviors of businesses. We offered the significant incentive of a $997 video training. Of course, it cost me nothing, but the perception of value is all that matters to increase responses. Through this survey, we were able to discover our audience's biggest frustrations, in their own words. I used respondents' exact statements as the bullet points in a webinar following this project.

We also leveraged the survey to get PR for our firm, as a lead magnet, and as a special gift for our Marketing Insiders Elite Members.

And we got new clients out of it, generating the only important metric—profit.

Money, intel, and PR? That is a valuable process.

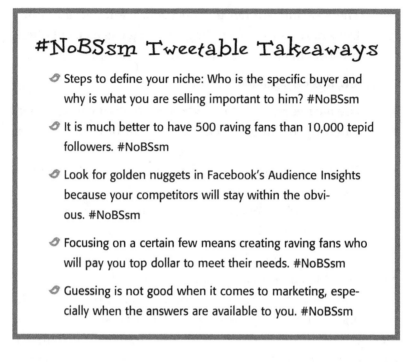

#NoBSsm Tweetable Takeaways

- Steps to define your niche: Who is the specific buyer and why is what you are selling important to him? #NoBSsm

- It is much better to have 500 raving fans than 10,000 tepid followers. #NoBSsm

- Look for golden nuggets in Facebook's Audience Insights because your competitors will stay within the obvious. #NoBSsm

- Focusing on a certain few means creating raving fans who will pay you top dollar to meet their needs. #NoBSsm

- Guessing is not good when it comes to marketing, especially when the answers are available to you. #NoBSsm

CHAPTER 6

Magnetic Leads

How to Quickly Create an Effective Lead Magnet

by Kim Walsh-Phillips

I talk about Facebook more often than any other social media channel. It has nothing to do with my personal affinity for the platform. It is not because of my deep-seated love of baby first step videos in my Newsfeed, or that I can catch up socially without leaving home, or that I can quickly share pictures of my girls with my family. (What can I say? I like efficiency and squishy babies.)

The reason I talk about Facebook so much for business is because of the results it brings my clients and my firm. We have tested advertising on LinkedIn and Twitter and haven't come close to the return on each lead and sale that we can with

Facebook. No other platform matches Facebook's digital data with prospect behaviors, lets you target your prospect list, or even comes close to Facebook's ability to build "look-alike" audiences, lists of people with the same demographics and behaviors as your list.

And no other network lets you scale up and down with such precision to maximize your return.

On Facebook especially, you will not be successful, especially long term, if you try to sell directly to cold traffic. Instead, give before you sell.

As Dan shared, your Magnetic Offer is something your best prospects would pay for, even if it weren't free. But, of course, all they need to do is give you their contact information. This is an effective way to start lifelong customer relationships with cold Facebook traffic.

Why Lead Magnets Work

When it comes to generating leads online, reaching out to prospects on social media and elsewhere isn't enough. Merely asking people for their contact information won't get you very far. You need to offer something of value in exchange, and it needs to be something worthwhile to your target audience. Put simply, you need to develop an assortment of lead magnets to walk your target market toward the sale.

Thankfully, you don't have to pour huge amounts of time, effort, or money into developing lead magnets. In fact you shouldn't.

For example, if I am going to offer a free guide about Facebook, I am not going to include every step-by-step on how to run an effective Facebook ads campaign because 1) There would be no reason for the students to continue to learn from me, and more importantly 2) they would be completely overwhelmed and most likely run away from the topic altogether. The guide can focus on one aspect of what they need, and give real value but not the entire story.

This isn't just about selling. It's about being effective for your prospect.

If it seems like too much work either to consume or execute, it generally does not test well as a lead magnet. Brands, speakers, and experts often think it is their obligation to tell prospects everything. But the contrary is true. You are doing a disservice to your target market if you give too much information. They will not be motivated to move forward to take action.

The reason is in our brain chemistry. Prospects want a quick win, giving themselves a quick dose of dopamine.

Dopamine is a neurotransmitter that helps control the brain's reward and pleasure centers. Dopamine also helps regulate movement and emotional responses, and enables us not only to see rewards, but to take action toward them. (Source: *Psychology Today.*)

Dopamine is one of our body's triggers for motivation. It is what propels us forward to action. It's behind all the actions in our day, such as getting out of bed and taking a shower to the more advanced actions like achieving goals. It is our reward trigger that makes sure we don't sit around like sloths all day.

It is your job to propel prospects forward into action. The moment they consume your lead magnet, they should get a quick dose of dopamine propelling them to continue along the path to a sale. Yes, this is manipulative. But necessary. Your prospect craves it.

If you have a product or service that meets the needs of your target market, then you have a moral obligation to purposefully work triggers to drive them to action. I believe there is nothing immoral or unethical about using triggers to drive your target market to take action in order to ensure they get what they need.

Our favorite lead magnets, because they have proven the most successful, include: guides, a who's who book, a step-by-step blueprint, an ebook, a gift certificate/discount code, video series, checklist, event tickets, webinar registrations, and contests.

GUIDE

Develop a guide focusing on something that matters to your target audience. Give people real value as a starting point to building your relationship to a point. It should have real content in it, with the main purpose being to drive them to the next step in your sales process.

To get started, make a list of the top 20 questions prospects ask you, and simply answer them. In this type of guide you are starting the sales conversion by answering what the prospect would have asked you if you met face-to-face. We developed one for our client, a granite and marble supply company, "Top Ten Questions about Granite." (See Figure 6.1 on page 77 and Figure 6.2 on page 78.)

A WHO'S WHO BOOK

This strategy serves a dual purpose because it feeds helpful content to the prospect AND it serves as a trust builder with your target market. You are showcasing who (besides you) chooses to work with you. An accounting firm might create "How 5 Businesses Cut Their Expenses by More Than 27%." A catering facility might offer "Ten of the Best Weddings in Our Town."

One of our successful client campaigns was for The Fertility Center. We put together "Stories of Hope" from its patients. Those struggling with issues surrounding fertility are hungry for information, and this book lets them envision the result they are looking for.

FIGURE 6.1: Atlantic Granite Landing Page

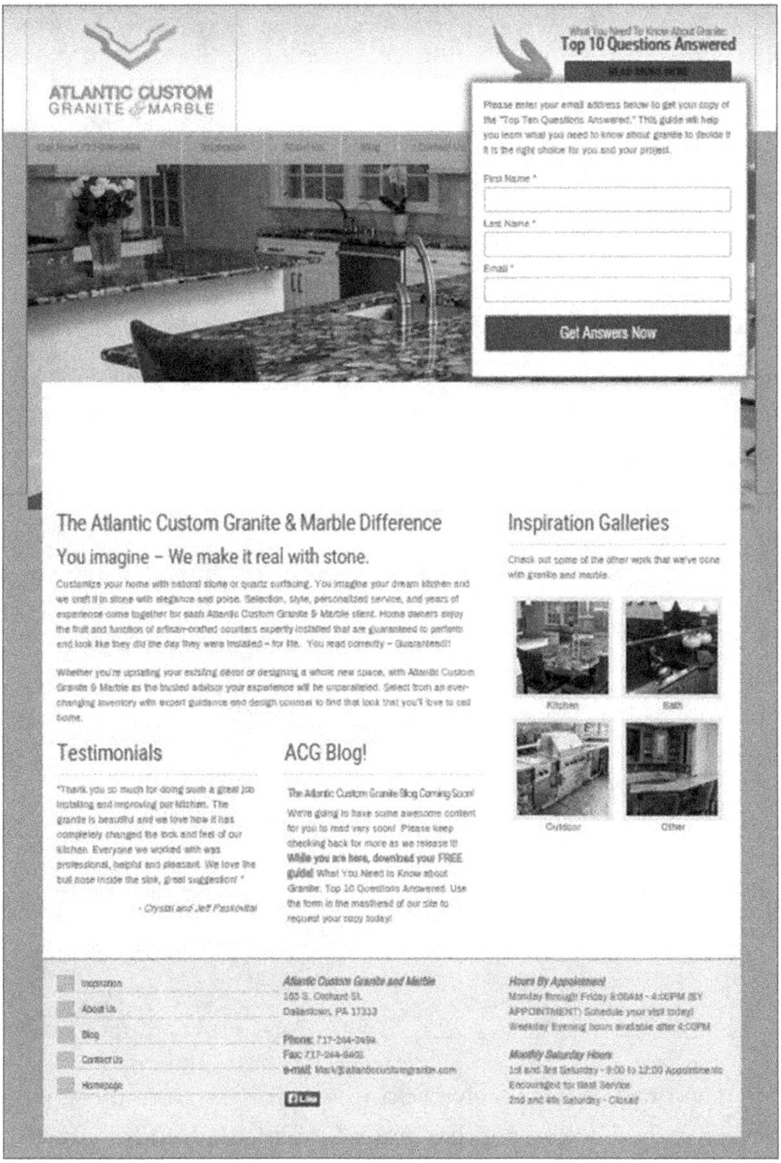

FIGURE 6.2: Atlantic Granite Lead Generation Magnet

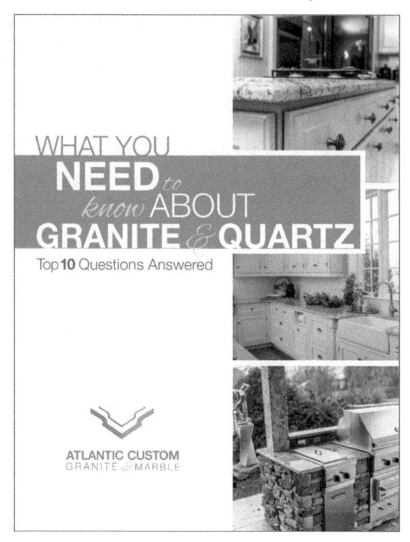

The practice has received positive feedback from those who received the booklet and has put new patients into the practice for less than $30 each. (See Figures 6.3 through 6.6, starting on page 79.)

FIGURE 6.3: The Fertility Center Landing Page

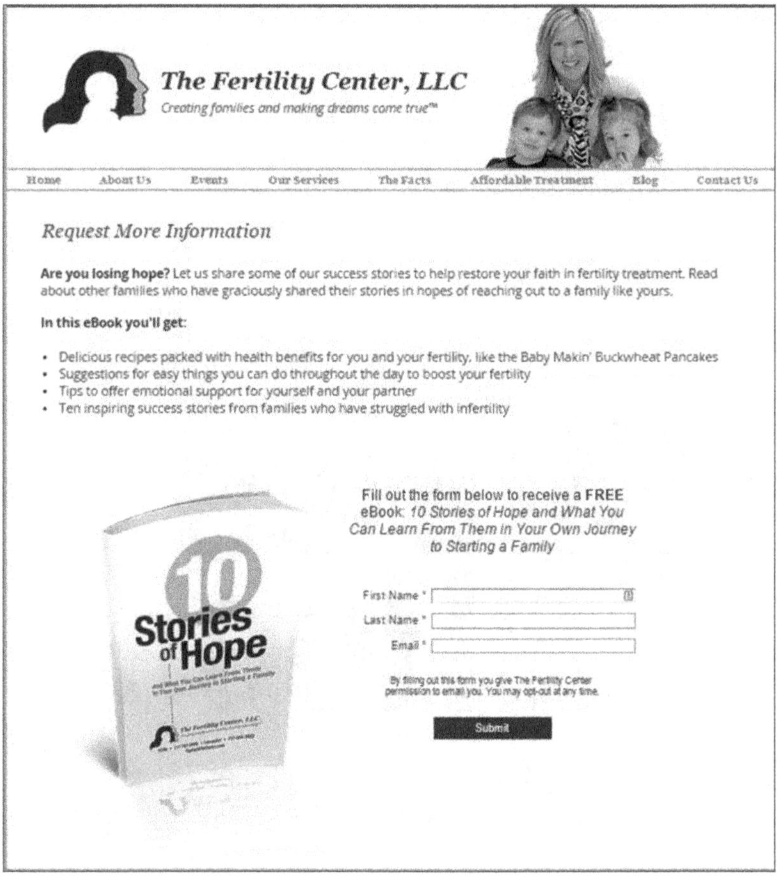

FIGURE 6.4: The Fertility Center "Stories of Hope" Book

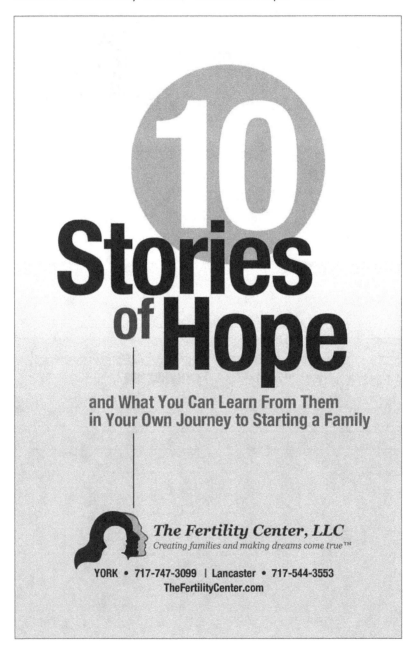

FIGURE 6.5: The Fertility Center "Stories of Hope" Marketing Funnel

Be in tune
with your partner:

You and your partner are going through this journey together. No one will quite understand your highs and your lows like one another. Use each other to lean on.

Now more than ever, it is essential to pay attention to your partner's emotional wants and needs. Remember that everyone deals with stressful situations and anxiety differently. If your partner is having an off day, offer encouragement and love.

Remember also that sometimes all we need is someone to listen. Give hugs and praise generously. Let your partner know that you are always there for support and resist the urge to retreat away from one another when times get tough.

Would you like a printed copy of this book
to keep on your nightstand?
Click here and we'll mail one to you.

18 | The Fertility Center

FIGURE 6.6: The Fertility Center "Stories of Hope" Marketing Funnel

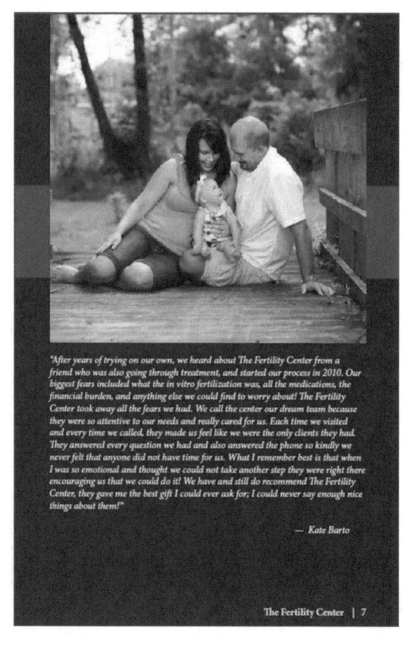

"After years of trying on our own, we heard about The Fertility Center from a friend who was also going through treatment, and started our process in 2010. Our biggest fears included what the in vitro fertilization was, all the medications, the financial burden, and anything else we could find to worry about! The Fertility Center took away all the fears we had. We call the center our dream team because they were so attentive to our needs and really cared for us. Each time we visited and every time we called, they made us feel like we were the only clients they had. They answered every question we had and also answered the phone so kindly we never felt that anyone did not have time for us. What I remember best is that when I was so emotional and thought we could not take another step they were right there encouraging us that we could do it! We have and still do recommend The Fertility Center, they gave me the best gift I could ever ask for; I could never say enough nice things about them!"

— *Kate Barto*

The Fertility Center | 7

Step-by-Step Blueprint

For example, we created a Facebook Ads Template (See an example at www.NoBSSocialMediaBook.com.) The document gives real value, but is a small sliver into what the prospect needs to be successful in Facebook marketing.

The copy is:

Uncover . . .

- *The blueprint for creating more effective Facebook ad images that can increase your sales conversions 3x or more.*
- *What to do to get the most out of your Facebook Ad Post Content. Use the copy examples to trigger an emotional response to take action in your prospect.*
- *How to utilize promise sentencing, calls to action, open loops and more as your secret hidden ad strategies the prospects won't notice but will drive them to action.*

eBook

Don't be intimidated by the prospect of writing an ebook. It can simply be a collection of your blogs or answers to the top questions asked by prospects. If you are writing a blog, take the last 30 to 50 of them, add an intro and a call to action at the end, and you have your ebook. When people are offered an ebook, they feel they're getting something of large value. This also sets you up as the authority and expert in your industry by being the author of a book. When you describe a prospect's problem effectively and ensure a solution for your niche audience, prospects will feel they're getting a bargain by simply having to provide their contact information.

Gift Certificate/Discount Code

Social media has the power to make people feel as if they are getting a deal in front of everyone else. Utilize this principle by offering a discount code or gift certificate to lure them in. Both discount codes and gift certificates have a higher perceived value than a coupon. It should be so enticing an offer that your prospect feels compelled to move forward. Remember this is part of your lead generation so the offer discount is really part of your marketing cost. (See Figure 6.7.)

FIGURE 6.7: Katie K Active Wear Landing Page

Katie K Active Wear (www.KatieKActive.com) used to offer a 15% discount code to anyone who signed up for their mailing list. We changed it to a $15 gift certificate toward a first purchase. It is conditioning prospects to make a purchase.

According to online shopping store Shopify.com, customers are 70% more likely to purchase again than noncustomers. The key is getting them to make that first purchase—and a gift certificate is an effective tactic for doing that.

Video Series

Some brands build their entire sales funnel around a series of videos. Internet marketing superstar Jeff Walker's entire business is based on these video launches. In my opinion, this is a dangerous place to start. While landing pages and reports can be changed quickly, videos aren't nearly as nimble. When just starting out, it may not be your best bet because they take more time and equipment to produce.

I have successfully used video for Facebook sales training launches and several of our clients such as Ron LeGrand and GKIC Insider's Circle have as well, but knowing the work and time needed, it is not where I suggest you start.

Checklist

People love instant gratification, and that's even truer online. A checklist offers the promise of useful information in small, easy-to-understand blurbs, so it tends to be a very effective lead magnet. Your checklist just needs to explain how to do something simply and logically. It can take many forms, including a flow chart, a cheat sheet, a process chart, or even an infographic. It is also a very valuable tool if given before a webinar or teleseminar as an outline of what you will be covering. It creates buzz and is a tease for your presentation. It also helps the attendee pay more attention becuase they are actively engaged while you are presenting. (Keep those hands busy working on something for you instead of texting or surfing the web!)

Event Tickets

This is another example of luring people in by offering them something at no charge they'd otherwise pay for. The event can be one you're holding yourself, or it could be some event that offers extremely cheap or discounted bulk tickets. From time to time, we get tickets to our clients' events and use them as lead magnets. When prospects realize they can get their hands on the tickets by merely providing their contact information, they're very likely to act. With this one, however, free isn't always the best. Test "no commitment" vs. asking for a refundable monetary reservation fee to ensure only those who plan on going register.

I've also charged a fee of $10 and donated it to charity. Ryan Deiss's Digital Marketer does the same thing each Black Friday with fantastic results. Last year it raised over $100,000. Make sure you tell the audience what the actual ticket value is, whether or not you are charging for it. (See Figure 6.8 on page 87.)

Webinar Registration

Webinars are one of the easiest ways to build your list. Most webinar software has landing pages and built-in forms to make the tech side quick. It doesn't require you to create a report or video series ahead of time. Of course they do require you actually create effective content, but since you are combining an opt-in with a sales opportunity, you can shorten your entire cycle.

Different lead magnets may be more effective with certain audiences than others, so test several for best results. Regardless of which ones you use, before you offer one, always ask yourself:

- Would someone pay for it if it wasn't being offered for free?
- Does it meet the needs of your target market?
- Does it set you up as the authority and expert?
- Does it help qualify your target market?

FIGURE 6.8: Digital Marketer "Black Friday Boot Camp" Landing Page

CONTESTS AS LEAD MAGNETS

Why would they enter this? No, really?

Contests can be an effective way to build your list and sales.

We ran one for this book and had over 1,000 people apply for a social media package and to be spotlighted in this book. (To see who won, see Chapter 15.) This gave us a lot of content for the book, new contacts on our email list, and hundreds of warm leads.

Engaging through a contest is effective.

This is the thought process behind "gamification," defined as the application of typical elements of game playing (e.g., point scoring, competition with others, rules of play) to other areas of activity, typically as an online marketing technique to encourage engagement with a product or service.

Put another way, make your marketing more "fun" so your prospects are eager to participate. Leverage gamification as a lead magnet to acquire new prospects.

However, do not run your contest directly on your Facebook timeline. While now "legal" by Facebook's rules, if you run your contest on your page, you cannot require people to give you their email address and/or like your page in order to enter. Instead, send your traffic to a landing page outside of Facebook (instead of using on the Facebook plugins to host the page on a Facebook tab). Move your prospects to a channel with the greatest chance of entering.

And importantly, give away a prize that also works as a way to qualify your leads. Instead of a generic iPad or Visa gift card, give away something your quality prospects would like, such as a gift certificate to your business, consulting time, a ticket to an event, merchandise, etc. For Bath Planet we gave away a bathroom remodeling and for One Hour Heating and Air Conditioning, a furnace.

Whatever your lead magnet is, use it to draw your lead away from social media in order to acquire people's contact information so you can nurture them into a sale. (See Figures 6.9 through 6.12 on pages 89 through 92.)

Start with one, optimize it, and move onto the next. See what your audience responds best to in not just opt-ins but in full conversions to customers.

Because in the end, the dollars generated through your lead magnet and the sales funnel that follows is the only metric that really matters.

For a speed method in creating lead magnets, visit www. NoBSSocialMediaBook.com.

FIGURE 6.9: No B.S. Social Media Marketing Contest
               Landing Page

FIGURE 6.10: No B.S. Social Media Marketing Contest Additional Landing Page Content

FIGURE 6.11: No B.S. Social Media Marketing Contest Opt-In Form

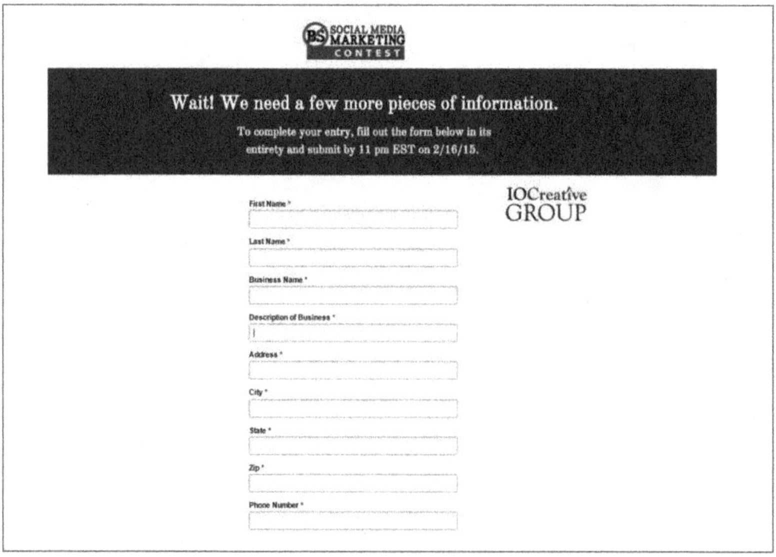

FIGURE 6.11: No B.S. Social Media Marketing Contest Opt-In Form, continued

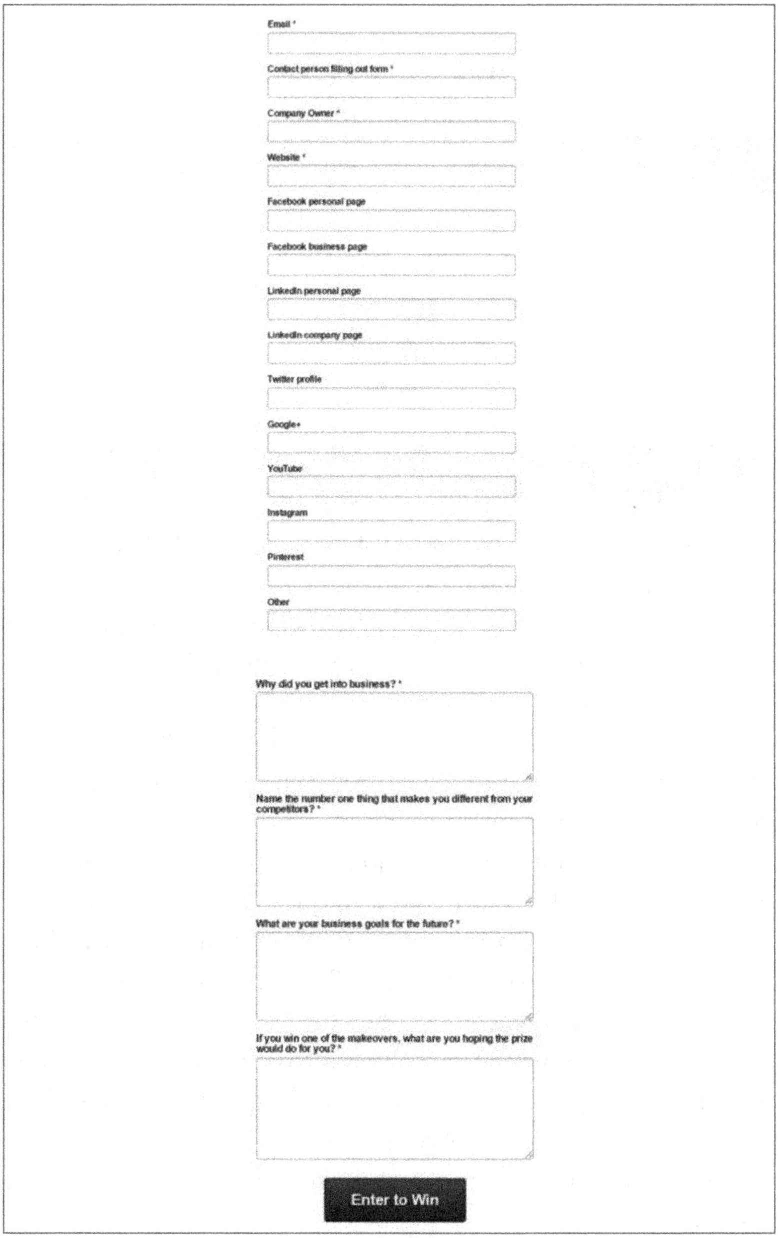

Email *

Contact person filling out form *

Company Owner *

Website *

Facebook personal page

Facebook business page

LinkedIn personal page

LinkedIn company page

Twitter profile

Google+

YouTube

Instagram

Pinterest

Other

Why did you get into business? *

Name the number one thing that makes you different from your competitors? *

What are your business goals for the future? *

If you win one of the makeovers, what are you hoping the prize would do for you? *

Enter to Win

FIGURE 6.12: No B.S. Social Media Marketing Contest Thank-You Page

And nothing has proven to give a higher ROI than social media marketing. Dollar for dollar, day in and day out, over and over again—you get the idea. Social media marketing produces a higher return per dollar spent than anything else.

How Do I Reach My Target Audience?

Once you have your lead generation magnet ready, it is time to get your perfect prospects to fill it in.

After new email subscribers join our list, they are offered the opportunity to ask me a marketing question. I am often asked a question about choosing their exact target market. I've been asked, "How do I reach seniors?" "How do I reach an affluent group?" "How do I reach small-business owners?" or "How do I reach owners of Sugar Gliders?" (which by the way are the cutest nocturnal flying creatures you ever did see and the niche of one of our www.FBSalesFunnel.com students).

How do you reach any specific market you are looking to conquer?

In 99% of cases, I have found Facebook to be the best place for mass marketing sales with the highest ROI. From small business to large business, business to consumer, and professional services, Facebook continues to outperform other media when targeting people for generating leads and subsequent sales.

Why?

Because Facebook combines behaviors with data mining to give you access to exactly who you are going after without having to buy a list.

Facebook partnered with data giants Epsilon, Acxiom, and Datalogix to allow brands to match data gathered through things like shopper loyalty programs, sweepstakes, credit card data, and government records.

You can access this information using Facebook's Partner Categories.

What Are Partner Categories?

Partner categories are a targeting option you can use with your ad to identify and reach the right people with the right message on Facebook—based on their activity outside of Facebook. For example, you can use these targeting options to show your ads to people who have taken actions that indicate they may be shopping for a new car.

Partner categories are available as a targeting option to advertisers in the United States. (See Figure 6.13 on page 94.)

The information is gathered from a host of both online and offline consumer activity.

By using a Facebook ad rather than buying a list, you can now target the exact prospect you are going after, like people who are interested in vacationing in Utah who are likely to move in the next year and have two young children.

Facebook also acquires their information on behavior, demographic, and interest data from its users' behaviors.

FIGURE 6.13: Partner Categories

Additionally, Facebook collects data from external sources such as the U.S. Census, warranty cards, registration information, the Department of Motor Vehicles, public record information, survey data, sweepstakes, and other offline sources.

As a consumer, it may feel kind of creepy to know that Facebook collects so much personal data. As an advertiser, it's fantastic. Facebook uses the data it collects to provide you with deep demographic targeting.

Currently, Facebook's demographic targeting offers thousands of behavior and demographic categories. The ten examples below are courtesy of www.SocialMediaExaminer.com.

Ten examples that provide a glimpse into the power of Partner Categories:

1. Household size of 6 (8,842,800 users)
2. Upscale department store credit card user (34,618,400 users)
3. Home office supply purchases (2,638,300 users)
4. Aftermarket vehicle purchase over 48 months ago (11,952,800 users)

5. Baby food and products buyers (10,497,100 users)
6. Casino vacations (4,242,000 users)
7. Dog owner (12,643,500 users)
8. Fitness buyers—runners (5,950,600 users)
9. Teacher/educator (223,000 users)
10. Donate to veteran causes (7,016,400)

Segment Interests to Optimize Effectively

We optimize ads daily, and one of the key ways we do this is by narrowing the targeted audience of each ad. If you want to sell tennis racquets, you could target fans of the U.S. Open, Nike Tennis, and Andre Agassi plus those who like tennis. But if you combine all of these, you will never know which is getting you the best return. We generally always start with a look-alike of the client's best customers plus one partner category. When we find one that performs well, we begin to add another category to see if it improves results. (For more on testing, see Chapter 14.)

Play around with each of the main options (demographic, interests, and behavior), run some A/B tests, and determine which avenue works best for your business. This is the kind of marketing none of your competitors are doing but can give you an incredible ROI. Most who read this book won't take action, but if you do, you will quickly grow your return on investment.

Now go find your equivalent of the Ohio Family with six kids that likes HGTV that converts really well for one of our financial planners.

You have been challenged. Be different than most and accept.

Get Your Target Market to Opt-In

by Kim Walsh-Phillips

I am fascinated by the story of Amazon and its founder Jeff Bezos. I am also one of their Prime Members and a company stockholder.

Jeff Bezos got the idea to start Amazon after he came across the fact that Web usage was growing at 2,300% annually. He had just turned 30 years old and been married for a year. When he told his wife he wanted to quit his job and do this crazy thing that probably wouldn't work since most startups don't, she told him to go for it.

Interestingly, Amazon's initial public offering went nuts in 1997—but then came the crash.

According to Business Insider, "For a while, analysts called the company 'Amazon Bomb.' But Amazon survived for two reasons: Users kept coming to the site in bigger numbers, and Jeff never promised shareholders anything but a long-term vision." Since then, Amazon.com has expanded beyond selling books to selling almost everything, from clothes to bird cages to a grossly dramatic replica of five pounds of human flesh, for example. (And some day when you have time on your hands, check out the reviews for Sugar-Free Gummy Bears. It's interesting because people love it and hate it for the same reason, it's a gastric nightmare! It has 1,400+ (humorous!) product reviews.)

By 2009, Amazon was up 5,000% since its IPO. And I am a happy stockholder.

(If you want to read more about Amazon's story, check out *The Everything Store: Jeff Bezos and the Age of Amazon* by Brad Stone, [Back Bay Books, 2014]). It is a very candid telling of how Bezos created a new disruptive way of doing business.)

You may not be trying to create the next Amazon.

But if you offer a quality product or service you believe in, people have a need for what you offer, you want to get more customers, clients, or patients, and you want to increase sales to your current customers, clients, or patients, then you are going to need your target market to respond to your ads.

When you have determined who you are going after and narrowed your target market, established your unique selling proposition and brand message, and have a working sales funnel, it is time to put some money in the game and launch.

When you are ready to launch your ad campaign, be sure to avoid these mistakes.

- *Do not boost your post.* Doing so is like turning your money into a paper airplane and sending it into the sky with the hopes it will bring you money back. Facebook puts the "Boost Post" button below every post you have in order to entice you to click it and spend money with them. You can't blame them. Just like Vegas, they want to give you opportunities to spend your money. But there are much more effective ways to advertise on Facebook.

- *Do not target too broadly.* Make sure your copy and images speak to a specific audience. We've seen businesses set up their audience to be very narrow but then use the same image for every audience. Being broad is a quick way to waste your money.

- *Do not make the ad about you or your product/program/service/ event.* Ads that speak directly to your target market and share why someone should click on the ad (or play the video or Like your page) will perform a lot better.

- *Do not copy other ads you see on Facebook.* Most of the people doing social media marketing are doing it terribly, terribly wrong and are not seeing measurable success.

Instead, read the next chapter on how to write an effective ad.

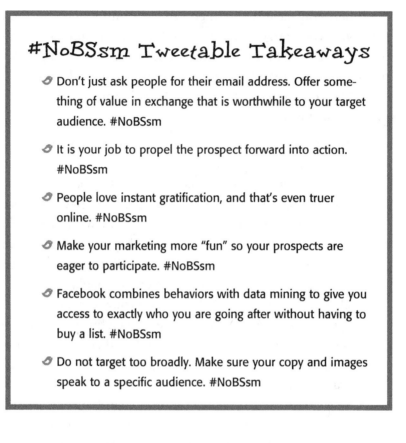

#NoBSsm Tweetable Takeaways

- Don't just ask people for their email address. Offer something of value in exchange that is worthwhile to your target audience. #NoBSsm

- It is your job to propel the prospect forward into action. #NoBSsm

- People love instant gratification, and that's even truer online. #NoBSsm

- Make your marketing more "fun" so your prospects are eager to participate. #NoBSsm

- Facebook combines behaviors with data mining to give you access to exactly who you are going after without having to buy a list. #NoBSsm

- Do not target too broadly. Make sure your copy and images speak to a specific audience. #NoBSsm

CHAPTER 7

Build Your Tribe

How to Set Up an Effective Ad on Facebook

by Kim Walsh-Phillips

I love data. Diving into a pile of numbers and discovering hiding treasure makes me (almost) as giddy as finding a good pair of Gucci shoes on clearance. My firm is responsible for millions of dollars in ad budgets for our clients, and it is our responsibility to manage those dollars wisely. For every dollar given to us, our goal is to give more than a dollar back in return.

The core of Facebook's effectiveness is its advertising platform. It is a very crowded advertising marketplace. Facebook boasts more than 2 million active advertisers (meaning they have used the platform in the last 28 days).

This is where direct response marketing can provide a strong competitive advantage. Most marketers (including those on Facebook) haven't the faintest clue how to write a direct response marketing ad.

Simply put, you need to make the message about them, *not you*. Tell them why they should care and why they should respond right now.

Here's how to take DR strategies to the Facebook platform (see Figure 7.1):

FIGURE 7.1: Breakdown of an Effective Facebook Ad

1. *Write a headline that addresses the "you."* You want the person looking at the ad to feel like you are speaking directly to them.
2. *Be willing to be controversial.* You want to tell the person seeing your ad why they should pay attention.
3. *Speak to your perfect prospect.* Don't try to be everything to everybody. Tell them what makes you different than anybody else and worth their time.
4. *Use Open Loop and Ad Congruency strategies.* The copy below your ad image should have two different strategies involved. First, it should be an open loop so that the text runs off the pages, enticing the readers to click to read the rest of the content. Second, it should have precisely the exact copy you would see on the landing page when people click on the ad. This is called ad congruency and it gives you a higher likelihood of opt-ins and sales conversions.
5. *Look at the camera and smile pretty.* If you are featuring a person in your ad image, the ad image that tests best for us is one that the person is looking straight at the camera with a smile.
6. *Try a red shirt.* We have tested different clothing colors and have found our red shirt strategy to work 75% of the time. Red shirts seem to test better than any other color of clothing.
7. *Be clear and concise.* Use your text to tell your target prospect what the outcome will be if they click your ad while making sure to fall into Facebook's guideline of no more than 20% text in your ad image.
8. *Show the reward.* Include a photo of the free report, coupon, video, or whatever they will get when they click through to the next page. They should also see this image

when they arrive at the landing page. This will dramatically decrease your landing page bounces.

9. *Build proof with your link.* Facebook allows you to change the URL display that is shown in your ads. Make sure it matches your brand and your website to give confidence to the viewer.

10. *Tell them exactly what you want them to do.* Use your link to give a clear call to action. Tell your viewer exactly what you want them to do with your ad.

Testing is really the key to ad optimization, starting from the best foundations. See more on testing in Chapter 14.

The more ads you run, the more data you will have to sift through to discover hidden treasures of qualified prospects. Once you discover the perfect message and marketing and media match, your job is clear—scaling up.

Going After Local Search

by Graig Presti

Side note from Kim: *As Dan Kennedy has said, "One is the most dangerous number." When you depend on only one source of traffic for your lead generation and sales, you are risking your company's future. Most of our clients having success with social media have expanded into these online search and reviews, with success. Graig Presti of www.CustomerAttractionSecrets.com or www.PatientAttractionSecrets.com for medical businesses was the obvious choice for this chapter. He has worked with many of Dan and my private clients to secure a position of strength online. He gets direct response, online search and how it ties into social media to produce a high ROI. In this section Graig shares why online search matters and should be incorporated into your overall marketing plan.*

You should rely on FACTS, not theory.

FACT: Google has overtaken Traditional Media to become the most trusted news source on the planet (2015 Edelman Trust Barometer).

For these few pages, forget about your website. It is no longer about a fancy webpage you paid thousands of dollars for. It's about using online tools outside of your website to increase phone calls and traffic, and produce more revenue for your business.

A lot of clients ask me how they can get greater response from their current direct mail, print ads, lead generation (offline and online), and increased internal referrals. My answer is always the same: Get your "Google house" in order!

Regardless of your offer, copy, or the media source, every single prospect is going to dig you up on the internet before they take action, make a phone call, or opt-in to a web form.

They're going to read your reviews, watch your videos, read your press releases, and pay attention to your online branding (or lack thereof). They need to trust you and believe you are the only choice in town or the best in your industry. Leave no stone unturned. It's no longer just about ranking on Page 1 of Google, it's about establishing credibility and relevance. You need to give the prospect undeniable proof to trust that yours is the go-to company.

Why Google Reviews Matter

One of my clients, Robert from Chattanooga, Tennessee, leveraged 125 Google reviews. His closest competitor had only 22. Robert's company looked like the expert 'go-to' business in his city. The result: He had to blow out the back of his building and add more space—and staff—just to accommodate phone calls and traffic from local search marketing alone. In just a year, Robert doubled his business.

No matter what industry you are in, you can use quality reviews to leverage trust and credibility from new prospects.

Google reviews and local internet have an impact on every form of new customer attraction.

- Reactivation campaigns
- Direct mail
- TV
- Radio
- Newspaper
- Public relations
- Billboards
- Internal referrals

In this day and age, every new customer will look you up on the internet. Like it or not, when people want to know if YOU are reputable, Google has become the most trusted resource.

Google reviews holds the key to your company's future success and possibly even survival.

Businesses with the most five-star Google reviews tend to get all the new customers.

Other third-party review sites like Demandforce and Yelp *do not count!* Since Google controls search results, Google pushes these third-party review sites to the bottom.

But it's not just because Google wants Google to be on top. It's because those third-party review sites just don't look credible. In a recent focus group of 25,000 random customers of random businesses throughout the country, one result dominated: Customers do not click on third-party review sites because they look spammy.

Folks don't trust random links on the internet anymore.

But they do trust (and read) Google reviews.

Here's the Problem

If you have only a few Google reviews (or they're not current), customers are going to skip ahead to another business with more five-star Google reviews. Those same people will call your competition. That's why a Google review system is vitally important to your company's future success.

Perception is reality, especially when friends or colleagues have been taken advantage of by shady marketers. It's no longer an option to sit on the sidelines and NOT have a consistent and quality online review presence.

According to IA/Kelsey and ConStat, 97% of consumers now use *online* media to shop *locally*.

Do you understand that number—97%? This means only 3% of people are not using the web to look you up. If you're not doing the right things online, you're not being found.

A further 85% of local internet searchers follow up with a phone call or visit to the listing that stands out best (ComScore), and 90% of searchers won't look past Page 1 of the Google search results. If you ignore the ramifications of these statistics, you will miss out not only on quality search-driven internet leads, but also on warm prospects who would directly reach out to your company.

If you're not on Page 1, you're not even being seen.

You're Actually Invisible

In local business right now, you are either doing it right or doing it wrong. There is no middle ground. Competition is stiff, and those who track data and follow up win.

Do you currently know how many customers you're getting from the internet? The average New Customer Value of people coming from the internet is twice what you normally see through other media. If your average new customer value is $1,500 offline, then a customer from the internet is worth $3,000—double! The reason is because new online customers are ready to move forward with your product or service *immediately*. Because you're attracting someone who is *pre-interested* and *pre-educated* in your services, they are ready to spend money.

- If your roof is leaking, you need a roofer.
- If your tooth hurts, you need a dentist.
- If you need tax help, you are going to look for an accountant.

The reality is that your customers are going to a computer, typing in something about their problem or treatment need, and picking someone from the search results.

Some 85% are picking the companies that stand out the most.

Because you cannot be sitting in front of the computer 24 hours a day—nor can your staff—managing your Google presence needs to run on a zero-time model. Here is a checklist to help you get started:

- Do you have a Google customer review attraction system that gets you ten or more five-star reviews each month?
- Do you have a Google Business page that "wows" your prospective customers?
- Do you have a video testimonial system that gets your best customers "bragging" about you online, and talking about how awesome your business is?
- Do you have a "branded" business YouTube video channel with keywords specific to your services and geographic location?
- Do you have a Google mobile site featuring converting offers to call your business and take action?
- Do you have professionally written press releases on "third party" media sites online—like CNN and local news media—bragging about your company?

The one thing the top 1% of businesses know that the other 99% don't is the fact that TRUST beats everything else.

When it comes to attracting new customers and getting them to stay, pay, and refer, it doesn't matter how hard you work or what school you attended or what certifications you have. If your customer doesn't trust and respect you, you've got serious problems.

But if your clients trust you, they'll do whatever you want them to.

The fastest, easiest, and cheapest way to gain trust is to garner rave reviews from other people who already trust and respect you—because while prospects might not trust you, they do trust what other people say about you.

The best part is Google is willing to do this for you, for FREE!

Google AdWords

Would you like to cut your marketing costs, while finally beating that competitor who can consistently outspend you? You know the person I'm talking about. There's one in every city and he's all over Google.

You are now going to pay 45% less than your competition.

You want to generate online conversions, phone calls, and ultimately sales. To double your new customer flow from online search, you need to know the exact words your customers are searching.

However, even if you already have some Google reviews and you're ranked on Page 1 for some keywords, you need to beware of the impact of *negative term search*. Every day I see businesses rank for negative terms like "WORST DENTIST IN [City]" because of an online paid ad!

This is a "negative keyword," and it happens when words like "worst," "unbearable," "painful," and "rip-off" are used in your advertising. Regardless of the reality, Google ranking and placement from *negative* keywords can destroy your credibility with potential customers.

The Only Thing That Matters to Google Is Relevance

When you achieve message-to-market match, not only will more potential customers reward you by picking up the phone or placing an order, but Google will also reward you (literally) by giving you lower ad prices.

For example, when someone searches for cosmetic dentists, they don't want to find orthodontists. You want to make sure you have a proper message-to-market match. Most businesses and media companies have no clue how to insert offers and online ads that are 100% Google-compliant and actually convert ideal prospects to paying customers.

The Top 1%

Most people aren't aware 98.6% of businesses' Google ads get banned in under 48 hours. Even the people who place those ads aren't aware of it.

In the city of San Francisco, one of the highest keyword searches is for "bridges San Francisco."

What people are actually looking for is the Golden Gate Bridge, but a very large ad agency once actually paid to put a dentist in an ad for "bridges San Francisco."

While dentists use the term "crown and bridge" it's not relevant for people searching information about the Golden Gate Bridge, or the Bay Bridge, or even the San Mateo Bridge.

When Google sees your ad as irrelevant, it gets devalued. You burn money on ads which may get you a bunch of impressions, but will never convert to useful traffic, new clients, or sales.

Worst of all, Google will punish you for such ad tactics. Your ads will cost more. Your account could even be shut down.

If Your Ad Gets Clicked On, It's Relevant

The higher your click-through rate (CTR), that is, the more folks who see your ad click on it, the less you will have to pay to be in the position you want. The lower your CTR, the more your ads will cost while your position of relevance plummets.

It's Darwin at work, a deliberate natural selection that weeds out bad advertisers and rewards good ones.

Remember: What's good for Google's customers is good for your business. When all the dust settles, what really matters is that your ads and your content are relevant to the keywords on which you bid.

THE KEY TO LOWER PRICES

There is an even more important secret to getting lower and lower prices, even while other businesses keep jumping into the game. *Your click-through rate is more important than how much you bid on the positioning.*

The click-through rate is the percentage of people searching who actually click on an ad. For example, if 100 people search, my ad shows up 100 times. If one person clicks through, I will have a 1% click-through rate.

If I'm paying $1 for Google position #2, the rest is just basic math. If your ad has a 2% click-through rate and good relevance, you may only have to pay $0.51 to jockey into position #2 and knock me down the list.

The moral of this story: If your ad is twice as relevant, you will pay 50% less.

The rules can be very simple, but the implications are huge. When you achieve high click-through rates, your new prospect contacts and sales go up, while ad prices go way, way down.

ONE WORD CAN MAKE A DIFFERENCE

You can often change the CTR of your ads by 50% when you change just one word. This is not unusual; it's not a fluke. ONE WORD can make the difference between being relevant on Google and being banned.

It's not about your main keyword searches anymore. It's about the niche-heavy work in your business. You don't realize it, but your competitors are getting 50% more phone calls because they are doing the right things, niching into their business and going after relevant ideal new customers.

Three Keys to the Google Kingdom

The key elements in your campaign's success are budget, keywords, and copy. How much can you pay overall and for each click? Which specific keywords do you want to target? And what should be included in the text of your ad?

You've got to get all these elements right to achieve the best results. Here are the ten steps for success:

1. Set your budget
2. Identify your keywords
3. Refine your keywords
4. Define your geography
5. Create effective ads
6. Place powerful headlines
7. Write persuasive text
8. Provide a call to action
9. Set up your account for best results
10. Track and monitor effectively

Follow the Rules

While you might think Google should be happy to take your money and not be bothered by the content of your ad, Google wants to make sure its customers are happy—because that's the difference between Google making money and Google making LOTS of money.

Your Google ads will be rated based on three things:

1. Click-through rate

2. Relevance of your keywords

3. Your ad copy and the content of your landing page

If your ad does not attract enough clicks, Google will assign you a low Quality Score. If your ad is not relevant to your chosen keywords, Google will assign you a low Quality Score. If your ad copy doesn't match the page you are directing people to, Google will assign you a low Quality Score.

The better your ad's Quality Score, the more likely you will pay less for your ads.

Need more help? Access free downloads (normally valued at $593) at www.CustomerAttractionSecrets.com or www. PatientAttractionSecrets.com for medical businesses.

How Paying for Likes Can Actually Help Your Business (and Other Shocking Insights)
by Kim Walsh-Phillips

I am very annoying to watch football with on TV.

Why?

I don't talk through the game, so that's not it. I don't ask what just happened in the last play, so that's not it either. And I do bring snacks to the party. In fact, I am a snack-toting champion.

The problem is that I can't stop myself from yelling at the TV during commercial breaks about the ridiculous amount of money wasted on branded campaigns with no calls to action or any level of measurement.

It was a few years into my marriage before my husband shared his concern for the level of anger I exude at the TV. (But seriously, did ANYONE test if Muppets driving around in your car would help sell one new vehicle? I wouldn't be surprised if the only one making money off that commercial was the ad agency that put it together.)

The same can be said of social media marketing. The fluff passed around is enough to spread on peanut butter sandwiches all across kindergartens from East to West Coast. Got a knife?

I don't care if you have one million fans. Did you get any sales from it?

What to Do Instead

We generally have one or more of the following four campaigns running for our clients. They are effective, ROI-focused, and produce more money than is being paid into them. Leverage these for your business to drive a high ROI.

Why Run a Likes Campaign

So first I say social media is all fluff and now I tell you to run a Likes Campaign?

I know. I know.

But here's the thing, Likes Campaigns can be very worthwhile if used correctly to attract qualified leads and grow your business.

Why run one?

Create social proof that others believe in your product or service. When restaurants start seating guests for the night, they seat them at tables in front of the window first because customers always help to attract new customers. The same is true of building social proof for your business. If you have 24 fans on your page and you profess to be popular and in demand, these messages are not congruent.

I am not an advocate for spending thousands of dollars on building ads, but I am a proponent for buying fans until you reach the 500 to 1,000 mark for a sense of legitimacy. In addition, if you use look-alike audiences, your ROI goes up with fans who are matched well to your perfect prospects.

This allows you to develop an inexpensive list of leads you can target on your next campaign. In all our Facebook Ads results, we see a trend that Facebook fans convert at a higher rate and lower cost-per-lead than other marketing channels. If you invest wisely in your Likes campaigns, you can develop an inexpensive lead funnel, especially if you also collect email addresses.

As you grow your fans, continue to target them in your opt-in and ad offers and track your cost-per-lead and cost-per-sale. The results will clearly show if this method is truly "like-able" because it's based on revenue, not fluff.

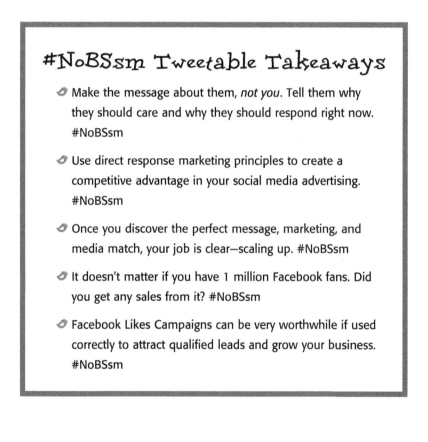

#NoBSsm Tweetable Takeaways

- Make the message about them, *not you*. Tell them why they should care and why they should respond right now. #NoBSsm

- Use direct response marketing principles to create a competitive advantage in your social media advertising. #NoBSsm

- Once you discover the perfect message, marketing, and media match, your job is clear—scaling up. #NoBSsm

- It doesn't matter if you have 1 million Facebook fans. Did you get any sales from it? #NoBSsm

- Facebook Likes Campaigns can be very worthwhile if used correctly to attract qualified leads and grow your business. #NoBSsm

CHAPTER 8

Everything Else

What About LinkedIn?

by Kim Walsh-Phillips

LinkedIn is the one network I am asked about most often. Some business professionals are more comfortable in that space because it appears to be, well, more professional. The problem is, LinkedIn's users are not nearly as conditioned to click on ads on LinkedIn, making mass marketing more difficult. But, all is not lost.

Yes, You Should Be on There

Yes, it is a powerful tool. Several of my firm's accounts came through my LinkedIn profile, and our clients receive messages on the network with valuable opportunities. But I have not found it to be effective beyond one-to-one sales and hence, not scalable.

Having done a lot of testing with its network ad options, we have yet to see a return anywhere near what we can get on Facebook regardless of the industry or sales funnel. That said, LinkedIn can be very effective for authority positioning and for making one-to-one sales, so I do recommend using LinkedIn's free tools.

Repeat after me, "Free qualified leads are good."

Do Not Use Your Selfie as Your Profile Picture

When I was on LinkedIn recently, I noticed a very disturbing trend—"selfies" being used as profile pictures. (In case you missed this pop culture term, a selfie is a photograph one takes of oneself.)

I understand it is a trend and I maybe should relax a bit, but frankly, I would have a hard time doing business with Mr. Off-Center-Looking-Up-At-An-Angle-Arm-Extended on a business networking platform. To me, when a selfie is used, it says two things: The person has no one on his team that could take a simple picture, and the person failed to recognize how home-grown pictures adversely affect their brand.

Old school or not, here's the thing, your brand stays with you no matter what else changes, so take it seriously. You may not think how you appear to others matters, but it does.

Proof That Your Personal Brand Matters

We have nine seconds to grab someone's attention and make a marketing impression, according to research by Sally Hogshead, author of the branding book *Fascinate* (Harper Business, 2010).

If you take into consideration how quickly people can scroll through their newsfeed, the time is cut in half. What do you want your picture to say about you? What do you want your prospects, clients/customers/patients, and future employees to think of when they see your photo?

Tips for a Good Profile Picture

If you want to step up your game, here are a few pointers for any social media profile photo:

1. Look straight at the camera.
2. Smile.
3. Hire a professional photographer if you can. If you can't do that (like only if you are stranded on an island by yourself,) use a camera remote. Here's one I like that lets you shoot video or take pictures as needed: Don't use the standard gray backdrop everyone else has. Do something to get your picture to stand out, such as using a photo from one of your news stories or a photo of you engaged in what you do for a living. Just remember the first two recommendations above.
4. I may get beat up for this one, but women, I recommend you get your hair and makeup done professionally. Most good salons have the ability to do camera-friendly work. This isn't about looking like someone else. This is about looking like the best you, and for photos, I leave that to the professionals.
5. Do not use a selfie as your LinkedIn profile picture. (See Figure 8.1 on page 118.)

Say "cheese" and get your brand working for you. Like my favorite line from Mad Men goes, "If you don't like what's being said, change the conversation."

FIGURE 8.1: Don't Be This Guy

Five Easy LinkedIn Tricks for Quick Sales

1. GET INTRODUCTIONS

To quickly build out your prospect list, utilize your network tree by leveraging LinkedIn Recommendations. These ensure your client or customer really knows the person you are asking for an introduction to. Here's how:

- Make a list of your top customers and/or clients
- Go to their LinkedIn profiles
- Check to see if they have any recommendations
- Make a list of those who recommended them to see if any of them would be worth having a sales conversation with
- Write an email to your customer and/or client asking for a simple introduction to this other person

Here's a sample:

Hi Tom,

I hope this email finds you well. I wanted to say thanks again for being such a great client. We enjoyed working with you on _____ (project) and were glad to see (successful outcome).

I was hoping you might be able to help me. I know how busy you are, so if you are too busy I certainly understand.

But I saw _____ (name) recommended you on your LinkedIn profile. Great recommendation by the way. I was wondering if you wouldn't mind doing an email intro? I am looking to increase my knowledge of this industry's needs and contacts and am just looking for a quick intro so I can connect.

If you are agreeable, here's email copy you can cut and paste for the email intro:

I wanted to offer a quick intro to our _____ (name of service and your title), (your full name). (Your first name) and her team have worked with us to (write what you have done for the client). (Your first name) asked me for an introduction to someone else in the (x industry) so I am connecting the two of you. She is researching our industry's needs and building out her network of contacts.

I encourage the two of you to set up a time to talk.

If not, no problem. Thank you again for your business and I look forward to working with you on (future project).

Best regards,

Your name

Of course, if you get the introduction, be sure to say thank you! And I don't just mean with an email. I love to give unique thank-you gifts that surprise and delight.

A few of my favorite sources are www.beau-coup.com, www.NeimanMarcus.com, and www.HenriBendel.com.

2. START A CONVERSATION

Scroll through your newsfeed for postings about job title changes, career moves, and work anniversaries. Post a positive comment publicly, and then dive into a private conversation using LinkedIn messaging. Ask additional questions about the change, what the person's role is, and what the plans are for the future. Start this first email just talking about them. As the person responds, work to identify opportunities where you might fulfill needs. Do not sell in LinkedIn, though. Instead, request to have a conversation offline and begin your sales dialogue there.

3. CONTACT PEOPLE YOU MAY KNOW

Scroll through the list of "People You May Know" suggested connections, and as you are adding to your network, jot down those you'd like to be in your sales pipeline. Each day, message five of these new contacts to thank them for their connection and ask about their position and role at their firm. As in number 2, do not sell on LinkedIn, but instead, request to have a conversation offline. LinkedIn's built-in CRM is a powerful tool for managing this process.

4. HAVE A POSTING FRENZY

Take advantage of LinkedIn's Long Form Posts to promote your authority to your entire network. (See Figure 8.2 on page 121.) Do this quickly, so you can focus on selling and not writing. Simply breathe life into old content. Start by writing an introduction to a

FIGURE 8.2: LinkedIn Long Form Post

blog post or article, and post the introduction as the Long Form Post.

I repost our blogs in the LinkedIn Long Form Post and include links in the article to opt-in to our mailing list. This has moved LinkedIn up into our top ten sources of mailing list opt-ins.

5. IF YOU WANT TO TRY ADVERTISING: SPONSOR AN UPDATE

Using "Sponsored Updates" from LinkedIn's advertising platform can get your messaging in front of key contacts quickly. These are run from your company page. You can focus your target market on geographic location, industry, title, and keywords, just to name a few. To see if this is worth ongoing investment for you, start small and analyze results before spending a lot.. With the analytics report, you will receive metrics for: Impressions, Clicks, Interactions, Followers Acquired, and Engagement.

Feel free to connect with me on LinkedIn and let me know what your best practices are: www.LinkedIn.com/KWalshPhillips.

Unnecessary Distractions

by Kim Walsh-Phillips

As a marketer, there is always a reason to be distracted. There is a new network, app, or program to try, strategy to implement, or campaign to copy. You could literally spend all your time flitting from program to program, dabbling instead of dominating. But you are doing yourself and those around you a disservice if you allow yourself to be distracted by unnecessary channels or opportunities.

To keep my focus in check, I have to constantly put blinders on. And, for good reason.

When the cold of winter breaks, my girls and I love to drive along the ocean road near my house, windows down, sunroof open. We sing loudly to whatever the Disney Radio station serves up. We can drive for a very long time before this gets old. Hair whipping, heads bobbing, and laughter ensuing, with each beat on the radio, all three of us, ranging from 2 years old to 40, smile ear to ear as my girls yell, "Louder, Mommy!"

Moments like this are my "why."

They are the reason each minute I spend working needs to be meaningful, efficient, and profitable. Because when I say yes to more work, I am saying no to another minute driving with the windows open. I cannot let the newest fad or shiny object distract me from my center. Instead, I zoom in on whatever will get me the highest return on my investment of money and time at ALL times.

We have yet to find another network that gives the same return as Facebook with any type of paid advertising. Go deep in that space before you spend time on any other distractions.

If you are comfortable with the return Facebook is giving you and you are utilizing your LinkedIn profile for maximum value, then I have a few recommended additional strategies for other networks.

Google+

This network has not taken off as media speculated it would. Google has stopped automatically giving every gmail user a Google+ account. And it would be easy to believe every other article declaring the network as dead. But there is something important to remember—Google loves data, because it can profit from it. Google+ provides them with a lot of user data. I would be surprised if the platform ever fully dissolves. Why does this matter for you? Google likes its own platform when it comes to search optimization. It ranks postings on Google+ fairly high in search results. As long as this platform exists, use it to simply repost your blog content and include links to sign up for your newsletter and lead magnet. It amounts to free traffic and authority building for you and your business.

Twitter

I have heard reports of businesses making a lot of money with their Twitter platform using advertising. I don't know any of them. Through testing we have done for my firm and clients, I have yet to see measurable profitable results from the platform.

I will give Twitter's sales team credit. It is persistent—by CALLING me a lot. If its ad platform really worked, wouldn't it be able to reach me in my Twitter Feed? At least once?

I have one use for Twitter that is very profitable, though. That is using it as a platform for building trust and authority in order to get media coverage and radio/podcast interviews.

Here's why. The larger and more engaged your network is, the higher your Klout score is, and the higher your Klout score is, the better chance you have getting booked as a guest on higher profile media outlets and podcasts. (The Klout Score is a number between 1 and 100 that represents your influence. The more influential you are, the higher your Klout Score. Find more about that at: https://klout.com/corp/score.)

This is because media wants to cover you if they believe you have a large platform to share your coverage.

Follow other industry leaders you find on Klout, and often they will follow you back and begin to share your content if it is valuable to them. Use Twitter to share your thought-leadership with posts to your blogs, articles, and images you have already created for Facebook and LinkedIn. There are a lot of platforms out there to automate this process as well and increase your follower count organically.

Instagram and Pinterest

Of the two photo sharing sites, Instagram is harder to monetize because it doesn't allow links in your photo posts except in the comments section. Pinterest does allow links in your posts as well as advertising to interests. There are Instagram and Pinterest experts out there, of which I am not one, so there are probably better people to listen to on this one. Because more networks would be a distraction for me, I simply repost my photos from Facebook quotes on these networks because it increases my Klout score.

YouTube

Although Facebook has surpassed YouTube in the number of video views annually, YouTube is still a strong source of traffic. Google owns YouTube, and Google gives its own content a higher weight in search. If you are engaged in this network, use it similar to a blog. Post consistently with your overall sales funnel in mind. Do not sell. Entice the viewer to take a next step that should be outside of YouTube. There are some video geniuses that are worth checking out if you want to expand your YouTube ROI. A few worth checking out are James Wedmore, Andy Jenkins, and Mike Stewart.

My best advice to you is to stay away from other networks until your core marketing channels are running at optimum speed. Anything else is a distraction from your why.

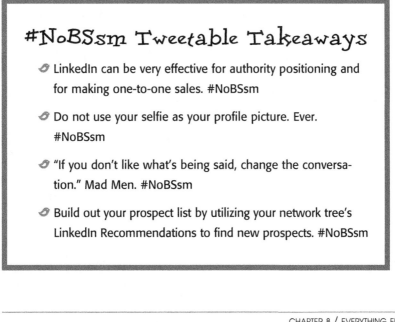

#NoBSsm Tweetable Takeaways

- 🐦 LinkedIn can be very effective for authority positioning and for making one-to-one sales. #NoBSsm

- 🐦 Do not use your selfie as your profile picture. Ever. #NoBSsm

- 🐦 "If you don't like what's being said, change the conversation." Mad Men. #NoBSsm

- 🐦 Build out your prospect list by utilizing your network tree's LinkedIn Recommendations to find new prospects. #NoBSsm

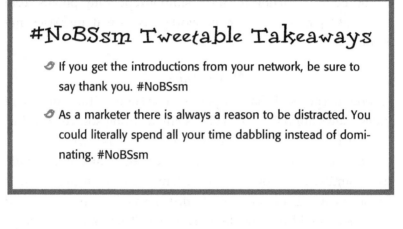

#NoBSsm Tweetable Takeaways

- If you get the introductions from your network, be sure to say thank you. #NoBSsm

- As a marketer there is always a reason to be distracted. You could literally spend all your time dabbling instead of dominating. #NoBSsm

CHAPTER 9

The Magical World of Email

The Monetizing Magic, Crafting Effective Emails

by Kim Walsh-Phillips

Once you get your prospects to opt-in to your list, what is the best thing to do with them?

Maybe you are old enough to remember when DOS email programs finally evolved into HTML and images and text could fill a page and be sent in a second to your entire list. That was a monumental change in the way we communicate, because suddenly you could share one message to thousands of people instantly without the need to purchase any media.

Businesses thought they hit the jackpot because they could market without spending money and without putting out much effort. They believed people would pay attention to those messages and respond to them. They believed that despite all of the other businesses using this same channel, with similar messages, theirs would stand out. And most still do believe this.

Here's how email marketing might be killing your business:

1. *Your best customers/prospects don't want email from you.* Did you ever check to see if your best customers like getting messages from you? Are you making the messages about you or them? Is there value in receiving this content?

2. *Your subject lines are all about you.* Do NOT use your email subject line to promote the latest and greatest product, event, or service you are offering. Use the subject line to entice the reader to open the message and read more.

3. *Your emails are not about your target market.* Your email recipients don't care about the "what." They only care about "why" it might help make their life better. Check your messages and make sure they are focused on the right audience.

4. *Email is all that you do.* When you don't use other market- ing channels, you lose credibility with your audience. Go beyond email with supporting marketing through print, new media, and targeted broadcast advertising and news- letters. (For more on newsletters, see Chapter 12.) The more channels you can hit geared toward the same target market, the more credible and effective you will be.

5. *There is no call to action in your email body.* People are too busy to figure out what you want from them. Tell them exactly what you want.

One of our clients, GKIC Insider's Circle, has a large (and very responsive) list. I interviewed its Director of Marketing Mike Stodola about its strategies and some of the biggest mistakes businesses can make when it comes to email marketing.

Mike Stodola has been in the direct response marketing world since graduating from college and immediately becoming an entrepreneur. Using Dan Kennedy and GKIC as a guide, he grew his real estate business so fast that at the age of 24 he opened his own brokerage firm, and in less than 18 months the marketing systems he put in place kept over 30 real estate agents busy on appointments.

He's worked with a wide variety of brick-and-mortar entrepreneurs and sales professionals to grow their businesses through effective automated direct response marketing. These have included everything from pizza shops to personal training, from insurance agents to medical sales reps. Mike never thought he'd work for anyone, but when GKIC moved to Chicago, his passion for what its systems had done for him and others swayed him, and he's been a key member of the marketing team ever since.

Through various marketing strategies, Mike's increased online promotions by over 112% and has been instrumental in implementing a variety of successful online and offline marketing campaigns that generated over $100,000 in revenue in just a few days. Mike will show you keys to implementing and automating marketing systems in your business so you can be more profitable and spend your time on high dollar-per-hour activities.

Kim: What are some of the mistakes people make when it comes to email marketing?

Mike: There's a lot of mistakes, but the biggest one is writing email copy that reads like a broadcast. Don't forget the recipient is not sitting in an audience in front of the computer. There's only one person who is actually reading it. You want to write every one of your emails like it's a personal communication, one on one. That's who and what it is to the recipient. Whether you are sending 10 or 10,000 emails, you need to engage the single reader who's looking at it.

Kim: Do you have any tips on how people can get in the right mind set to just speak directly to one person?

Mike: A lot of times people make it too corporate. You want to make it personal. I would literally write out an email to one person, such as: "Hey, Kim. I am doing this cool thing on Thursday. Love for you to check it out." Something like that instead of getting all corporate, being very formal, and doing a bunch of formatting.

If you wouldn't normally talk to the people you are interacting with in a formal, stylized manner, then don't do that via email either. Really write an email to a single person. Then, just modify it slightly to the whole group.

The second mistake people make is writing boring emails. That's the biggest sin in all of marketing. If you are talking about you, you, you, or your program, your webinar, your product, whatever it is you have—that's a huge mistake. You need to focus entirely on the reader of the email.

Kim: What are some tips and tactics you use when writing a subject line?

Mike: The whole point of the subject line is to get your subscriber to open the email. It's got to be engaging. It has to be exciting. It has to arouse curiosity. As long as it does one of those, the subject line has done its job.

Wait to create it until after you've actually written the email. Once you've crafted a personal story, talked about the outcomes, and outlined what the person reading the email is going to get, you are going to find a good subject line inside of what you have already written. Just follow the rules: Arouse curiosity, excitement, or engagement.

It used to be that people would put the RE: in the subject line, like they were responding to an email or a forward. Avoid this! People are used to that and right now a lot of email systems are flagging that as spam. We don't want to trick people—ever. Good marketing doesn't need to use a Black Hat strategy.

What you can do, though, is tell people what they are going to get. Put it in brackets in the subject line: [video] or [pictures]. Help them see it will be something more than text inside. Or you can talk about a big takeaway they're going to get—a FREE webinar or access to a product you want them to engage.

If you're a restaurant owner, your subject line could read, "How to get the perfect Filet Mignon [video]," so people will open it. Even better, you can give a time frame or a price to add specificity.

All the rules that apply to headlines apply to email subject lines because that's really all they are.

Kim: When your email's goal is for readers to take some type of action, what's your process for writing that email?

Mike: Same as the headline, you have to be entertaining, engaging, or invite curiosity. Mix it up. If you have a lot of casting, you are going to have three different emails. One could be a personal story so it's engaging. Tell a little bit about the background and the struggle and how you overcame it. Really get personal with this. And you might have another that speaks to the results of others with your product or service, and another one that offers a tip or strategy.

One thing we did recently at GKIC—with one of our highest open and click-through rates ever—was an email with a video link. It showed how someone got over 100,000 people to respond to one of their offers in 24 hours. It was an incredible success story. We really just shared that excitement and said, "Hey, if you want to know how to do this, you have to click here."

The engaging one is where you step into the shoes of your ideal customer, client, or patient and figure out what they really want. What's the big takeaway? Too often we focus on what we're selling in our email—like a steak and vegetable dinner—when what the prospects might really be looking for is a romantic evening with their spouse.

That's what you should be selling. They want to get the feeling back, the date night feeling. If you can figure out what your ideal client really wants, you are going to get a much higher response and engagement level in your emails.

Kim: Can you talk more about how that 100K in 24 hours email was structured?

Mike: This was an email we sent out for one of our referral partners (an affiliate, if people are familiar with that term). During an affiliate launch, the main partner typically drafts an email all the referral partners can forward to their lists. There could be ten other people sending out that exact email, so at GKIC we wanted to make ours different.

Since the video was written in the affiliate's voice, we took the results they had in the first 24 hours and told people, "Don't watch the video for the actual content, but watch what they're doing from a marketing perspective because they have gotten 100,000 leads in 24 hours."

It was GKIC contrarian. Our pitch conveyed *process,* not *content.*

And it got one of our highest open rates ever.

Kim: So you made them feel like they were going to see something others wouldn't have access to?

Mike: Yes, and to increase click-throughs we employed another strategy as well. Right now, the ability to embed video in email is not widely available. We took a screen shot from the video and then put a little play button on top of that (using Snip It, a free tool from Windows). Of course when readers click on that image, they think they are clicking play, but it really just takes them to the page with the video.

Images (and images with play buttons) always have higher click-through rates.

Kim: Can you just share a few tips to increase email deliverability?

Mike: If your email provider sends you 99% junk mail, you're probably going to switch, so providers have implemented things to improve the user experience. Promotions and social folders are one example. But people check their social and promotions much less regularly than their primary folder, so we are always fighting to stay in people's primary folders.

In order to accomplish that, you need to get people opening and engaging with your emails. One of the things email providers look at is your click-through rate. If you have a link, and a lot of people are clicking through, it says, "Hey, maybe this isn't spam because we see X percent of people and X percent of people are taking action with this."

Having pictures and links to other pages definitely helps this.

Secondly, email providers can see how long viewers stay on the click-through page. You want to make sure you are taking readers to something relevant, something they like. You want to point them to good content. Our very best emails, with our highest level of engagement, point to our blog. Some 90% of the time, it's written content, and it takes anywhere from three to eight minutes to read the entire post.

One other thing you can do to help yourself is called list hygiene. This is not just for the big guys, but even the little folks out there. If you see someone's not opening your emails again and again and again, the email provider sees that as well. The providers are going to start saying, "People aren't interested in this." Before that happens, every 30 to 90 days, you should remove unresponsive people from your email list. Don't send emails they won't open anyway. It affects the deliverability of your message to people who really do want it.

If you have good marketing, you shouldn't be afraid of losing people. If they are not opening your emails, they are probably not your right target anyway, at least not through that specific media channel.

Kim: So you recommend purging people who haven't opened up an email for a certain period of time so your open rate goes up?

Mike: Yes. You can probably double your open rates just by removing people who haven't opened for 90 days. That's huge to the email providers. When they see a much higher open rate, it keeps you in good standing. All the big ones out there are doing this. If you are not performing list hygiene and really keeping on top of your open rate, it's something to start paying attention to.

Kim: Do you have any P.S. strategies? How do you use the P.S. in your emails and your marketing?

Mike: There are three different ways we use a P.S.

The first is for email linking to a content strategy (like a blog). We use a P.S. to introduce a secondary offer. For instance, if our blog is about the ten best headline formulas, we give a link to click over to the blog. Because we have a lot going on or in case the reader doesn't need the headline formulas, in the P.S. we will provide a different offer. We might tell them about an upcoming webinar or a promotion. It could be a product, seminar, or an event we can tie in. Or it could just be, "In case you forgot, we have our Super Conference coming up at the end of April. Click here now for all the details." A lot of people scroll down to the P.S. even if they don't read the emails.

The second way we use the P.S. is a teaching process. Tell them what you're going to tell them. Tell them, and then tell them what you told them. If our email went through all the details on a specific product, the P.S. is just going to be a quick two to three sentences recap of the big transformation people will get when they click to the sales page and purchase.

The final way we use the P.S. is an engagement strategy where we introduce a new strategy or a new bonus or a new topic in the email. It's a teaser for the future. This works the best in a lot of our follow-up systems. If you come to GKIC and download a report, we will follow up with you for three to five days, and will use the P.S. to introduce what tomorrow's email is going to be about. It might even give you a free report or a useful tool. We want to start training people to read all the way down to the bottom of our emails. That's why we use this primarily in our initial contacts. We want to provide something valuable in each email as well as create a teaser. If folks read our emails the first three to five days in a row, it builds a habit. We provide value, and our readers stay engaged.

Kim: You walk them through the path you want them to take.

Mike: Absolutely. Because most people don't use a P.S. in marketing, even though these get a very high click-through rate—second only to the very first hyperlink in the body copy of the email. Take advantage of any of these three P.S. strategies, and watch your email engagement climb.

For more email strategies, visit http://tinyurl.com/NoBSsm EmailSecrets.

What Disney VIP Treatment Can Teach You About Email Marketing

by Dan Kennedy

As a fan of Disney, I think one of the greatest services it offers is a VIP guided tour.

This allows you to do things such as skip to the front of the line, get led in through secret back doors, and basically do more in one day (and in great style) than most may ever imagine.

It's a premium service, so as you can imagine, there are people who say the price is exorbitant. These are the same people who complain about having to wait in long lines at Disney and only having time to go on four attractions during the entire day.

Maybe if they considered that you can, for example, go on 12 attractions in the time it takes others to go on one attraction, they would see the value. Maybe they'd realize in the end with a guide you can do in one day what it takes the average person multiple days, even a week, to do.

I see this in business all the time. People look for the easiest, fastest, or cheapest route without considering the whole picture.

Email marketing is a prime example.

Many businesses think, because it's so easy to use, they don't need to put as much thought, time, or planning into it as they do with direct-mail campaigns.

Then these same people complain about their poor open rates, declining click-throughs, and deflated results.

If you want better results, you have to consider the WHOLE picture. And you have to invest in making your emails better.

For instance, one key disadvantage of email is that there are a lot more emails flooding your customers' inboxes every day, many more than there are pieces of mail being delivered to their regular mailbox.

That means a lot more competition for eyeballs.

So you don't want to be sloppy about what you are sending.

Rather than firing off an email in ten minutes and blasting it out to your entire list without much thought or consideration, take the time to establish a plan with response or conversion goals so you know exactly what you want your audience to do before you ever write your email.

And make sure you've included the core elements needed in each email you send.

Consistency is also a factor. While you can do a campaign in the mail at random times, once you start sending emails, you should deliver them consistently week in, week out without exception.

If you send email in a hit or miss, random fashion, and go missing from their inbox, people will forget about you in a heartbeat—even if you return to a regular, predictable schedule at a later date.

This doesn't mean you can't send emails at other times apart from your schedule. If you take care of the readers on your email list by sending valuable, relevant emails at regular intervals, they will pay attention at other times too.

There are many strategies you can combine with your email marketing to improve your results and increase your profits too—in many cases, well beyond the standard ROI you see quoted in studies.

In fact, rarely do I consult with a client where there aren't untapped opportunities within its email strategy, including ways to combine email with other media to get higher response.

Strategies to use with its opt-ins can separate the looky-loos from hyperactive buyers, increase profits, improve click-throughs, or even create more loyal customers, clients, or patients.

Split-test your subject lines, layout, email length, time sent, call to action, and so on, and then examine your results to see what is working and what isn't.

There is no free pass to the front of the line. If you want your emails to be the first thing your customers want to open, you have to invest time and resources in making them worthy.

Effective Emails: How Obama Did It

by Kim Walsh-Phillips

No, this isn't a political chapter. I will leave that up to Dan.

Regardless of how you feel about voter results, businesses can learn a lot from what the Obama team did with emails and how they did it.

An article released by *Bloomburg Business Week*, "The Science Behind Those Obama Campaign E-Mails," gives an insider guide to the tactics and outcomes of the Obama fundraising campaign. While most of the attention during the campaign was on outside groups raising money, this email machine outperformed any PAC 10:1.

Here's what Obama's people did and how you can learn from it:

- They split-tested EVERYTHING, sometimes testing more than 18 variations on small batches before sending out the winning message to their list of millions.

  Business Lesson: Never assume you know best. Everything should be tested in small batches before the big launch.

- The more personal the subject line seemed, the better it did. The email that consistently did well for them had a simple subject line of "hey."

  Business Lesson: Do not assume you know what will work best in a subject line. Sometimes "spammy" sounding emails do better than all others. (That is why spammers use them, after all.)

- The best open-rate email was sent out with the subject line of "I'm Sorry." It outperformed any message before it in the past 11 YEARS by 25%.

  The emails came directly in the President's name, giving them a sense of authority and importance.

  Business Lesson: Determine who your target market trusts the most and utilize that voice in your messaging. Do not have your emails come from the organization, but from a person. This doesn't mean you have to give your personal email out. Use another address, but have your name on the display line.

- Sending out more messages did not have negative consequences. The reverse was actually true. Their unsubscribes were few, and their dollars raised increased.

  Business Lesson: As marketers, we worry about sending out too many messages and tend to back away when one or two complain. The research of the Obama team showed that overall, sending more messages did not have a negative consequence. In fact, they got better results. Most likely, your marketing needs to be persistent beyond your comfort level to achieve the best results. Don't believe it? Test it.

While most companies want their marketing to be a certain traditional way of communicating with lackluster words paired with glossy photos, the Obama fundraising machine once again showed that you cannot assume what strategy will work. Testing, personalization, differentiation, and persistence are key.

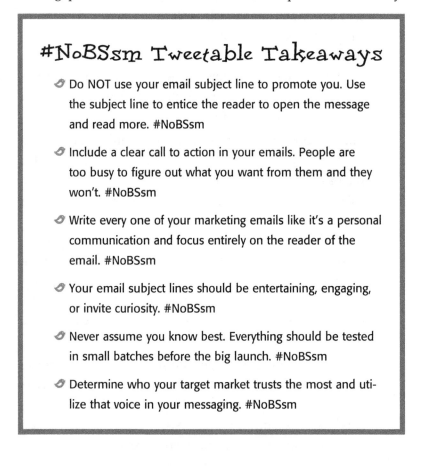

#NoBSsm Tweetable Takeaways

🖊 Do NOT use your email subject line to promote you. Use the subject line to entice the reader to open the message and read more. #NoBSsm

🖊 Include a clear call to action in your emails. People are too busy to figure out what you want from them and they won't. #NoBSsm

🖊 Write every one of your marketing emails like it's a personal communication and focus entirely on the reader of the email. #NoBSsm

🖊 Your email subject lines should be entertaining, engaging, or invite curiosity. #NoBSsm

🖊 Never assume you know best. Everything should be tested in small batches before the big launch. #NoBSsm

🖊 Determine who your target market trusts the most and utilize that voice in your messaging. #NoBSsm

CHAPTER 10

Make It Your Nature
to Nurture

How to Nurture a Prospect Through Facebook Even If They Never Opt-In to Your Email List

by Kim Walsh-Phillips

If you are driving straight to the sale with cold leads, then you are leaving a lot of money on the table.

Why? Because going straight to the sale means you will only close people who are ready to buy right now and from you.

People are made up of two types, Divers and Skimmers (courtesy of Andy Jenkins). Divers jump right in when they see something they like. Skimmers need to test the water first with their pinky toe, talk to their friends about what the temperature is like, and slowly enter the pool. Unfortunately, only 15% of buyers are Divers.

By structuring your marketing and sales funnel as **Magnet → Opt-in → Monetize** (MOM), you are able to bring in qualified prospects at each phase of decision making and nurture them into a yes. This brings you the greatest chance of closing the deal when the sales portion of the message occurs.

The problem becomes a matter of what you do if your prospects won't opt-in. For whatever reason, they won't give you their email address. It might seem impossible to nurture them into a sale. Those leads are lost forever, or at least that used to be the case.

Using Website Retargeting, you can nurture a prospect from a cold lead to a sale without ever sending him or her an email. Facebook's Website Custom Audiences allows you reach out to people who otherwise would be lost.

Facebook's Website Custom Audiences gives advertisers the opportunity to create Facebook ads that reach website visitors— visitors to any page or to a specific page. You can do some pretty ninja-like things with this feature: customize sales messages, reinforce a purchase, or nurture a prospect to a sale without an email address.

You Can Still Get The MOM Formula Without An Opt-in.

I'm not suggesting you should ignore list building. But you also shouldn't ignore those who aren't yet comfortable sharing personal contact information.

With Website Custom Audiences, you can target ads at people based on how far along they've moved in the funnel. How? Because they are getting cookied (a short line of text that a website puts on your computer's hard drive when you access that website) and Facebook is tracking it. (I know, a bit creepy as consumers, but fantastic for us marketers.)

1. Develop Dual Messaging

Let's use an example of my Six Social Media Secrets free report offer. (See Figure 10.1 on page 143.)

FIGURE 10.1: Six Social Media Secrets Free Report Offer

Once people opt-in to your list, you can begin to show them valuable content in their newsfeed in order to nurture them before making the sale. Or you can offer a special offer, product program, or service right after they opt-in, sending the message via email and in their newsfeed.

With messaging in more than one channel, you increase the depth of your targeting and give a greater likelihood of response.

Think of this as your sales funnel. Warm them up, so that over time they build trust in you and are more likely to purchase from you. And it can be kept very simple.

1. Create an ad driving people to your free report.
2. Create an ad targeting those who visited the landing page but didn't opt-in.
3. Create an ad targeting those who do opt-in.

The second ad is targeted only at those who visited that landing page today and didn't convert. The messaging in that second ad understands that the targeted users know what the free report is, but may need further convincing. So prompt them to ask any questions they may have about the report in the comments.

In testing for the third, when we lead with one or two valuable tips before asking for the sale, we convert more overall sales at a higher profit. Of course, you should do your own testing and see what works best for your market.

2. Create a Website Custom Audience for Each Page

For the above example to work, you need to create a Website Custom Audience (WCA) for each page of your sequence.

In this example, I target anyone who went to my free report, but didn't see the thank-you page for opting in, meaning they didn't provide their email address. (See Figure 10.2 on page 145.)

Duration is up to you. Clearly, the shorter the duration the greater the relevance. But, of course, the shorter the duration, the smaller the audience (and the smaller the budget you can assign).

Create a WCA for each landing page of your sequence. This way, you can create Ad #2 to reach anyone who saw Landing Page #1, for example; and then Ad #3 to reach anyone who saw Landing Page #2.

But you can also use this method to reach people who have seen specific pages of your website. If you are a home remodeler, you could send a gift certificate (others may call this a coupon) to those who visit your gallery page of Before-and-Afters. Or if you sell products, take a page from Amazon's playbook and send follow-up messages with the product they left behind.

If you are a service-based business, try sending a free white paper offer to someone who visited your "About Us" or "Services" page. Utilize your Facebook newsfeed as an extension of your sales funnel.

FIGURE 10.2: Facebook Custom Audience to Target People Who Landed on the Free Report Page but Did Not Opt-In

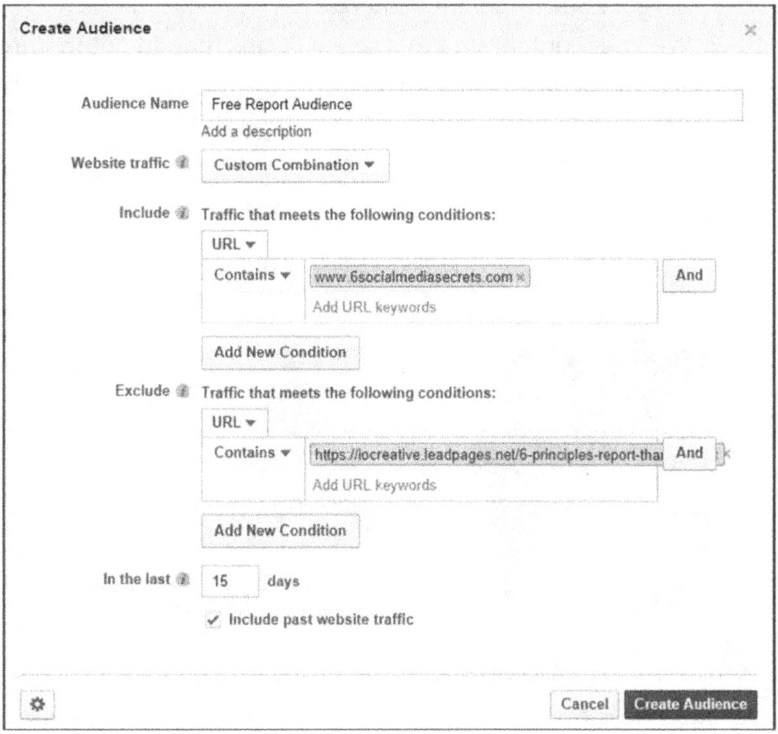

Here is an example:

1. Lead Magnet: Target all website visitors.
2. Landing Page #2: Target visitors to Lead Magnet.
3. Landing Page #3: Target visitors to Landing Page #2.
4. Landing Page #4: Sell to visitors to Landing Page #3.

3. Nurture Before Asking for the Opt-In

With increased mistrust of online brands, Facebook's Relevancy ranking affects your ad cost and reach distribution. We have been experimenting with Facebook's ad retargeting to offer content before asking for the opt-in or sale.

The results have been pretty spectacular.

Here's our campaign:

1. Target Look-Alike plus interest.
2. We offer content first in a series of tips that do not require an opt-in. (See Figure 10.3.)

FIGURE 10.3: Facebook Ad Without Required Opt-In

Tip #1 tells them the reward they will get when they click on the ad as well as a sneak peak into the first tip.

As in Figure 10.4 on page 147, tip #2 congratulates them for opening tip #1, and tells them why to click again. This same

FIGURE 10.4: Facebook Ad for Tip #2

strategy repeats for the next two tips. (See Figures 10.5 and 10.6 on page 148.)

The final in the series gives them a bonus free report to gain their opt-in. (See Figure 10.7 on page 149.) Once they opt-in, they are invited to sign up for an upcoming webinar. This is the monetization step.

Start with value, and walk your prospects to the sale. M + O + M. After all, MOM does know best.

FIGURE 10.5: Facebook Ad for Tip #3

FIGURE 10.6: Facebook Ad for Tip #4

FIGURE 10.7: Facebook Ad Congratulates and Rewards Those Who Clicked on All Four Tips

Nurture Leads Into Sales: The Engagement

by Kim Walsh-Phillips

After a first date, 99.99% of couples are not ready to get married.

And I am not sure I could be friends with the other .01%.

Most sane people need to date for a while to build trust, develop a strong connection, and make sure the other isn't a complete psychopath. (The third one is a fairly accurate description of a lot of the people I dated while living in South Florida.)

The same goes with nurturing your relationship with new leads from Facebook. They just met you, and the majority of them will not be ready to make a purchase right away. But they are your treasure chest for profit. The unconverted leads already identified themselves as interested in what you have to offer. They are no longer cold leads as they already received at least one thing of value from you.

Of course you have the option of passively sitting and waiting for them to convert into a sale. It's a bad option, but that is how a lot of businesses operate. They focus on lead generation only and don't give any attention to turning those valuable warm leads into a sale.

Most businesses aren't like Cynthia Samuels of Inspired Business Services offering high quality content each week via a free ezine once people sign up for her list.

Inspired Business Services' mission is to unlock the potential of every individual and company by providing them with the business tools needed to thrive. They provide clients with the resources and support needed to market and grow the business of their dreams. Inspired Business Services also provides the critical information needed to attract, hire, assess, develop, and retain top talent as clients' businesses grow.

Or like Livewire Digital, sending an industry trends and technology report to their list each week.

Livewire's mission is to enhance your business's revenue and reduce costs by providing your current and future customers (as well as employees) with self-service information and documents through secure, easy-to-use, multichannel delivery systems, including kiosks, websites, digital signage, and mobile applications.

Engage Effectively

Because Elite Digital Group and I are known for being direct response social media marketers, we often have prospects who are also direct response marketers. We love working with those who already understand marketing to sell, instead of spending money on branding or awareness-only campaigns.

Leave that to the big advertising agencies or the graphic designers-turned-marketers. They have plenty of ways to waste their clients' money.

There is occasionally a conflict with our clients and prospects though. We can sometimes find ourselves in a battle to explain that you can't just sell on social media. You have to take time to engage as well.

If you sell only, your costs will be higher for each click and your sales will suffer if they come at all. Sell only and you won't be successful.

Engagement in-network carries multiple benefits.

BUILD TRUST WITH YOUR FOLLOWERS THROUGH CONNECTIONS AND CELEBRITY POSITIONING

Social media is similar to dating. To develop lifelong customer relationships, you need to build trust over time. Offering engaging and valuable content is an opportunity to demonstrate that you are THE expert in your industry.

GROW YOUR REFERRALS

When people interact with you, their social networks see it. This is one of the most powerful things about direct response social media networking as opposed to any other type of marketing. Referrals are built into the platform. Businesses are smart to consistently pay attention to this fact and utilize it to its fullest ability.

CONDITION THEM TO RESPOND

If you have an engaged audience with people paying attention to what you say and interacting with you, then they are ready to buy as soon as you are ready to ask them for the sale. The more your networks are engaged, the more likely they will respond to your calls to action to purchase later on. Lose them with irrelevant content or a too heavy sales pitch too soon and you can lose them forever.

INCREASE YOUR FREE REACH

When it comes to Facebook, the more comments, likes, and shares you get, the higher your engagement level is and the more Facebook will show your posts to your network for free. If you can keep that engagement level up when you aren't promoting anything, when it comes time to promote, you will have more reach into the newsfeeds of your target audience.

Strategies to Create Engagement

In *Jab, Jab, Jab, Right Hook: How to Tell Your Story in a Noisy Social World*, Gary Vaynerchuk says, "It's hard for a business to strike the right balance among competing priorities of sales and engagement. Success comes with engagement first and sales second."

(I didn't agree with all of what was in Gary's book and thought some sections contradicted others, but I do agree with the book's main premise. There were enough clever marketing strategies to make it worth the read.

Start with value and only then ask for the sale.)

CREATE ORIGINAL VISUAL CONTENT

Social media is a visual, quick-paced medium that requires you not only compete with other businesses, but also with content being produced by your target market's friends and family, all of which is being shown on the same information feed.

To get the attention from your prospect away from "What Aunt Mary is making for dinner tonight," create original free content that invites the reader to share.

This is your opportunity to establish yourself as the thought leader and THE expert in your industry, so create visuals out of your quotes and blog posts. I recommend taking time to pull together 90 quotes and designing them internally or outsourcing them to freelancers. You will then have three months of visuals you can continue to rotate on your newsfeed.

I provide social media support to my church as part of my mission work. While listening to one of my favorite sermons right from my phone (using the mobile app Word Swag), this post was created (see Figure 10.8):

FIGURE 10.8: Tower Hill Church Ad Created Using Word Swag

Quotes for The Fertility Center offer encouragement to those who may be struggling with fertility issues. (See Figure 10.9.)

FIGURE 10.9: The Fertility Center Ad Created Using Word Swag

That's 302 people reached for free on a page that only has 398 total fans for Tower Hill Church and 535 people reached for

a page that only has 712 fans of The Fertility Center. Ignore what you are hearing. Organic reach is NOT dead.

We also pull quotes from my blogs and create multiple images, putting them on rotation. Here's an example (see Figure 10.10):

FIGURE 10.10: Blog Quote Used as Featured Ad

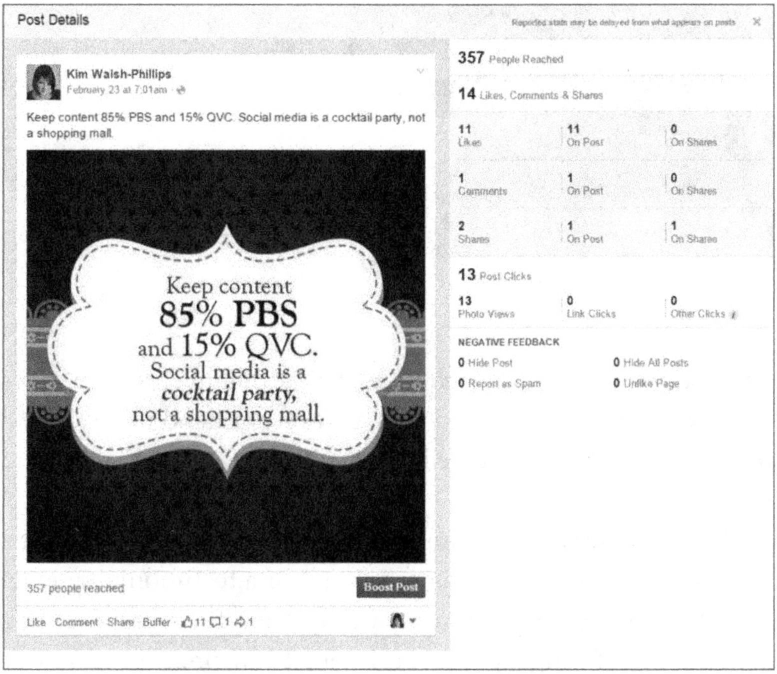

See Figure 10.11 on page 156 for one from a GKIC Leader.

FEATURE YOUR CLIENTS, CUSTOMERS, OR PATIENTS IN A Q AND A

Your audience is interested in the people who choose to do business you. It's your "Who Says So Besides You."

Feature them, their stories, likes, habits, and hobbies along with photos and a few quirky facts to give your audience engaging content while building trust with your prospects,

FIGURE 10.11: GKIC Leader Quote Used as Featured Ad

because they see other people just like them. This also gives your customers a reason to give you recommendations. When they are featured, they will share it with their friends and family.

The customer feature also works well in heavily regulated industries because you are not asking for a testimonial or even to talk about what your company did for the prospect. You are simply offering up human interest information from one person who chose to do business with you. (See Figure 10.12 on page 157.)

Build the customer Q and A in a system for ease of use and systemization. If you have an automated marketing program in place, like Infusionsoft, then create a series of questions that are sent automatically when customers gets to a certain point in their customer life cycle with you. Even if only a small percentage responds, you can expect to have rotating posts throughout the year.

FIGURE 10.12: GKIC Insider's Circle Featured Member Charlie McDermott

ASK QUESTIONS

The simple act of posing a question on social media is the quickest and simplest way to signal that you're looking for input. Being willing to ask for feedback and listen to what is and isn't working not only helps your business grow, it also builds loyalty.

Oreo cookies, at over 40 million engaged fans, is very successful at this. Nabisco infamously ran the cookie or crème campaign—getting over 1 million people to answer on the Oreo Facebook page. It was a campaign to engage millennials and obtain contact information for its customers.

USE FILL-IN-THE-BLANK POSTS

Fill-in-the-blank posts are a go-to way to increase engagement. An example from our client is:

Fill in the blank: I am a ____ woman. (See Figure 10.13 on page 158.)

FIGURE 10.13: Fill-in-the-Blank Posts Inspire Increased Engagement

GET PERSONAL

Occasionally share something about your life that is more personal in nature. It could be a picture of your pet, you and your family on a great vacation, or your staff gathering for a brainstorming meeting where you include shots of your white board after you've solved all the problems of the world. When you share some of your authenticity online, generally your fans respond well to it. Here are a couple of examples (see Figures 10.14 and 10.15 on page 159).

FIGURE 10.14: Share Some Personal Posts to Build Authenticity

FIGURE 10.15: Fans Respond Well to Personal Posts

Examples of posts that are "behind the scenes" and help build trust with an audience.

WRITE A PHOTO CAPTION

Post a funny or unique photo of your company or your products at work or another photo you find online and ask people to make up their own caption. These posts can be smaller giveaways where the winners get coupons or other prizes. It's a tried-and-true way to keep your visitors entertained.

We recently did this for Ron LeGrand, and the results were phenomenal.

From my Account Manager leading this project at the time, Mary Lorson:

When our client shared a quirky photo of himself looking at a horse, we saw an opportunity. We posted the photo on Facebook, and took a lighthearted approach with this post: "Okay everyone, this photo is BEGGING for a good caption. We'd love to hear your ideas!" (See Figure 10.16.)

FIGURE 10.16: Ron LeGrand Photo Posted with Request for Caption to Inspire Engagement

We posted our own comments to keep the mood light, and provided replies or "Likes" for each suggestion to keep engagement high. After the first few days we "spontaneously" suggested that since suggestions were so good, we should hold a contest. Two days later, we announced the winning caption would win a customized T-shirt, and created a link to keep the contest legal. In the next few weeks, we created only

two additional newsfeed posts, with links back to the photo, reminding people of the contest. Over the 20 days the contest ran, we received more than 70 entries and 24 Likes, all without any media spend. (See Figure 10.17.)

FIGURE 10.17: Overwhelming Engagement to Ron LeGrand's Photo Caption Contest

FIGURE 10.17: Overwhelming Engagement to Ron LeGrand's
Photo Caption Contest, continued

FIGURE 10.17: Overwhelming Engagement to Ron LeGrand's
Photo Caption Contest, continued

FIGURE 10.17: Overwhelming Engagement to Ron LeGrand's Photo Caption Contest, continued

FIGURE 10.17: Overwhelming Engagement to Ron LeGrand's Photo Caption Contest, continued

> **Stephanie Iannotti** When Ron LeGrand talks everyone listens....even the horses!
> October 12, 2014 at 5:35pm · Unlike · 🖒2

> **Donnie Strode** "Excuse me, could you tell me where the 'PRETTY HORSE' Seminar is?
> October 12, 2014 at 6:51pm · Unlike · 🖒5

> **Rick Resch** Now that is some real horse apples. I mean real estate!
> October 14, 2014 at 12:37am · Unlike · 🖒2

> **Rick Resch** Quit your smiling, did you do that or did I do it, Mr. Ed?
> October 14, 2014 at 12:42am · Unlike · 🖒1

> **Dana Schmidt** "Its OK! It was just a nightmare...I DID NOT personally guarantee the ranch. You do know who I am, correct??...RON LEGRAND!"
> October 15, 2014 at 10:48am · Unlike · 🖒1

> **Dana Schmidt** "But RON..You said we would be here forever!" "Do you know how much that NON refundable LEASE OPTION FEE is??"
> October 15, 2014 at 11:09am · Unlike · 🖒1

> **Ron LeGrand** ⊕ Go Dana! Judging this contest is going to be TOUGH.
> Commented on by Mary Larson Vergenes [?] · October 16, 2014 at 7:50am · Like · 🖒1

> **Roberta E. Eastman** Do I have a horse. I mean house for you!
> October 16, 2014 at 9:15am · Unlike · 🖒2

> **Dana Schmidt** "Relax! I was just horsing around...NO-ONE Lease-optioned the ranch..."
> October 16, 2014 at 10:17am · Unlike · 🖒3

> **Francisco Mancera** "yes, you remind me the one that i know_____."
> October 17, 2014 at 4:58pm · Unlike · 🖒1

> ⋯

> **Frontier Acquisitions** "Don't worry Ron, I have a VA to take care of that "Minutia!"
> October 17, 2014 at 7:23pm · Unlike · 🖒2

> **Rachelbuyshouses** Ron's systems work in a both stable and unstable market. His students have unbridled enthusiasm and biting at the bit to make offers. Old school investors will change their tack when they see Ron's strategies. With a hot-to-trot mentor who will ride y... See More
> October 20, 2014 at 8:41pm · Edited · Unlike · 🖒3

> **Seceder.com** Horsie: "What did you just ask me?"
> Ronnie: "If you'd mind if we nickname your left backside Hillary, and your right one Clinton."
> Horsie: "Would I get a Lewinsky out of the deal?"... See More
> October 18, 2014 at 12:39am · Unlike · 🖒2

> **Joe Trometer** "Horse Sense to Profits", "Get on Your Horse and Run With It", "Western Style Real Real Estate Winners Circle".
> Our Horses have a huge place in our American heritage...... See More
> October 18, 2014 at 4:30am · Unlike · 🖒3

> **Don Shade** Well at least they got the right ends of the subjexts
> October 18, 2014 at 10:13am · Unlike · 🖒1

FIGURE 10.17: Overwhelming Engagement to Ron LeGrand's
Photo Caption Contest, continued

FIGURE 10.17: Overwhelming Engagement to Ron LeGrand's
Photo Caption Contest, continued

LINK YOUR BLOG

Social media should be your most important tool for cross-
promotion on the internet.

A great place to start when creating content is to write a
list of the Top 25 Questions you get from prospects. Record

FIGURE 10.18: Ron LeGrand Viral Post Example

yourself answering these questions and send the recording to a transcription service. You will then have 25 weeks' worth of blogs.

If you have the budget, I recommend paying to promote your posts so more people are exposed to your value-rich content. This will serve as a cornerstone to building your network and establishing yourself as the number-one authority and expert in your niche.

FIGURE 10.18: Ron LeGrand Viral Post Example, continued

FIGURE 10.19: Blog Promotion

I promote my blog every week on Facebook to my Facebook fans. This has doubled our overall website traffic each month. (See Figure 10.19.)

SHARE AN INDUSTRY ARTICLE

You should always make building credibility a priority, especially with social media. Showing that you're on top of industry news solidifies your place in that industry. It makes your company feel more legitimate and more knowledgeable. (See Figure 10.20 on page 171).

However, don't simply post a link to the article. Lazy marketers do this, and it doesn't work. If this is all you can do, then don't bother being on social media.

FIGURE 10.20: Share an Industry Article

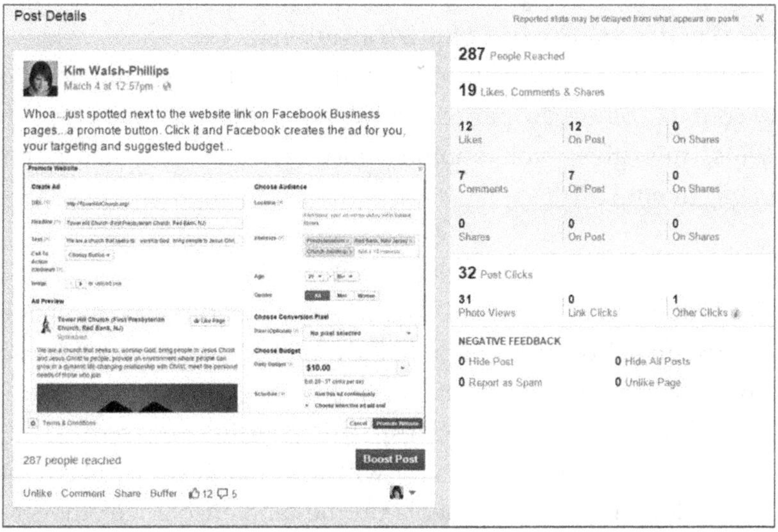

Instead of being a re-poster, add your comments, and ask a thoughtful question as to what the reader thinks about the information shared. This makes you a thought leader and content curator.

Other effective things to share are articles that are new or trending. The reason for sharing is to help keep your fans ahead of the curve, and then they are more likely to respond and share. Commentary is still required for engagement.

ASK TRIVIA QUESTIONS

A trivia question about your business or your industry can be a fresh way to keep your audience coming back. Offer a prize that is relevant for your perfect prospect, such as a gift certificate toward a purchase or a book by you or a supporting author. This can create page engagement AND give you potential leads.

To make sure this happens despite how crazy your week may get, systematize the process using a form tied into your CRM and a set schedule of prize awarding.

Make sure to announce the winner each week publicly to encourage others to participate in the following week's post. (Plus, this gives you another post and another chance for engagement.)

Single Out a Fan of the Week

Celebrating your fans and followers is another way to create engagement. You can randomly pick someone each week, choose from those who engaged most, or put a requirement in place, such as those who answered a specific question on a post.

Singling out a repeat visitor will add a sophisticated layer of interaction to your social media profiles and encourage others to do the same. As an added bonus, this is another strategy that has built-in social sharing.

Use Humor

Oreo cookies is fantastic at this. Unlike a lot of product and brand pages, its pages do not take themselves too seriously.

Example 1: A humorous exchange between Oreo and Kit Kat. Oreo is owned by Nabisco, and Kit Kat is owned by Nestle, so they are direct competitors.

First, someone tweeted this:

Can tell I like chocolate abit too much when I'm following @kitkatand @oreo hahahahahah

LauraEllen (@Laura_ellenxx) March 11, 2013

Two days later, Kit Kat's social media marketers responded with a clever challenge to Oreo with an image of a tic-tac-toe board and a Kit Kat "x" in the middle.

Several hours later, @Oreo responded with and image of the Kit Kat "x" being eaten and the tweet:

"Sorry @kitkat we couldn't resist. #GiveOreoABreak"

In another campaign, Oreo cookies had a goal to engage millennials. The strategy was to become more relevant with the Millennial crowd by re-imagining pop culture through the eyes of Oreo. The program, Daily Twist, used daily events and trends to come up with a new image each day such as Comi-Con and New York Fashion Week. The campaign reached more than 230 million people for free.

Post Behind-the-Scenes Photos

Your Facebook fans want to feel as though they have a "backstage pass" to you and your business. Post photos of your team at work, setting up events, planning a new product, etc. (See Figure 10.21 on page 174.) They will eat this content up and it will help to strengthen their relationship with you.

This is also an effective strategy to develop buzz and interest in your events and product launches. Get them excited before you ever even put your resources on sale.

Be Controversial

Being at one extreme or another is a tactic publishers like Huffington Post use with much success. Make it work for you.

Stand out in a crowded marketplace, calling out your shared enemy with your fans. (See Figure 10.22 on page 175.)

A few more engaging ideas:

- *Restaurant*: How do you dress your burger? Photo competition
- *Accountant:* Biggest cost reduction you put in place this year
- *Furniture*: Room in need of a makeover

FIGURE 10.21: Share Behind-the-Scenes Photos

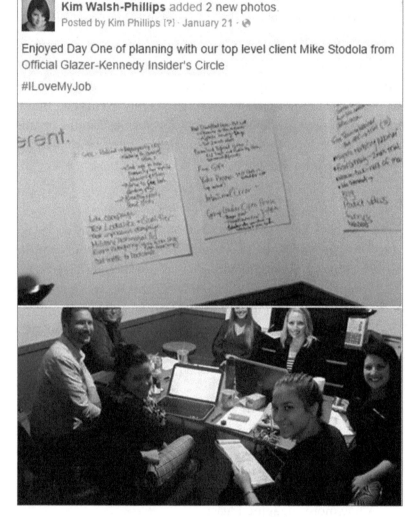

- *Lawyer*: How would you judge this case?
- *Any business*: A picture of one of your customers along with a fun fact about your product or service or question.

All are interactive and entertaining, but stay focused on the topic of authority and target market.

FIGURE 10.22: Be Controversial

> **Ron LeGrand**
> March 3 at 12:03pm · ✿
>
> "Flipping is illegal." Morons will love to tell you this, so let me tell you why they say this (and why you won't be going to jail): http://ow.ly/J9kuX
>
> 472 people reached   **Boost Post**
>
> Like · Comment · Share · 👍 10 ↩ 3

GET YOUR FANS INVOLVED

For The Fertility Center, we have found two types of posts to be most effective:

1. Inspirational quote images that are sharable. These range in topics from staying strong in trying times to believing in miracles and keeping a positive outlook.

2. Question or fill-in-the-blank—Asking questions can be a dicey game. Some audiences respond very well to questions, while others may hear crickets. The best advice is to keep it as simple as possible. A recent question we asked on The Fertility Center page was: It is the little things that brighten the day. Fill in the blank "Today, ____ was my silver lining."

But the most effective thing we have done was to get its fans involved.

When we were looking for patient stories for an ebook we put together, we turned to Facebook. We posted "Calling all past patients! Would you be willing to share your journey to inspire and help others struggling with infertility? If so, just send us a private message saying 'I want to help!' and we'll get you all the details!"

The response was absolutely overwhelming. Within an hour we had more than we needed for the ebook, and we gained brand ambassadors who were willing to help answer questions potential patients ask on The Fertility Center's Facebook page. (See Figure 10.23.)

FIGURE 10.23: The Fertility Center Engaged Fans to Get Involved

There was no shortage of loyal patients who had been helped by The Fertility Center. We weren't asking them for a referral. We weren't asking them for a testimonial. We were asking if they would be willing to respond to a few comments on the page.

We knew that if the response came from a past patient, someone who has walked that same path, it would mean so much more than if it came from the company. Here's an example:

Comment from Lauren: My husband and I haven't been able to conceive a child on our own. We are losing hope and don't think we can afford fertility treatments. What can we do?

Response from Company: Lauren, we have so many patients who have the same concerns as you. We'd love to have a conversation with you about your financial options.

Response from Past Patient: *Hi Lauren—I totally know how you feel, your story sounds very similar to mine. You have to keep the faith, that's what we did, and then we found The Fertility Center and everything changed. We now have a healthy baby boy and couldn't be happier. I know how tough it can be, but the staff at The Fertility Center really helps ease your fears. Oh and they have a lot of different financial options too. Make sure you tell Kathy at the front desk "hi" for me. She's so sweet. Best of luck to you!*

Over the years, The Fertility Center's Facebook page has developed into somewhat of a self-propelled online support group where fans can turn to each other when they need support and also share times of joy. While it's important that the company keep a steady presence of commentary on the page, in situations like this one it's best to take the back seat. Engaging for engagement alone is not a profit-driven tactic and should be avoided at all costs. Used as part of a well-thought-out and optimized sales funnel, it is a vital component of an effective digital sales strategy.

#NoBSsm Tweetable Takeaways

- 🐦 Using Website Retargeting, you can nurture a prospect from a cold lead to a sale without ever sending him or her an email. #NoBSsm

- 🐦 Use Facebook's Custom Website Audiences for ninja marketing: customize sales messages, reinforce purchases, and nurture a prospect. #NoBSsm

---

#NoBSsm Tweetable Takeaways

- Engage with your followers to build trust and nurture them into a sale. #NoBSsm

- Start with value and only then ask for the sale. #NoBSsm

CHAPTER 11

It's the Little Things that Count

Effective Content 101:
An Interview with Ahava Leibtag

by Kim Walsh-Phillips

Once your direct response social media marketing campaign is up and running, you are going to need a lot of content. What should you include to get the best results?

Digital content expert Ahava Leibtag shares what works best in digital content and the mistakes many marketers are making.

Ahava is passionate about content and prides herself on tackling the toughest content projects from health care to higher education to hip hop. Seriously. And she has more than 15 years' experience in writing, messaging, and marketing. President and owner of Aha Media Group, she is also a well-recognized content expert and the author of *The Digital Crown: Winning at Content on the Web.*

Kim: What are some mistakes you see frequently?

Ahava: Three potential areas: people problems, process problems, and technology problems. Very often, there's overlapping.

Lots of businesses are running in these silo camps. They have not learned to integrate their marketing departments well. Unfortunately, many older companies and big academic medical centers and universities are still set up with old school marketing departments. They're really having trouble making inroads. They do not come at a project from the perspective of "Who are we talking to? What are we trying to say? When are we going to say it? How are we going to say it?"

Rather, they're saying, "Okay, you go write a brochure, and you go write web content, and you buy the billboard, and you get the advertising campaign going."

They're creating duplicate work, which they're paying dearly for and not seeing any return on investment.

It also creates confusion for the customers because they're receiving so many different messages on so many different channels.

It's important for these companies to recognize the problems can be fixed, but the work flow and process will also need to be redesigned so future projects don't suffer the same fate.

Kim: When you have that conversation, what is generally the response?

Ahava: "We know." That's always their response. In fact, I've never gotten, "Oh wow, that's a surprise." They all say,

"We know." In fact, a lot of times, they'll say to me, "How did you know that?"

They know. They all know. They're all frustrated by it almost on a daily basis. I talk about the spectrum of dysfunction wherever I go. What I find fascinating and a little bit scary is that the bigger and more established the brand, the worse the dysfunction. Think about it. In order to get a company to grow to a certain size, you need to go through all these things that entrepreneurs go through. You have to start thinking about departments and silos, and who is producing what, and whose role is it to do this, and does it make sense for it to be like this.

Then they look at the talent and the workforce that's out there. They don't have people with integrated training, so they have to select people who are the best fit.

Very often, they engage me to reorganize their process and re-engineer it. We've had a lot of success doing that.

When I go in for reorganization I say, "My feeling is that you create roles. You can't focus on the people you have currently. You create a role and you write a job description. If the people who are currently in these roles don't fit, they either need to be retrained, moved to a different role, or they need to leave."

That's where I get the surprised look. "You can't come in and fire people. We're not going to do that." My response is, "You don't have to fire people, but don't be surprised if you keep doing what you're doing and keep getting the same results."

Companies have to really start to ask themselves, "If we can't produce what we need to produce with the team we currently have, what are we going to do? We can't keep employing people or keep them in roles if they're not the right people."

The reason I'm so hardlined about it is that I want to qualify my leads. I want to make sure I'm working with people who are most primed for success.

If people aren't ready to make those hard choices, then they're not ready for my type of content strategy, internal workflow consulting. They just won't have success with it because they're not willing to say, "Okay, we really need to rethink what these people are doing."

I always say you should give people a year to offer different training programs and compensation. But at the end of the day, I think there needs to be an understanding that at some point, we're going to have to make some tough decisions.

I might only be able to solve up to 10% of a client's problems on any given engagement. As a consultant, a lot of times, clients hire me because they want to point the blame at somebody when they can't solve the problem. That's very often why they bring in a consultant.

This is why I've shifted my business toward teaching. We teach you how to build the tools. I have a four-step proven methodology for doing this. Trust and vulnerability comes out best when I'm in tandem with the client and working with them as partner instead of telling them what to do. It really does have to be a lot of heads getting together and trying to figure out what's the best solution for a particular challenge.

Kim: Would you mind sharing another mistake marketers make with content?

Ahava: The second mistake is people are still just talking about themselves too much and not thinking about the pain points of the end user or the person they're trying to reach. I downloaded a white paper yesterday and read the whole thing. I was shocked at how poorly this white paper was put together. It had a soft beginning that told stories and gave you a couple of stats. Then three pages in, it started on that hard sell of why their software platform was the one to go with. I was actually kind of embarrassed because the think tank who helped them distribute the white paper is a really well-known content marketing group

I thought to myself, "Did anyone read this before it went out?"

This is exactly the opposite of what you're trying to do with a white paper. You should try to address what the customer's pain points are, not try to sell them on your particular software or why it's the best.

I see it over and over again in companies' tweets, in companies' Facebook pages. There's still so much focus on us, us, us, instead of about the customer.

Kim: Do you have any suggestions of what folks can do to help get that voice out more, that's more focused on their prospects and not on them?

Ahava: A sales technique I've used that really helps me is this. After I talk to somebody and I get the feeling they're interested but lukewarm about the next step, I'll say, "I just want to leave you with one question, if you could tell me what do you think your most pressing content challenge is at this moment?"

A lot of times, the answers they give me turn into newsletter and blog posts. This is how I find out what people are really freaking out about right now, currently in the marketplace, and how can I respond to those questions and give them the answers they need. This helps them feel like, "You know what? This person gets it. I'm going to go talk to her because she knows what's going on."

I also think you need to be smart and have a traditional marketing mix.

I allow myself one newsletter per quarter to present a case study about something we've done. It's clearly a sales email. It opens well but I never get any requests from it.

The requests I get are from the emails that answer the most popular questions on people's minds.

One more tip is that what you think is bothering people is way more detailed than what's actually bothering people. Folks are usually much more high level than what your solution provides to them.

Whatever you're thinking, reel it back ten steps to the more basic form of that challenge, and then you've probably got yourself a really good idea of what's going on with your customers.

Kim: Can you give us an example?

Ahava: I'll give you a personal example. What I sell is sometimes referred to as both content marketing and content strategy. The two are actually very, very different. When I start to try to explain it to clients, I see their eyes glaze over. I was busy thinking about internal work flow and editorial calendars, personas, and messaging architectures. It took me awhile to figure out that really, people just want to know, "How do we create content?"

A lot of times, you see the flip side though. Clients come to you and say what they think they need. It's like a doctor whose patient walks in with 400 pages printed from the internet and says, "You need to replace my hip." Clients announce, "We need this," or "We need that."

When I'm listening I ask myself, "People, process, or technology?" What I find out is that the way they diagnose the problem is far more complicated than the problem itself. They're so familiar with the problem, that they've turned it into an 80-point diagram.

That's where the brilliance of bringing in a consultant is really important. It gives a different perspective. You just want somebody who is going to look at it differently than you do.

The whole problem is really just asking, "What am I trying to sell? What's the simplest extrapolation of that idea?" The best content strategy solution is often the simplest question to provide that answer.

For more from Ahava Leibtag, connect with her on Twitter @AhavaL and AhaMediaGroup.com to sign up for her free newsletter, *Content Ahas,* and check out her fantastic book, *The Digital Crown: Winning at Content on the Web.*

Why Micro-Commitments Matter

Kim Walsh-Phillips

It is fairly obvious that those who know you will be more likely to respond to an offer than someone who has never heard of you before. The same is true of your social media audience. They see so many messages in a day from people they don't know, connect with, or care about that they completely ignore. They don't have time for nonsense or to figure out why they should buy from you. After all, that's not their job. It's yours.

Before you go for the sale, start from a position of value with your target market. First, let them know why you are a good match for their needs, why you are an expert in your field, and why they should pay attention to what you have to say. They will care because you are leading with messaging that is all about them.

And that's all they care about.

The Year of the Blog

Each year the media declares it is the "Year of the Blog." When researched, we found articles spanning back to 2004. This is so misguided.

Some of the titles:

- 2004 *"The Eyes of the Nation: The Internet; Year of the Blog? Web Diarists Are Now Official Members of Convention Press Corps"*
- 2005 *The Daily Whim: "Another Year of the Blog"*
- 2012 *Non-Profits, Year of the Blog. Here's Why You Can't Afford to Wait Any Longer*

A blog is just a channel. It is your content in a digital medium. You still need to have effective messaging in order to get a high ROI. Remember, for every channel, your customers and prospects are the ones holding the remote control. Do not give them a reason to hit the mute button.

What is true now is that your social media marketing efforts will crash and burn if you don't offer content as part of the equation. And there are many reasons to develop great content.

Google Search

Great SEO (search engine optimization) can no longer be manipulated with thousands of hidden pages or meta tags. Black hat tricks may work at first, but can make you lose an incredible amount of time and money later.

At one point, German car manufacturer BMW was blacklisted by the search giant Google. Google's top rule is that companies should design websites for users and not search engines. BMW admittedly used "doorway pages" in order to boost its web traffic. For this offense, the car manufacturing giant saw its top ranking numbers dive drastically to a zero ranking.

Google has been paving its way through social media and making more of a name for itself in that social realm with Google+. From this platform, author ranking has become a key feature. Building your author rank with Google+ will allow you to gain trust and rank higher in the Google-sphere by the content you produce all over the web. The more your content is +1'ed or shared, the higher your rank and trust from Google will elevate.

Some of the things they are looking for include:

- *Click-through rates.* Once people come to your site, do they click around? Do they engage with your content in any way? *Tactic*: Offer links in your blog posts and ask for comments and questions at the end of the post.

- *Scroll rate.* Do your visitors go below the fold when they visit your site?
  Tactic: Break paragraphs and images up on your blogs so they are only partially visible on the top third of your web page. Entice your viewer to scroll down to see what else is on the page.

- *Time on page.* How long do they spend engaging with content on your page?
  Tactic: Include multimedia resources such as audio files to listen to or videos to watch that support your blog content.

- *Bounce rate* (obvious sign for Google that your stuff stinks). This is if someone comes to your page and immediately leaves.
  Tactic: Make sure your ads match what viewers will see on the landing page you are inviting them to go to. Speak

directly to viewers letting them know that this page was meant for them.

- *Spelling and grammar.* Proofing does matter! Google is looking for content churned out by robots and checks for this by checking the grammar and spelling to make sure it is good.
  Tactic: Make proofing part of your blogging strategy. And do yourself a favor and have it be someone else. We are never good at seeing our own mistakes. I have a full-time proofer on staff, but if you don't produce enough content for that to make sense, use a freelancing resource or site like Grammarly or ProWritingAid to get your content checked.

- *Facebook advertising.* Facebook requires that you have relevancy for your audience. While there are numerous metrics to distract an advertiser who is trying to determine what is working and what isn't, the relevance score tries to balance the positive and negative into one single metric. It provides insight into what Facebook is seeing and why an ad may be delivering the way it is. This means the content can't be spammy garbage that is unwanted by your audience. You raise your relevancy by offering great content to identify your target market, and only once they have been nurtured do you follow up with them as a lead.

- *Thought leadership.* LinkedIn gives preferential treatment to long-form posts and will share them beyond your connections to build your follower count. This content is also SEO-friendly and can help your search engine ranking.

- *Establishing trust and authority even more.* Your goal should be to become THE expert and authority and leader in your marketplace. You want to create a channel of one. It should go without saying, but to be the thought leader in your market, you have to share your thought leadership.

- *Identifying qualified leads.* Blog content with clicks campaigns are an inexpensive way to identify qualified leads with any advertising you do. Once leads come to your site, you can then easily retarget them or get them to opt-in for your mailing list or blog. Social Media Examiner releases a blog once per day and through organic traffic only, it has been able to grow its opt-in email list to over 350,000 people. Their goal is to sell tickets to two annual events: one virtual and one in-person. Through this blog strategy, they have grown into a multimillion-dollar company.

So a blog? Yup, it's not optional. It is the core foundation of an effective direct response social media marketing strategy.

To turn marketing into revenue, engage your audience in content that is useful before you start to sell. Use your content to build trust, bring attention to a problem, agitate the problem, and then sell your solution. This works much better than agitating first, which more closely describes Thanksgiving Dinners with an ex-boyfriend's family and not how you want to market on social media. Creating a content plan is not difficult if you first set some goals, stick to a schedule, and commit to it throughout the year.

Set Goals

With an integrated content plan, setting goals for what is to be sold requires a specific and detailed approach. It is important to begin with a clear vision of your desired outcome, then create content which supports it.

Do you want to fill a workshop or seminar? Encourage prospects to schedule a sales conversation? Book your catering orders? Decide first your overall goal for your content. In this step, also determine the date the sale request will take place and any incentives you will offer to drive the sale home.

We use our blog (www.iocreativegroup.com/blog) to offer value to our audience, establish ourselves as experts and authorities in the marketplace, share case studies to build trust, and to get more leads for our business.

Our blog and weekly email is both the first and final step of a lot of our prospect requests. They come in through reading the blog, stay on our list for a few weeks, months, or even years, and then contact us to schedule a conversation.

Some of my most popular blog topics were all of the how-to variety:

1. Five Ways To Attract New Clients, Members, or Customers from Facebook
2. How to Increase Your Website Traffic Without Spending a Dime
3. Five Ways Facebook Can Grow Your Business While You Take a Holiday Break
4. How to Build Your Audience Quickly and Cheaply Using Facebook Impression Ads

After you develop your goals, create a schedule and stick to it. Whether it be once a day or once a week, consistency and commitment are key. Create your schedule based on one you can stick to in order to build your audience and generate those all-important raving fans.

Creating an Effective Blog

To blog in a way that is most effective and will give you the best end result, begin with the end in mind.

First, think of a blog as the editorial in your media channel. This is your owned media. You control it and you can use it any way you like no matter how big or small your audience is.

This is where you can appropriately express your opinions on a subject matter as they might affect your target audience. Content should focus on your prospects' interests and pains to zero in on what they find important. The following are steps to creating an effective blog.

Create a Blog Brand Voice

A blog should have an overall tone or theme, or be presented in one person's voice. Focus your brand around your Unique Selling Proposition to reinforce why you are different from everyone else and how you can help solve your prospects' pain.

Do not spend time trying to be everything to everyone. That will not create raving fans or turn traffic into buyers. Align yourself with a specific message that reaches a specific market.

For the work we do for GKIC Insider's Circle, we stay true to its voice and do not try to appeal to the masses. It is a marketing organization that primarily targets brick-and-mortar businesses and members who come from a sales background. Its content is going to focus frequently on salespeople and big corporations making stupid decisions, MBA marketing types who are removed from reality, and Madison Avenue ad agencies. It is clear who its market is and who its messaging should target.

For a few examples see Figures 11.1 through 11.4 on pages 192 and 193.

Create an editorial calendar to plan topics that are complementary to your overall sales goals and communications strategies. Entice the reader of each blog post with a sneak peak into next week's blog topic. Make sure to stick to your schedule and post consistently.

After you have established your goal, move to the next step.

FIGURE 11.1: GKIC Ad Aligns its Message to Reach a Specific Market

FIGURE 11.2: GKIC Ad Tip

FIGURE 11.3: GKIC Ad Tip

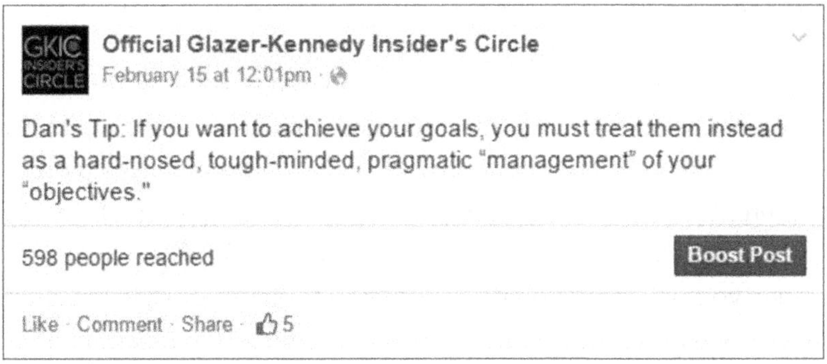

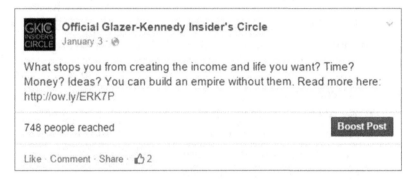

FIGURE 11.4: GKIC Link to Blog Post

CREATE A THEME RELATED TO YOUR SALES TOPIC

For example, look at magazine subscriptions. For many, each month, the magazine has a certain theme. For example, a sports magazine might have a preview of March Madness in its February issue. That February issue has lots of other things in it but it has a whole bunch of material related to college basketball.

In order to achieve your ultimate goal of a sale (or many sales), your role will shift to one of publisher and content provider while your prospect gets to know you.

When I wanted to sell tickets to an event focused on customer retention, I developed a monthly theme around this topic: "Why

Customer Retention and Growth Marketing Is Important to The Success of Your Business."

CREATE WEEKLY SUB-TOPICS THAT FIT EACH MONTHLY THEME

Your next step is to develop four subtopics that relate back to the overall theme of your monthly topic. Each week will focus on a different aspect of your overall theme, and all will lead toward week four (or day four if you conduct this for four days in a row) when you will make the offer to your audience with a call to action. This weekly content planning will ensure fresh, relevant content is always being added to keep readers interested and engaged up until the point of sale. Like two of my favorite TV series, *The Blacklist* or *Scandal*, each episode leads into the next. Here too each blog will lead to the finale of the item you are going to sell.

For our firm's example, the four subtopics I chose were:

- Your customers are 66% more likely to buy from you than noncustomers.
- There are no costs in selling to your current customers.
- Those who currently give you money should not be treated the same as those who don't.
- How do you thank your customers each year?

DEVELOP SUPPORTING CONTENT

One of the first things to do before writing any content is to make sure you do some research. Take a look at Quora, LinkedIn Answers, Yahoo!Answers, or other similar Q and A networks where you can find lots of people asking questions that relate to your specific industry. Identify their frustrations, objections, and pain points to address in your content creation. Bonus: You get the exact copy that people use when describing their pain points. This is usually quite different than the way those in your industry refer to it.

Researching these questions may create some ideas and directions for content. Also, take a close look at the links to content within the answers to these questions. Follow these links to see what others in your industry are doing with their content online. (Spying can be fun and profitable! Just keep those dang binoculars hidden.)

You may also want to set up and conduct a survey, or call your existing customers and prospective customers to find out what needs are unmet. When you begin to write your content, keep those unmet needs in mind. Use the information you collect to create a veritable library of remarkable content that is designed to help your customers get what they can't get anywhere else. Storytelling, testimonials, and providing something of value that meets people's needs should all be included in your content.

Each post can be anywhere from 350 to 2,000 words. The length should depend on how long it takes to fully get your point across. I have found my shorter blogs perform better with email list opt-ins and driving calls to action, but the same isn't true for some of our clients. Test what works best for your specific market and be very wary of anyone who tries to tell you there is one end-all-be-all for every market.

Write Social Media Posts

Once you have your content written, use this content as the source for your social media posts for the month. Engage your social network in an ongoing conversation focused around your topic theme on LinkedIn, Twitter, Facebook, and other networks.

This way, all of your content is created with your sales strategy in mind. All of your posts and articles are about walking your prospect towards the sale.

A guideline for content/sales online is that your content should be 85% PBS and 15% QVC, meaning that you shouldn't self-promote or sell more than 15% of the time. If you post one update per day (recommended), then in each month, you should have no more than four self-promotion posts.

For my firm's example, posts were pulled from the four weekly blogs.

AUTOMATE PUBLICATION

On-time and consistent delivery is an essential part of making this plan work.

To ensure this, schedule all content in advance. The last thing you want is to have a blog post or social media deadline sneak up on you with no idea of what content to use. Use a service like TweetDeck or HootSuite to pre-program all your content on Twitter, Facebook, and LinkedIn. Schedule your blog posts and emails ahead of time in your application as well.

For blogs, you should post new, relevant content at least once or twice a week. Your readers should also know the day you typically post and keep to that schedule. Alert readers via email about any new posts on your blog and promote these posts in your social media network.

For our firm, I was able to set up all of the content ahead of time and the system ran smoothly in spite of the fact that I was out of town for most of the month visiting private clients and for speaking engagements. (Marketing automation rules.)

PUBLISH CONTENT

This is when it starts to become fun. Launch your content and start to analyze the results. A/B test different times of day to send messages and post content, different subject lines to get your emails opened, etc. Tweak your remaining content appropriately.

Ask yourself if your content is useful to customers before publishing.

While your goal is the sale, the process of getting there includes being useful to your audience.

"Youtility is marketing so useful, people would pay for it. It's a necessity for all businesses now, forced to compete for attention not just against other companies selling the same stuff but also against everyone and everything. In this hyper-competitive era, you don't break through the clutter by shouting the loudest, you get noticed by being truly and inherently useful."

—Jay Baer, author of *Youtility: Why Smart Marketing Is about Help Not Hype* (Portfolio 2013)

It is FINALLY Time to Sell

On day or week four (depending how long your series is), it is time to ask for the sale.

You have spent the three previous posts engaging your target market where they are. They are now interested in the topic you are focused on and are seeking a solution to the problem you have agitated. You have essentially led them to this moment when you reveal the solution. And, since you spent the previous posts providing useful content, you will be seen as the credible source for the solution.

When you are ready to sell, do not just make an offer to purchase something, attend something, or request something. Beyond the thing you want your target market to do, give them a deadline and an added incentive to do so. Creating a sense of urgency is an important part of driving your audience to action. Neiman Marcus, for example, gets me in with an exclusive 24 hour *Prada Sale*. (Or they would, if they would ever put Prada on sale—hint, hint, Neiman Marcus.)

When it was time to ask my audience to register for an upcoming seminar, I added an incentive of a free white paper if they registered by a certain date. This workshop sold out.

The payoff is a long-term, credible, relevant online presence that increases traffic, builds connections within a community, and creates a strong brand awareness for your product or service.

Consider a campaign example from one of our clients, Chanhassen Fitness Revolution (http://chanhassenfitness revolution.com).

When going after cold traffic, we first ran ads to a blog post about exercising:

FIGURE 11.5: Chanhassen Fitness Revolution Ad Drives Cold Traffic to a Blog Post

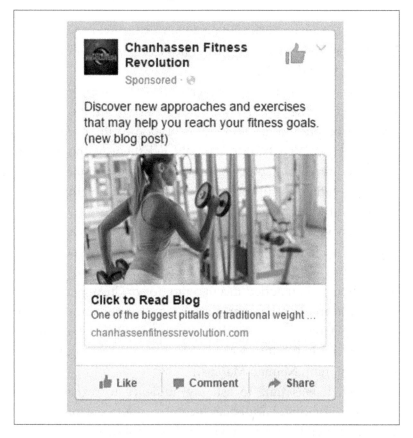

Then, we retargeted with an ad about the 21-day boot camp:

FIGURE 11.6: Chanhassen Fitness Revolution Follow-Up Ad Retargets Traffic to an Offer

And we then sent traffic to its landing page. See Figure 11.7 on page 200.

And then we sent them to another landing page to finish the signup.

We have tested this "connect first and sell second" strategy time and time again, and the total cost per lead and success rate always beats going after cold traffic directly.

FIGURE 11.7: Chanhassen Fitness Revolution Takes Warm Traffic to a Landing Page

Another example of an effective campaign:

1. Step One (see Figure 11.8 on page 201)
2. Step Two (see Figure 11.9 on page 202)

Sometimes your prospects will need an extra nudge. When you are going after completely cold traffic on Facebook, your audience may need more nurturing to turn into a sale. It is then that a micro-commitment campaign may be the solution. This is

FIGURE 11.8: Facebook Ad Drives Cold Traffic to a Blog Post

where through a series of content first, lead magnet second, and offer third you can turn a cold lead into a lifelong customer.

How to Run a Micro-Commitment Campaign

1. Develop blog content that would appeal to your target market.
2. Develop a "lead magnet" giving your target market something of value such as a free report, ebook, video series, etc. (For a step-by-step "how to" on creating a Lead Magnet, visit www.NoBSSocialMediaBook.com)
3. For at least four weeks, run your blog content and lead magnet to your perfect prospects, targeting fans of your Facebook page, your website traffic, and fans of other similar pages.

FIGURE 11.9: Facebook Retargeting Ad Drives Warm Leads to a Live Online Event

4. When you start to run your main offer, focus on the warm leads you have created:
   - Facebook fans
   - Website traffic (retargeting using Website Custom Audience)
   - Email list

When we went straight to cold traffic, our cost was $3.00 per webinar attendee and our show-rate was 20%. When we changed this strategy to a micro-commitments plan, our opt-in decreased to $.87 each and our show rate was over 50%.

Even if you add in the $1.23 it takes for us to get someone on our email list, we are ahead of the game by using this formula.

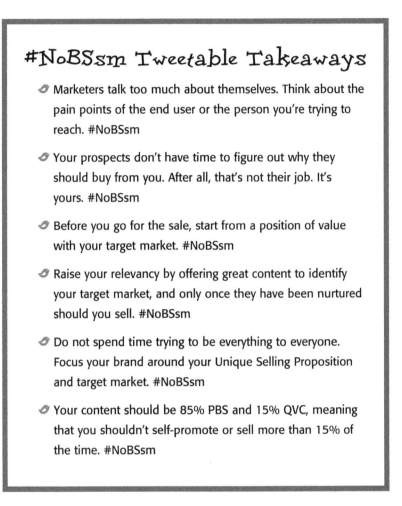
#NoBSsm Tweetable Takeaways

- Marketers talk too much about themselves. Think about the pain points of the end user or the person you're trying to reach. #NoBSsm

- Your prospects don't have time to figure out why they should buy from you. After all, that's not their job. It's yours. #NoBSsm

- Before you go for the sale, start from a position of value with your target market. #NoBSsm

- Raise your relevancy by offering great content to identify your target market, and only once they have been nurtured should you sell. #NoBSsm

- Do not spend time trying to be everything to everyone. Focus your brand around your Unique Selling Proposition and target market. #NoBSsm

- Your content should be 85% PBS and 15% QVC, meaning that you shouldn't self-promote or sell more than 15% of the time. #NoBSsm

CHAPTER 12

The Biggest Secret in Social Media Is Offline?

The Cost of Not Following Up

by Dan Kennedy

"The reports of my death have been greatly exaggerated."

—MARK TWAIN

Today, the death of "old" media and offline media is wildly and foolishly exaggerated. For a wide variety of businesses, newspapers, print magazines, merge-mail like Val-Pak, the new USPS' Every Door Direct-Mail, printed catalogs, even the Yellow Pages directories not only continue to work, but provide improved and improving returns on investment.

A local marketer utilizing FSI's (Free Standing Inserts) in his city and suburban community newspapers consistently gets an 8:3 to as high as an 11:3 ROI from them. That means he gets $8-$11 for every $3 spent. He cannot match that ROI from any online or social media, despite being smart about it. While his two chief competitors exited this "dead media," he stayed and doubled his ROI.

One of the media most often, most vociferously pronounced dead is the printed and mailed customer newsletter. Bloggers and social media experts love to conduct its funeral. They are *dead wrong*. Their opinions—and that's all they are—are ignorant and dangerous.

Personally, my business empire has not only been built with print newsletters as its foundation and a centerpiece around which everything else orbits, they continue to be the chief reason my companies enjoy TCV (Total Customer Value) 2X to 20X above all our competitors (and yes, I know their numbers).

Well over 50% of my high value private clients rise up out of the newsletter subscriber base. It would cost me a fortune to find them otherwise. You might judge my business "unique," however, my model has inspired literally thousands of people in a wide range of consumer and B2B categories to aggressively invest in their own print newsletters for their customers, clients, patients, or donors—and all report significant improvements in retention, ascension, frequency of purchase or patronage, and referrals. Many are in their 3rd, 5th, 7th, 10th, 20th year of continuous use of their own print newsletters, and wouldn't stop their use of this "dead media" under any circumstance.

One of the very best at it is Annette Fisher, founder and operator of Happy Trails Farm Animal Sanctuary, a thriving and growing animal rescue operation. I suggest you go to www. HappyTrailsFarm.org, look around, make a donation to get on the newsletter list, and treat each newsletter you receive by mail as a master class in session. The best B2B model is, un-humbly said, the one I created and still contribute to, obtainable at GKIC.com.

Another demonstration of how very much alive the oft-pronounced dead print newsletter is can be found with Shaun Buck at NewsletterPro.com. Shaun's company creates and produces semi-custom and custom customer/patient newsletters for dentists and orthodontists, day spas, specialty retailers, and other small businesses, and in total, mails more than 1.5 MILLION of these for his clients every year. It *is* expensive, in raw terms, for these businesses to print and mail such monthly newsletters. Shaun has a 98% retention rate year to year with these clients, and they can't *all* be fools. They *must* be getting positive results. Shaun eats what he serves, too, and has grown his own businesses by 4,000% in a very short time by mailing newsletters. You'll hear from him later in this chapter.

So, in this age of digital media and proliferate social media, with abundant opportunities to post and distribute the same content you'd put into print newsletters or even the exact same newsletters free of cost, why the devil are so many business owners still creating, producing, printing, and mailing real newsletters?

Didn't they get that memo from Al Gore? "Hey, look, I invented the internet!"

Print newsletters arriving by mail, opened, physically handled, read, clipped from, saved, and shared have positive effects that *cannot* be replicated online.

First, customers recognize and appreciate the fact that you are investing real money in communicating with them, providing information and entertainment, and expressing appreciation for them. This engages reciprocity, and for in-depth understanding of that, I recommend reading Robert Cialdini's books.

Second, consumers place a higher value on printed publications. One 2014 survey conducted by a major newsletter publisher I work with found that over 80% of respondents indicate they *always* read the print newsletters and magazines they subscribe to or receive free, regularly, from businesses they have relationships with. Those same respondents said they read ezines, blogs, and other digital media included in paid subscriptions only about 20% of the time. *That's a 400% differential.* You can't win if your output never gets read. Frankly, a whole lot of online communication is killed with the delete button and has no value placed on it whatsoever.

Third, print newsletters have a much longer shelf life. It's very common for me to hear from somebody just getting around to reading one of my newsletters sent months ago or even after revisiting an issue from years ago, then asking about products or services. How often do you think somebody settles into their comfy chair for an evening and reads email or blog posts from months ago?

A client of mine who is a financial advisor and wealth manager recently had a new client bring him over $9 million to invest and manage, after being on a prospect list and receiving a client newsletter every month for five years. An article about teaching kids to respect wealth before they inherit it rang his bell. He read it in an issue of the newsletter four months after it had been sent. My client could have gotten nothing else from mailing his print newsletter to his entire list for those five years and still come out ahead financially from just this client and the several referrals he'll certainly obtain.

Fourth, print newsletters are a great place to profile, feature, showcase, and give recognition to customers, clients, or patients. It's meaningful to people, to see themselves *in print.* I get a lot of thank yous from the GKIC Members and my clients when I dispense atta-boys and recognition in newsletters. One of the grand masters at doing this, and driving referrals by doing it, is a long, longtime follower of mine, Dr. Greg Nielsen, a chiropractor. You can find him at: www.docnielsen.com.

Of course, none of this works if you commit the ultimate marketing sin: being boring. A great newsletter is never much about your basic deliverables, products, services. It shouldn't be technical. Look at what makes popular magazines thrive:

- *Human interest stories.* They can be about your own adventures, about your customers, and about celebrities that somehow relate to what you sell. The long-standing giant *Reader's Digest* was built on and lives by its human interest stories.

- *New, unusual, and fascinating information.* Information people are motivated to repeat to peers and friends, thereby supporting word-of-mouth advertising for you. It's called a NEWS-letter for a reason; it's supposed to contain news. If you want to see the most successful newsletters built of "many short bits" of fascinating and new information, look at the publications by Boardroom, notably BottomLine Health (http://bottomlinehealth.com) and BottomLine Personal. (http://bottomlinepersonal.com). My friend, the late Marty Edelston, created this now-giant publishing company from a tabletop in his spare bedroom. The most successful topics that he made his bones with include "Foods Never to Eat on an Airplane" and "What Big Drug Companies Don't Want You to Know About Cancer."

- *Opinion.* Yes, care must be taken. But if you have a personal relationship with customers and your personality is linked to your business or you operate in a business where trust and affinity matter, then people are interested in your philosophy, ideas, and opinions, and can be motivated by shared values.

  By the way, the best work on "being fascinating," as a person, as a marketer, and with content, has been done by my friend and colleague Sally Hogshead. Both her books are important reading. You can learn more at www.how tofascinate.com.

- *Useful tips.* "How to" relieve a sudden headache (from a chiropractor), remove pet stains from carpet (from a pet store or a carpet cleaner), ready your car for a long trip (from an auto service shop or an insurance agent), grow giant tomatoes (from a lawn care company), etc.

You also want to incorporate limited but direct promotion, such as introduction of new products or services, lead generation offers of free information about a different specific product or service each month, and seasonal "preferred customer" offers.

It is my firmest conviction, based on solid and overwhelming evidence, that nothing can "glue" customers to your business like a good print newsletter mailed to them frequently, on a regular schedule.

You can, of course, link and integrate it with online and social media in many ways. Extensions of short "teaser" articles, videos, tools, contests, and surveys can be housed online and driven to by the print newsletters. Engagement, comments, and contest participation can occur on Facebook or other social media sites, pushed by the print newsletter and reported in the newsletter. The circular possibilities are endless. Addition, multiplication, and integration are all, as Martha Stewart says, very good things. But subtraction of the proven and reliable print newsletter from your media mix is just dumb.

Nurturing Prospects into Sales and Retaining Customers Through Newsletters
by Shaun Buck

Side note from Kim: *Why include a chapter about print newsletters in a book about social media? Because once you bring in a lead, your job is to do EVERYTHING you can to nurture them into a customer and to have them keep buying from you for life. Dan shared earlier in this chapter, "So, in this age of digital media and proliferate social media, with abundant opportunities to post and distribute the same content you'd put into print newsletters or even the exact same newsletters free of cost, why the devil are so many business owners still creating, producing, printing, and mailing real newsletters? Print newsletters arriving by mail, opened, physically handled, read, clipped from, saved, and shared have positive effects that cannot be replicated online." Shaun Buck, president of The Newsletter Pro, www.TheNewsletterPro.com, is my go-to expert for newsletters and the no-brainer choice for this chapter, and on the following pages he does an excellent job of connecting the dots.*

A few months back, I was sitting in the audience of the largest internet marketing conference in the world when one of the main presenters took the stage and told us he was going to reveal the latest and greatest "new" thing in internet marketing during the next presentation. After a short 15-minute break, I, along with 3,000 or more other marketers, anxiously awaited the big reveal.

The presenter took the stage once more and repeated his promise of letting us in on this big new idea. I opened my laptop, prepared to take notes, and after a few moments of monologuing, he dropped the bomb we had all been waiting for. "The biggest new thing in internet marketing," he said, "is direct mail." At first I wasn't entirely sure I heard him correctly, but then, almost on cue, he repeated it. This time there was no mistake; at the world's largest internet marketing conference, the main presenter had just told the audience that generating a new lead via social media, and immediately taking that lead offline with direct mail, was "the new big thing."

I couldn't help but laugh to myself at the thought that offline marketing was considered "new." After all, the United States Postal Service can trace it roots back to 1775! But for many of the marketers in the room, the new idea wasn't offline marketing; it was generating a lead online and following up with that lead using offline media.

The Case for Online Lead Generation with Offline Marketing

How could offline marketing be considered a "new" idea? Offline marketing was around for decades, if not centuries, before online marketing was ever invented, so why did it seem like such a novel idea to so many of my fellow audience members?

When it comes to online marketing, the idea of spending money on offline media after you have acquired a lead from social media can be hard to swallow; it could even feel a bit counter-intuitive, but let's look at the reality of the situation.

Shortly after waking up each morning, you sit down at your computer and open your inbox—sound familiar? You're instantly flooded with dozens of new messages ranging from spam to special offers to important memos. (Isn't it a good thing our computers no longer say "You've Got Mail" every time we get a new email?) The first thing you do is search for any and all emails you can instantly delete without ever having to open them, in hopes that you can get your number of emails down to a manageable level.

As a business owner, here are a few email stats you need to know:

- The average commercial email deliverability rate is just 67%.
- The average open rate is 9%.

- The average time spent reading each email is 3 seconds.
- The average person gets 147 emails per day (according to a recent study by *Forbes* magazine).

According to the USPS 2015 fact sheet, the average delivery point (household, business, P.O. box, etc.) only receives 3.92 pieces of mail in their mailbox each day. Compared to the average 147 emails hitting inboxes per day, you are marketing in a vacuum with direct mail.

Can you imagine 147 pieces of mail showing up in your mailbox each morning? If they were all checks, it would be cause for a celebration! But if they were bills, commercial mailers, or advertisements, you would likely start to dread going out to the mailbox each day.

I'm not suggesting that you don't use email in following up with your newly acquired leads or that you don't continue to optimize them through social media, but I am saying digital marketing alone is leaving a massive amount of money on the table. Let's look at how complementing your current email efforts with a prospect-nurturing campaign can drastically increases sales.

The Path to More Customers

How long do you follow up with someone who inquires about your product or service after the initial inquiry? If you're like most businesses, it's not long.

The following stories illustrate the importance of the follow-up.

First Story

My company, The Newsletter Pro, is a print newsletter company that specializes in custom content and design. Our average clients range from $1 million to $100 million in annual revenue. One of the many ways we generate new leads is by exhibiting at trade shows, but it's not always easy to find a trade show that fits in with our average client. On the rare occasion that I do come across the perfect show, I usually do anything I can to get us in.

Most recently, I discovered one of those rare gems and immediately inquired about exhibiting. I had a good conversation with a salesperson and even received a follow-up email, promising more information to come, but that was over six weeks ago. I haven't heard anything since. If it was like any other trade show, they probably had an exhibiting fee between $5,000 to $10,000—a fee we would have willingly paid. How much is the lack of follow-up costing this company?

Second Story

I recently visited Disneyland with my oldest son, Brandon. I had Brandon when I was 16 years old, but, at 18, he's now the oldest of five boys. We were there for the first leg of a high school graduation trip I had promised him last spring, and in between riding Splash Mountain 20 times and eating a ton of Dole Whip, I convinced him to join me for a timeshare presentation put on by Disney Parks. I had sat in on one years ago and remember being blown away by the presentation. It was a really great learning experience, plus my wife and I have been considering buying a Disney timeshare (with four little guys running around, we spend a lot of time in Disney parks).

From the moment the salesperson walked in the door, I knew this was not going to be the same presentation I had seen before. At 35 years old and accompanied by an 18-year-old kid, the salesperson immediately judged my ability and willingness to buy. My 90-minute presentation was completed in less than half that time, this including a tour of the mock Hawaii property. The salesperson didn't ask me any qualifying questions, like "Where do you work?" or "How do you plan to pay for the timeshare?"

If he had, he would have found out that I own the largest full custom print newsletter company in the world and mail millions of pieces each year. He would have learned that I have a team of 35 employees, four young kids, and a serious commitment to Disney. In fact, he would have discovered that I was ready to lay down the cash for a timeshare right then and there, but he judged this book by its cover and, in doing so, he lost a huge sale. In the months that followed, that salesperson made one very brief follow-up phone call and promptly marked me as a "bad lead" in the system.

If you think the above examples are rare, or unlikely to happen to your business, think again. Disney is arguably one of the best marketing companies on the planet, and even they failed at landing the follow-up sale.

There are many reasons leads don't turn into customers. Hundreds of books have been written on the subject, but the number-one reason leads don't turn into sales is due to the lack of follow-up. Just because you are ready to sell a prospect and turn him into a customer doesn't mean he is ready to buy.

- 18% of prospects are ready to buy right now
- 82% of prospects take greater than three months to make a buying decision
- 61% of prospects take greater than one year to make a buying decision
- 44% of salespeople are only making one follow-up call after a meeting

When you look at those facts, does it make you wonder how many sales you're leaving on the table? What would happen if you implemented a follow-up process that would continue to nurture your leads until they were ready to buy?

Here is an example of a near perfect prospect follow-up sequence:

Many years ago, when I was in my early 20s, I was looking to buy a franchise. Being the nerd I was (okay, am), I requested UFOCs (now called FDDs, or Franchise Disclosure Documents) from dozens upon dozens of franchisors. At the time, I was 9 to 12 months out from making a purchase, but I wanted to research my options.

Within six weeks of requesting these UFOCs, all communication had stopped with every franchisor but one. This single franchisor called occasionally, but her primary way of following up was with a monthly print newsletter. Now, as a guy who creates hundreds of newsletters per month, I can tell you it was one of the best newsletters I have ever seen. Each edition featured a cover article either about herself or a fellow franchisee. When it was franchisee, they most often talked about how excited they were to be a part of the business or how fast their franchise was growing. They talked about their upcoming convention and all the exciting benefits of attending.

Each time this monthly newsletter hit my mailbox, I immediately opened and devoured it. I even forced my wife to read it so we could chat about it over dinner. This franchisor reminded me each month who it was, what they did, and why I should be excited about its opportunities. I ended up buying a franchise nearly six months earlier than I had originally planned—primarily so I could attend the annual convention.

The above story lends itself to an important question: Why did I buy early? Was it because she sent a newsletter? Was it the follow-up? Was it something else entirely?

Because I'm a self-acclaimed newsletter guy, you might assume I'm going to give all the credit to the newsletter, but the newsletter was just the vehicle used to deliver the message. The reason I bought early was because of the relationship I had developed with the franchisor, a person I had yet to meet face to face. After months of receiving her newsletter, I felt I knew and liked the person I was getting into business with. I felt connected to the franchisees and the business model the corporate office was selling. I was excited about the opportunity and truly believed this franchise was going to benefit my life and the lives of my loved ones.

It all comes down to this: People want to do business with people they know and like. When you take the time to build a relationship with your qualified prospects, and both educate and entertain them through the buying process, you will close more sales at a faster pace. You can accomplish this by inviting your customers over for Sunday dinner each month, but unfortunately that's not a scalable technique and it could very well lead to a divorce.

In years past, you could simply send an email, but with the average person receiving 147 emails per day, that's no longer a viable option. On the other hand, with the average person receiving 2.7% the number of direct mail pieces per day as they do emails, a print newsletter, delivered directly to your prospects and customers, can have a huge impact on conversions, retention, and referrals.

Now that we have a plan for turning your social media prospects into new customers, let's look at the single biggest mistake entrepreneurs make *after* the sale.

Congratulations! By now you've managed to create an ad, get your ad approved by the powers that be, convinced someone to click on your ad, redirected them to a landing or sales page, encouraged them to take a positive action, and ultimately, with some nurturing and follow-up, persuaded this lead to make a purchase. Your job is done, right? Wrong. It has only just begun. Right about now is when most entrepreneurs miss the boat. You have just done an incredible amount of work to make a sale—now is not the time to forget about your new customer. As Dan Kennedy would say, "The purpose of making a new sale is to get a new customer." If you implement a long-term relationship building a value-adding system, these new sales will turn into repeat sales, long-term customers, and referral sources. But that begs the question, how do you begin to build that relationship?

The first step is to stop participating in customer neglect.

Many businesses are treating their customers all wrong. But in most cases, it is not even the business owners' fault. They are just copying what they have seen other companies do.

There are two very common customer neglect scenarios. The first: The business successfully lands a sale, but never communicates with the new customer again. Can you imagine? Who would do this? Well, as I pointed out earlier in this chapter, businesses and salespeople alike abandon customers and prospects all the time.

"We live in the single most difficult time in history to make a first sale, but we live in the single easiest time in history to make a second sale." —Perry Belcher, cofounder of Digital Marketer

The second and more common type of customer neglect is to land a new customer and then bombard them with nothing but bills and sales material. Like any red-blooded entrepreneur, I'm all for selling, but the "buy or die" strategy some employ is not my cup of tea. When I see a business that's always selling but never adding value outside of those purchases, it reminds me of that friend or relative—you know who I'm talking about—the one who never calls unless they need a favor or a cash advance. I have one family member I tend to dodge simply because they constantly suck both the money and the life out of me and never add extra value. Most entrepreneurs have at least one of this type of person in their life and work hard to avoid them, but many of us also are this person to our customers. Crazy, right? You don't want to be known as an annoying pest to the people who have proven they are willing to spend money with you.

Both of these very common business practices are killers when it comes to overall customer lifetime value and referrals— they even interfere with additional short-term sales.

Once you get a new customer, you must immediately pivot and start focusing on the long-term retention of that new customer. Remember, people do business with people they know and like. Businesses that live and breathe that phrase thrive.

- A 5% increase in customer retention can increase profits 25% to 125%. (Bain and Company, *Harvard Business Review*)
- The probability of selling to an existing customer is 60% to 70%. The probability of selling to a new prospect is 5 to 20%. (Marketing Metrics, a think tank)
- Companies that prioritize the customer experience generate 60% higher profits than their competitors. (*Leading on the Edge of Chaos*, Emmet Murphy, and Mark Murphy)

If you take nothing else from this chapter, make sure you get this point: The real money and long-term growth for your business is in increasing the relationship you have with your existing customers. Nothing can maximize profits faster.

The single best vehicle I have found for building relationships, increasing lifetime value, and skyrocketing referral rates is a monthly print newsletter. Dan Kennedy himself has said, "My single biggest recommendation is the use of a monthly customer newsletter. Nothing, and I mean nothing, maintains your herd better."

If you have tried a newsletter before and determined it didn't work, it's probably because you did it wrong. I can confess that my very first newsletter was horrible. To make matters worse, I mailed it for over two years. You can see an example of this awful newsletter in my book, *Newsletter Marketing* (2013). To help prevent you from making the same mistakes as so many others, let me give you a few guidelines when it comes to "what not to do."

Mistake 1: Ineffective Content

Every communication you send shouldn't be about your business. You need to focus on subjects that will interest your customers (even if they don't interest you). When I look at dental newsletters, most of the time the newsletter is all about dentistry; how implants work, the signs of dry mouth, and what a cavity really looks like. In all honesty, if I was that interested in dentistry, I would have become a dentist! We work with a good number of dentists, but reading about and seeing before-and-after pictures of dental work is frankly scary, boring, and could be a form of cruel and unusual punishment (a clear violation of the 8th Amendment of the Bill of Rights, I might add).

The same goes for all businesses. Would you want to read a newsletter about newsletters? What about a newsletter from your dry cleaner about getting grass stains out or from your plumber about unclogging clogged toilets? Do you want to know what people really want to read? Just check the second most visited site on the internet: Facebook. People are interested in *you* and what's going on in your life. If that wasn't true, Facebook wouldn't exist.

Mistake 2: Sending an Email Newsletter Only

People have way too much email, which means way too much competition in their inbox. The USPS found that a print newsletter can linger around a home or office for up to four months. Granted, an email might linger in someone's inbox for four months, but by then it's extremely unlikely that it's going to be read. How many emails do you refer back to from four months ago? Don't be cheap here, your customers know email is free, and because of that, they're likely to pay little to no attention to your email newsletter. If a customer is not worth spending $1.00 per month to maintain a relationship with, you might be in the wrong business.

Mistake 3: Not Mailing Monthly

I have a small percentage of people who ask us to mail quarterly newsletters; however, as a company we have decided not to take on those clients. As I write this, we send out over 3 million print newsletters per year. We have offered a quarterly service in the past, but after a lot of data crunching, we determined that quarterly newsletters simply don't work. When you send a quarterly newsletter, your customers simply won't realize it's a regular publication. A monthly newsletter requires about six months to see best results—on the other hand, a quarterly newsletter might take years.

Think about it, how many close relationships do you have with people you only talk to four times a year? Even if you consider them a close friend, how close can you really be? Relationships need to be nurtured, and once a quarter just isn't enough.

Using a newsletter to create relationships, increase customer lifetime value, and skyrocket referrals is a complicated subject with many moving parts. For a more in-depth look, I'd like to offer you my book, *Newsletter Marketing,* for absolutely FREE! All you have to do is go to www.thenewsletterpro.com/nobs, fill in your information, and my office will mail you a complimentary copy on the next business day.

Want to know more about Shaun Buck or The Newsletter Pro? Visit www.TheNewsletterPro.com.

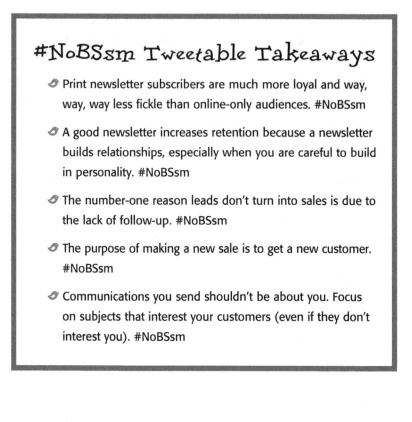

#NoBSsm Tweetable Takeaways

- Print newsletter subscribers are much more loyal and way, way, way less fickle than online-only audiences. #NoBSsm

- A good newsletter increases retention because a newsletter builds relationships, especially when you are careful to build in personality. #NoBSsm

- The number-one reason leads don't turn into sales is due to the lack of follow-up. #NoBSsm

- The purpose of making a new sale is to get a new customer. #NoBSsm

- Communications you send shouldn't be about you. Focus on subjects that interest your customers (even if they don't interest you). #NoBSsm

CHAPTER 13

Creating the Slam Dunk

Effective Calls to Action

by Dan Kennedy

The most common failure in struggling business owners is not product, place, price, or profitability. Their businesses basically work. They just fall down when it comes to selling. This is something of a lost art and a newly disdained activity. People want to send out proposals by email instead of getting face to face to present them. They want an iPad on the wall in their store to do the work of a live, human demonstrator. Sometimes, they hear customers say they prefer such approaches, but it's vital to realize that the customer is NOT always right. We must never surrender to expressed preferences that sabotage the most effective selling. For a lot more on selling, I urge getting a copy of another book in this series, *No B.S. Guide to Sales Success.*

The worst of all selling failures comes when it is time to ask for specific action. Most advertising peters out and meekly ends, without a clear and direct call to action. People are routinely permitted to wander around in stores, look at merchandise, and leave empty-handed without ever being put through an organized, scripted sales presentation that leads to a "close" or even having their names and contact information captured for follow-up. In social media, there is a cultural idea, and a fear, about moving people too quickly or definitively to an offer and a call to action—only somewhat justified by the interference of the gods of Facebook, Twitter, LinkedIn, etc. The fact is, there's no money made until somebody sells something, and damn little gets sold without somebody directly asking for the order.

My famous friend and colleague, the great Zig Ziglar, observed that "timid salespeople have skinny kids," and said that what separates the poorly paid professional visitor from the kingly compensated professional salesperson is asking for the order. All advertising, all marketing, all media—social and otherwise—must be engineered to get prospect and seller to a time and place where the order can be requested. Anything else is mere professional visiting.

In advertising, the vital skill is knowing how to ask your prospect to take action. Your experience in effectively closing in-person sales will pay off when you sit down to create effective advertising. The same techniques, words, phrases, and ideas used in personal selling should be used in your marketing.

A "Slam Dunk" Customer

If you're trying to target the entire world, you'd better be prepared to go head-to-head with big, dumb companies with billions of dollars to waste in the effort. Going after every possible person who could ever use your service is a fool's errand.

Instead, you need to figure out who your favorite clients are. Where do they come from? How do they act? What do they read? How much do they earn? What do they like to do for fun? What is it about YOU that they resonate with?

Get a grip on WHO this person is, WHERE to find him, and WHAT he really wants that only you can provide. And then figure out what PRICE you want him to be able to pay. This should be your first step to building a smarter lead-generation system.

An Easy Layup—Your Lead Generation Magnet

Give your leads a clear reason to contact you and get that reason in front of your "slam dunkers." Narrow down your perfect clients from the unwashed masses. This "thing" you're creating is an incentive to respond. It's your Lead Generation Magnet. It can be informational, like a report, guide, book, CD, or webinar, or it might be some other kind of "gift." Obviously, the more desirable your magnet and its offer, the stronger the pull it will have to your perfect prospect.

Here are a few Lead Generation Magnets that work very well:

- My friend Larry Levin, seen often on Fox Business News and heard on radio, offers his options trading technique that made him over $1 million—for free. If you'll just call his 800 number and leave your email address, he'll send it to you.
- My client Ted Oakley, a wealth manager seen in *Forbes* and other investor-oriented publications, offers his free book, *$20 MILLION AND BROKE*, for business owners selling or who have recently sold their companies.

- My client Arthro-New offers a free online video about chronic and arthritic pain relief featuring Dr. John Frank, M.D., and Super Bowl player and a free month's trial package (to move prospects to tele-reps).
- Doctors with local practices I've worked with offer books like *The Official Consumer Guide to Cosmetic Surgery* and *How To End Back Pain and Golf As If You Were 10 Years Younger—Without Drugs or Surgery.*
- A B2B consultant offers a "Special Research Report" on expense reduction and cost control case histories to hospital CEOs and CFOs.
- A company of which I was part owner taught people how to start homebased information-publishing businesses. It successfully advertised its Lead Generation Magnet in over 50 national magazines for years—its "little yellow book" was titled *How to Make $4,000 a Day, Sitting at Home in Your Underwear, with Your Computer.*
- My longtime client Ben Glass, a personal injury attorney in Virginia, creates and advertises many different free reports and books and is a master at using Lead Generation Magnets. You can take a look at www.BenGlassLaw.com. Ben is so good at this, thousands of lawyers all across the country use his LGM formats and models, and you can see that at GreatLegalMarketing.com.

Answer the WHY YOU Question

"Why should I do business with you rather than any other option—including doing nothing?" The answer is what I call your Unique Selling Proposition (USP). Your lead magnet should make dead certain that the factors that make you different are clearly spelled out. This provides fuel to your Call to Action (something else you need in your magnet, do NOT forget that critical piece) that compels them to act without hesitation, knowing that the benefit they want can only be found with your products/services.

Don't rely on hope, networking, or prospecting grunt work to get customers through your door or to your website. Create a lead-generation system that includes these key components to get them to raise their hands and ask for YOU.

The Seamless System Wins

Many big, dumb companies wind up with separate, separately ruled little fiefdoms. Advertising. Marketing. Social Media. Sales. Their princes view each other with suspicion. Often, they compete with each other for budget dollars. They don't respect each other's roles or value. The whole thing winds up a patchwork quilt, with big, ugly seams separating each patch. *You* probably can't afford this all-too-common level of corporate dysfunction.

In its place, you want a seamless system—a customer-centric system.

It's entirely about the customer, and totally designed and organized to move someone seamlessly from first point of contact along a single, well-paved and fenced-in path to the point of sale. If that point of first contact is in social media, terrific—but then you must move that person from the avenue through your driveway, onto your garden path, and ultimately to the point of sale.

Making the Sale
by Kim Walsh-Phillips

"Well, it was a gold bomber jacket. How could people stay away?" said art advisor Stefano Basilico after the sale. "I think we're going to start seeing a lot of bomber jackets come out at auction from now on."

This quote ran as part of a story on www.ArtNews.com after Christie's Auction House ran a record-breaking auction of contemporary art including Seth Price's Vintage Bomber 2006 that sold for $785,000, beating its high estimate by more than ten times.

That night, Christie's grossed $852.9 million. The artists included Cy Twombly, Ed Ruscha, Peter Doig, Martin Kippenberger, Elaine Sturtevant, and Seth Price. Seventy-five of the 80 lots on offer found buyers, for an impressive sell-through rate by lot of 94%.

Warhol's Triple Elvis [Ferus Type]) 1963 sold for $81.9 million and Warhol's Four Marlons made $69.6 million. An untitled Cy Twombly from 1970 handily surpassed its estimate, $35 million to $55 million, selling for $69.6 million with premium.

"The evening was primarily made up of people buying for themselves," Brett Gorvy, Christie's chairman and international head of postwar and contemporary art, said at the postsale press conference. He pointed out there were 500 bidders from 43 different countries and that new buyers were facilitated by recent "outreach" efforts in Shanghai, Hong Kong, and the Middle East.

"This was a collecting-buying pool tonight, rather than dealers," he said.

Christie's got it right. It wasn't inviting people to an art opening or gallery event. It was cultivating relationships with qualified art buyers from around the world in order to make a sale.

And it was record-breaking.

Many brands on social media stay in the engagement stage and never move onto the sale. They want "Likes" because it makes them feel good to have people connected to them.

Likes can't be deposited in the bank and won't pay your bills.

How you make the sale has to be determined BEFORE you create content. Using the famous Covey tactic, begin with the end in mind.

How to Do It Right

Michael Kors, world-renowned, award-winning designer of luxury accessories and ready-to-wear, did a fantastic job of incorporating a sales strategy into Facebook marketing.

According to its case study on Facebook:

> *Michael Kors launched a new sneaker product line. The launch, the brand's biggest new product launch, reached the target customers (women, ages 15 to 35) for the shoes—"decked out with luxe textures, metallic accents, and high-shine studs"— so Michael Kors decided it would make Facebook a key focus. The launch kicked off the brand's move into sneakers, and was part of a broader effort to attract new customers to the brand. The campaign primarily aimed to increase awareness and drive purchases of the new sneakers.*

It created an exclusive sneaker line of 500 pairs that sold out in a matter of seconds via Facebook, prior to releasing a full new line in its stores. In many locations, that second release sold out as well, no doubt spurred by the frenzy social media caused.

The overall results:

- Reached 36 million people in its target audience (Nielsen Online Campaign Ratings)
- Sellout of many sneaker styles in-store and online
- A 16-point increase in awareness of the new sneaker (Nielsen Brand Effect study), equating to 5.8 million incremental users aware of the sneaker
- A 16-point increase in association of Michael Kors with "Jet. Set. Go." (Nielsen Brand Effect study), equating to 5.8 million incremental users associating the brand with the message
- 1 million views of the sneaker videos attributed to the ads (www.adweek.com/socialtimes/michael-kors-limited-edition-shoe/417663)

We've used this same model for something a little less sexy than sneakers: furnaces.

For One Hour Heating and Air Conditioning in Omaha, Nebraska, we wanted to drive direct sales to a profitable offering but one that gave great value to its target market. Here's how you make a furnace sexy: Make your offer exclusive, special, and time-limited, and watch your audience behave differently. This offer was available for only 57 furnaces at a price of $981 (normally valued at $3,000) with the purchase of an air conditioning system.

When it's time to make the sale, if you've followed my advice and focused your attention only on your perfect prospects and spent time perfecting the skill of community engagement, your job will now be easy.

But how exactly does this happen?

Sometimes it's better *not* to ask for the sale of what you really want, but rather for the sale of something else entirely.

If you are old enough to have owned a Walkman, then you probably remember Columbia House's special introductory offer . . . eight records (or tapes or CDs or eight-tracks even!) for the price of one. Started as a mail-order business in 1955, Columbia House secured over 125,000 members and $1.7 million in net revenue its first year alone. Its model was, and still is with a DVD-only program, to give away its product with a small level of commitment in order to secure a customer.

The popular Asian restaurant P.F. Chang's ran a Facebook promotion in celebration of its anniversary. All of its Facebook Fans received a coupon for complimentary lettuce wraps with the purchase of any entrée. While of course this attracted a lot of new fans, the real success was that it drove 50,000 people into the restaurant for the offer, 40% of which were first-time customers.

Or in the business-to-business space, give a seminar on a topic of interest for your prospects and include one-on-one consultations as part of the event. Your attendees get a sense of what you have to offer in a trial run yet in the most-likely-to-purchase environment. Include a time-sensitive call-to-action introductory offer to your services or product to drive more prospects into your "upsell" marketing funnel.

Offering a transitional stepping stone is a strategic way to speed up your sales cycle and convert more leads into paying customers. How can you give your prospects a compelling reason to give you a try while ensuring they are committed and serious potential customers? Because if they aren't then they aren't worth pursuing any further.

Ever hear the saying that an idea is worthless without action?

Along those lines, a prospect is worthless without conversion. If you aren't actively turning your prospects into buyers, then you are missing out on a lot of potential revenue. It would be like closing your flower shop that is overflowing with red roses in inventory the day before Valentine's Day.

THE DIFFERENT METHODS OF CONVERTING YOUR LEADS INTO SALES

While there are many different ways you can convert a lead into a sale, here's how I have had the most success for our clients and firm:

- *Email follow-up sequence with a call to action.* Following up after a prospect doesn't convert means more than just emailing additional sales messages. It requires answering objectives and providing content to further nurture the relationship before making the sale.
- *Follow-up training event.* If you had a training event and your prospects did not convert, that does not mean it is a one-and-done deal. When we held our FB Sales Funnel launch in the fall, almost 500 people watched videos 1 through 4, but many did not convert until they attended a

follow-up live webinar. Give your audience different ways to learn and buy for the greatest ROI.

- *Direct-mail campaign.* If your prospect entered your marketing funnel through digital channels, it doesn't mean your conversation needs to stay there. Test taking your conversation offline to gauge whether or not that increases your conversion rate.

- *Facebook advertising.* Through Facebook's Ad platform, you can target your email list by creating a Facebook Custom Audience. Leverage this by uploading your email list and creating messaging specifically for those you targeted with your sales messages, yet did not convert, with a follow-up offer or piece of content.

- *Follow-up call.* This is the most effective, yet least often used method of sales conversion—the good ol' follow-up call. Our clients who utilize telemarketing as part of their sales process achieve a better ROI than those who don't. Sure, there is a time investment involved (which means more risk), but there's always risk when you're making money.

Loss Leaders

There are almost as many ways to structure your sale as there are things to sell.

GKIC Insider's Circle starts with a loss leader in order to get people into its membership. Most of its offer funnels start by offering a product that is worth more than the person is paying for it, plus two free months of membership. Yet, it knows it makes money on this. In fact, back when it used a three-month free membership program, it retained even more members. It chose to spend thousands a day going after leads because it is getting a high enough return on its investment.

This loss leader funnel is only advertised after the prospect has seen blog content, by seeing a content-rich ad, clicking on it, and going to the blog.

For some smaller entrepreneurs, loss leaders are not an option, at least at the beginning. Nonetheless, the goal should be to spend the most you can to acquire a high-quality customer so you can obtain them and keep them for life.

Like Dan Kennedy says, the one who can spend the most going after his target market wins.

What Do You Do to Make the Sale without Breaking Trust?

by Ari Galper

Side note from Kim: *If you head out for the night and ask the most beautiful girl in the room for her phone number and she happily gives it to you, that is the first step in successful dating. Following through, you have to actually call her in order to take her out on a date. The same is true with your social media marketing. Bringing in qualified leads is just the first step in increasing revenue. You then need to close the sale. Ari Galper, www.unlockthegame.com/NoBSGuruSecrets, is a master at selling. Many of my clients have used his coaching and training products to dramatically improve their results. I asked Ari to share some of his fundamentals of successfully selling and in this chapter, he does just that.*

So you've implemented everything you've learned in this book, and now you're moving prospects through a lead-generation process to a phone conversation with you or your sales team—to ultimately make the sale.

How are you going to make sure you are building trust with them?

What happens if you start to "sell" your solution, and they hold back from telling you the truth of their particular needs and problems?

What if you end up chasing them after the call only to hear them say, "I want to think about it"?

What if you end up burning social media leads by trying to sell the traditional way?

I'd like to introduce you to a new way of making the sale that keeps your integrity and values intact. You'll also be able to stop chasing "ghosts," prospects who express interest in your solution, but never tell you the truth of where they stand and never call you back.

Are you chasing any ghosts in your pipeline right now?

This trust-based selling approach is called Unlock The Game®. It is being used successfully by thousands of business owners and sales consultants in more than 38 countries and has been received as a "bombshell" to the entire sales industry.

Here are some of the core beliefs:

- The sale is lost at the beginning, not the end of the process.
- If your sales process starts with "pitching" your solution, you immediately signal the sales game is on and prospects will retreat to the point they are unlikely to move forward with your solution.
- If your prospective customers don't buy *how* you sell, they aren't going to buy *what* you sell.
- Once your prospects realize that you operate differently, they will open up to you. They will share important information about their budgets and timelines. They will explore options with you. If you can solve their problems, they will initiate the buying process.

How you sell makes a big difference.

Here's why, now more than ever, it's time to be open to a new way to sell. Traditional selling has become so artificial, potential clients put their guard up as soon as they sense they're being drawn into a process designed to get them to buy.

The traditional sales mindset has made selling a polarizing and dehumanizing process for both you (the seller) and your prospect (the buyer). It is a painful process of chasing people until they say "yes."

The Unlock The Game mindset is the core missing link many business owners and sales consultants have been yearning for. Once you consider adopting this new view of selling, you'll find it easy to incorporate—to begin to do less chasing while creating a sales breakthrough in your business.

Selling Can Become an Enjoyable Experience Again—Void of Pressure or Rejection

If you can view prospects as human beings instead of "targets," you'll see new and productive results immediately. You'll shift your attention away from *your* needs ("making the sale") to your potential clients' needs.

This means focusing on solving their problems. This will free you from the traditional sales conditioning that may be holding you back from your true sales potential.

Why is the mindset shift so necessary?

If you try to change your sales behaviors without first shifting your thinking, you'll eventually slip back into old habits. This can be frustrating if you're attempting to make permanent change. For years, business owners have tried to distance themselves from the negative "salesperson" stereotype by taking the "asking questions" approach. Through asking questions to uncover potential clients' needs, you make them feel that you care about them, and they stop suspecting you have a hidden agenda.

To be sure, this is a crucial way for you to learn how you can help potential clients. However, need-oriented questions will do little to make them feel comfortable with you if they suspect your questions are only part of a strategy to lead them closer to buying.

Unless you first change the intent behind your questions and unless you're sure your mindset is open—beyond the notion of thinking about the sale—there will always be an inherent conflict that makes it difficult for your potential clients to trust you.

The Unlock The Game mindset is based on three simple core principles:

> *Principle 1*: Let go of the traditional sales goal of "making the sale," and replace it with a new goal: to discover the truth of your potential client's situation.
>
> *Principle 2*: Stop defending yourself.
>
> *Principle 3*: End the chasing game.

If you understand and live by these principles, you won't ever slip back into traditional sales thinking again.

These core principles are like having your own "sales culture," just as organizations have their own "corporate culture." They will guide you to make decisions and sell in alignment with your new mindset or "culture."

Let's review these principles in more depth.

Principle 1: Discover the Truth of Your Potential Client's Situation

Let go of the traditional sales goal of "making the sale," and replace it with a new goal: to discover the truth of your potential client's situation.

"Going for the sale" has always been the driving factor behind selling. Most of us have a voice in the back of our minds after a sales call, *"Okay, things are looking good, he seems interested. Keep asking questions, and maybe he'll commit to setting up an appointment, and that'll bring me closer to a sale."*

The problem is, that voice is keeping you in *your* world and not in your potential client's world.

Your prospects can immediately sense you're not 100% focused on solving their issues. That can trigger suspicion that you're more interested in the sale than actually helping them solve their problem.

Discovering the *truth* of your potential client's situation is the most crucial part of the mindset, because if you remain in your own thoughts, it's difficult to genuinely help the other person prior to when they are ready to buy.

Sometimes, we don't always want to hear the truth (you know what movie that phrase came from) because it's not in line with "hoping" for a sale.

When you reach your prospect's truth, you may discover your solution is really not a fit for them.

As business owners and sales consultants, we want to believe that what we're selling is right for as many people as possible. But coming to terms with and feeling comfortable with the truth about whether you can help certain prospects allows you to eliminate false expectations and feelings of rejection associated with selling.

In other words, if you can get to a "no" as efficiently as you get to a "yes" (through trust-based selling), you'll find yourself spending more productive time with clients who are a perfect fit.

Giving equal weight to a "no" as well as a "yes" will help you untangle your conditioning from traditional selling—where it's always been about the "yes"—to creating the best relationship with your prospective client.

Principle 2: Stop Defending Yourself

When potential clients challenge us or bring up objections about our solutions, it's easy to react defensively. It's a natural reaction.

And when we hear common objections like, *"Why should we choose you over XYZ company?"* we often times overreact. We put even more pressure on the potential client to choose us and move forward to the sale.

Although our natural reaction is to "sell harder," this predictably only reinforces your prospect's mistrust.

Suppose the person you're speaking with says, *"We've been looking at similar services. Why should we go with you?"* Instead of staying locked into the traditional mindset and defending yourself or trying to persuade him, use trust-based language to diffuse the situation and re-engage the conversation: *"That's not a problem [relaxed, soft tone]. I'm happy not to make any assumptions that we are automatically a fit together. If you'd be open to it, how about we talk through each of your needs to see how we can address them differently so you have all the information you need."*

This response comes directly from our own trust-based language we created for virtually every sales objection and scenario.

When you let go of the idea that you have to use persuasive skills to "move" your prospect down your sales process, with all the subtle sales pressure that invariably includes, you no longer have to defend yourself ever again.

Letting go of defending and persuading frees you to explore whether what you have to offer will help solve your prospects' problems.

Principle 3: End the Chasing Game

Chasing prospects has been a basic pillar of traditional selling for decades. It's just part of the "game." The thinking goes, *"The more I pursue, the more I increase my chances of making a sale."* It comes from the traditional sales mindset, in which your primary goal is to make the sale rather than focusing on whether you can help a potential client solve a problem.

Chasing is so commonly accepted as a normal part of successful selling that even business owners who try to distance themselves from the negative stereotype of "selling" still find themselves pursuing potential clients.

Because most of us believe so strongly in our solution, we make the instinctive assumption that everyone who fits the profile of a potential client actually needs what we have. That assumption causes us to shift into "chase mode" whenever we meet someone who fits our profile.

We then try to create forward momentum by hoping (I call it using the drug "hopeium"!) that because this person fits our profile, the conversation will lead to a sale. Unfortunately, "hopeium" only creates false expectations that, in many cases, lead us to rejection and loss of the sale.

Chasing positions us to feel that we're bothering or distracting potential clients from their normal daily activities. It's easy to feel as if you're intruding on their time, and that can eventually take a toll on your sales self-confidence. With a shift to the Unlock The Game mindset, your thoughts no longer get caught up in premature expectations based on your own needs.

Instead, you'll discover what it's like to not make immediate assumptions about every potential client you speak with. You'll begin saying to yourself, *"Because I don't yet know the truth of this person's situation, I'm not sure whether I can help them or not, or even whether they have a problem, or whether they feel that solving that problem is a priority."*

Most sales consultants don't realize they could stop chasing by gracefully telling potential clients something as simple as: *"Would you be open to us circling back on our calendars to set up a time to chat again, so we both don't end up chasing each other?"* This is another way of asking to set up a next call without applying sales pressure so they respect you each step of the way.

When you've developed enough trust with your prospect using mindset and trust-based language, they will feel you're genuinely interested in helping them solve their problem and not there just to make the sale.

Like challenging-and-defending, chasing-and-avoiding is an "old mindset" game. Taking a personal vow to end the chasing game will take your sales results and peace of mind to a whole new level!

You see, chasing puts you in a subservient position to your potential client. It fuels the negative "aggressive" sales stereotype that so many of us hate and want to avoid at all costs.

The responsibility is on us to start new relationships with humility and the sincere intention of helping others instead of ourselves. A modest, unassuming manner makes it easier for potential clients to open up and begin telling us the truth of their situation so we don't have to chase them along the way.

The Sale Is Lost at the Beginning and Not the End

As you're reading this, thousands of business owners are reviewing their monthly sales pipelines, scratching their heads, and wondering why so many of their sales consultants' "leads" never pan out. And when they talk with their sales teams, the focus of discussion is usually centered around, *"What happened at the end of the process that caused the deal to drop off?"*

My hunch is that they're probably not discussing what happened at the *beginning* of the sales process that triggered the sales opportunities to disappear.

With the Unlock The Game approach, the emphasis shifts to building relationships that allow trust to emerge at the very beginning of the sales process, literally at "Hello."

That way, you can be sure you're operating with truthful information about your potential client's true goals throughout your presales relationship.

Humanizing the Sales Process

Subconsciously, many of us use words and phrases that categorize us as someone who has the intention of making a sale. This immediately associates us with the negative "salesperson" stereotype.

Common phrases such as *"I'm just calling to see if you'd be interested"* or *"I'm calling to see if you'd be willing to explore"* categorize us as someone with the traditional sales mindset.

At the end of what has been a good conversation, traditional sales conditioning kicks in and we attempt to close an appointment by saying, *"How about we set up a time to discuss the next steps?"* or *"How about we schedule a time to move things forward?"*

But those "closing" questions are a dead giveaway that you're really focused on moving things forward to reach your goal: the sale.

What if you attempt to move them forward and the prospects aren't ready yet?

What can you break between you and them? Trust.

Remember, the goal of this mindset is to build trust.

It's important to change to trust-based sales languaging that doesn't connect you to the negative sales stereotype. Rather than closing an initial conversation by pushing them to the next step, try asking (with a soft tone and relaxed voice): *"Where do you think we should go from here?"*

You'll be amazed what happens when you ask this question at the end of your initial sales conversations. Miraculously, they start opening up and telling you the truth, which is your new goal.

Here are more samples of our Unlock The Game trust-based language:e

- "Does it make sense to"
- "Would you be open to"
- "Is there anything I can do to make you more comfortable about how we might be able to work together?"

Trust-based phrases like these are a big relief to potential clients who may start to suspect that, as the conversation draws to an end, you're going to pressure them to move to a next step.

Trust-based language diffuses inherent pressure in the sales conversation and gives the other person the message that your thoughts are not about your goal—the sale. Instead, you're simply asking them how they're feeling so far and where they want to go next. Their response will tell you whether the two of you have really created trust.

You'll discover this kind of trust-based language also makes you feel much more comfortable because it makes rejection impossible. Instead of pushing a potential client for a "yes" or a "no," you're simply talking about the possibility of whether both of you are a fit together, without making any assumptions.

For more from Ari, visit www.UnlockTheGame.com/NBGuruSecrets.

Where's Your Hidden Money?

by Kim Walsh-Phillips

If you haven't yet launched a product, program, or service to sell or you are looking for supplemental income, then you are just like me a few years ago.

I have always been a public speaker, sharing my expertise in a (fingers crossed) entertaining way to audiences around the world. I have also always written a lot of content and used it to connect with my audience.

Until I was introduced to the world of information marketing, I didn't sell anything when I spoke. I would get paid by the event organizer and hope that someone in the crowd would become a client.

Fast forward to today where we have developed programs that teach people how to monetize their marketing (see examples at www.NoBSSocialMediaBook.com). While we run these programs and promotions readily as part of our overall business structure, I can also call upon them to bring us quick surges of cash.

Before I took my friends and family on the Disney VIP Tour in celebration of my 40th birthday, I ran a one-hour webinar and made enough money to pay for the entire trip without having to dip into my savings.

We can activate our list when needed to drive them to the sale because we have products waiting that we've developed with their needs in mind. This is the hidden money in our business.

Where Is Your Money Hiding?

The easiest place to start is with the hidden money you already have in your business. These are moneymakers that are sitting there, waiting to give you revenue. You'd be surprised how many there are.

FINISH YOUR ONLINE COURSE OR PRODUCT

If you are almost done, go ahead and launch the product. Set a deadline for yourself, and stick to it. If you want to be really aggressive, give yourself 30 days to finish the content and 30 days to build out a promotion. Or do something like the project I worked on with content-marketing superstar Ahava Leibtag, my interviewee in Chapter 11. She produced a webinar to give content and sell the program, and conducted the next three webinars live, recorded them and then sold the recordings.

GKIC Insider's Circle has developed a brilliant way to create products. It invites people to attend a livecast for free. The livecast is then recorded and sold during the program. It uses the sales funnel as the product. It also sells a product and membership during the livecast opt-in process that more than covers its production costs. And it can retarget anyone who opts in with future offers.

I have learned a lot over the years about getting people engaged on the webinar, keeping them engaged, and getting them to respond to your call to action to buy. A lot of the strategies I have found to work may be controversial as they are manipulative and persuasive. And they are. If you have a product or service that can help people, then you have a moral obligation to do everything in your power to get them to take action. Everything. This stuff is powerful, and so it is all about using your powers for good and not evil.

I've perfected my webinar selling technique over time and have a show-up rate of around 50% and a 100% engagement level throughout the whole presentation. I generally close 20% to 40% of those online.

In my pre-event promotion, I make a point of telling people to show up early in order to secure their spot. I get on the webinar early and welcome guests, telling them to close all other windows down and put their phone on silent. I let them know that I will be moving quickly and they will want to devote all of their attention to this training to get the most out of it.

In my welcome, I always have a slide that includes my headshot and media logos of where I have spoken to set up credibility. I also come on screen during the beginning, so the viewers can see I am an actual person. This creates bonding and rapport with my audience.

I start by asking an interactive question. I usually ask people where they are watching the training from and what snack and/or beverage they are enjoying. I announce these to the audience so they know the depth of the attendees.

As a key strategy, I call out a few people in my attendee list who didn't answer. This lets the audience know that they must pay attention and stay engaged or they are going to be called out on it. Anytime you see your attention rate go below 90%, ask a question and call out someone who doesn't participate. It will only happen once or twice, and everyone will be fully engaged.

I open with telling them the transformative value they will get by being on the training. I say, "You made the right decision being on here today because you are going to discover how to drive qualified leads and sales through Facebook. I am also going to share a few mistakes you are most likely making that's costing you money and a compelling, albeit controversial, landing page strategy." In this one sentence, I have given them intrigue, curiosity, and suspense, all tied around keeping them involved and engaged in the training.

Next, I share who this is for and who it isn't for. Here, I self-identify with the audience. I like to connect with them in a way that is uplifting and supportive.

I share what topic we are focusing on and why it is an issue now. People need to know why it is urgent that they address it right now. I explain what the consequences will be if they don't deal with this problem right now. I give instructions to take notes and tell them a few phrases that they should write down. This helps to keep the audience engaged and paying attention and sets up my authority as being in charge.

I then share my story. It is important every time that I share where I was before, how I found a solution, and how it got me to where I am now. I have to let the audience know that I wasn't always this successful. I understand their journey, and I want to share what helped me make a change for the better. I feel compelled each time to share with my audience how I struggled to survive for a long time and only once I discovered how to make direct response social media marketing work did our company turn around.

I then present problem agitation, sharing mistakes a lot of people make that they are probably making, too. Of course, I provide some real content. I have experimented and tested this multiple times, and have found that I should never give any more than three ideas, lessons, or tips to my audience. I am sure that doesn't sound like a lot, but anytime I have given more than three my audience is lost and overwhelmed. People are also much less likely to buy, and they don't leave my training nearly as satisfied. Giving no more than three gives a quick win they can take right then that feels good and they can move forward on.

I transition into the close with, "Of course you want to (outcome you have been talking about), and now you have two choices. You can either do it alone, wasting time and money as you figure it all out, or you can let me come alongside you, holding your hand every step of the way as you _____ (outcome)."

I finish by giving my offer, describing the transformative value of what will happen if they buy, not the products themselves. An advanced strategy that works very well is that I gave proprietary names to my strategies with course offerings and products. This increases the curiosity factor, the value of the course, and my authority.

I recognize early-bird buyers by name and thank them for signing up. This gives them the appreciation and recognition they deserve and encourages others to buy. Besides taking live questions, I also always add on a fast-action bonus. While there are those who will jump right in and buy, many need an extra push to get into action. Announcing the names and giving a fast-action bonus will help.

I never send out replays. I have a much higher showing rate and my overall sales have increased. But I do send out follow-up emails to those who attended. There are always a few stragglers who buy after the training ends.

To check out this strategy and see my process in action, sign up for a free Facebook sales training at www.FBSalesLaunch.com.

Follow this template as a starting point, and then test your own strategies to produce the best results. Between what I do for our firm, affiliates, and clients, I give over 50 webinars a year and I am still perfecting my process.

SELL A WEBINAR

Hold a live event online that you charge for and use the recording as a digital product to sell after the event. You can simply use PowerPoint or Keynote and GoToWebinar to deliver your presentation and produce the recording One of the courses I created this way is our LinkedIn Domination Course (http://www.lidominationworkshop.com). I hold it first as a live event and then sell the recording ongoing. That is, until I host the next live one and do it all over again.

WRITE AN EBOOK

The thought of writing a book may seem daunting. I get it. Writing this book is no walk in the park. (I do not drink nearly as much coffee when walking in the park as I have writing this book ,for example. And I may smile more when in a park.) But writing an ebook does not need to be daunting. If you have a collection of blogs, you could simply book them together, add in an opening and closing chapter, and voila! Your ebook is complete. Or if you want to start from scratch, there is a simple process to follow that can get your book done in one day.

1. Come up with a book theme. For example, for an accounting firm, the book might be "How to Increase Your Profit Without Increasing Your Sales."

2. Write ten questions to answer as part of that theme. Questions might include: What are the hidden business deductions I am probably missing? What company structure is most profitable? What employee classifications benefit my bottom line the most?

3. Write down three bullet points answering each question.

4. Record yourself answering each question, using your bullet points as your guide.

5. Send your recording to a transcriber. (We use www.InternetTranscribers.com but there are many out there that will work for you.)

6. Edit the final transcript.

7. Hire a freelancer on ODesk or HireMyMom.com to design the book for you.

8. Lift up your hand and reach over your shoulder to your back and pat yourself because you have your product and you are officially a published author.

9. You can either sell the book directly on your site or sell it through Amazon's Kindle publishing program KDP. If you want to add in a bonus, include an audible version of the ebook as well.

Offer Gift Certificates

If you sell products or services, a gift certificate can be an effective entry point to help pay for your marketing and get customers in the door. This is really a coupon with a higher perceived value. You are giving a time-sensitive reason for the recipient to act now in order to receive something of value. We run a campaign for a bath remodeler using this strategy.

PACKAGE THE HOLIDAYS

We all know to wish our fans on social media well on the big holidays, but have you ever thought how you could turn those holidays into a promotion? More creative than a 20% MERRYXMAS20 code, use the holidays as an opportunity for a unique offering.

A lot of the messaging for The Fertility Center is centered around women because we've found that the female partner is doing the majority of the research in family planning. But that doesn't mean that we can't focus a bit on the dad-to-be as well. For Father's Day we developed an exclusive package that none of its competitors were even coming close to. The Quick Start Paternity Planner included a miniconsultation, a semen analysis, and weekly fertility-boosting tips. (It was an email that the company was already doing, so it wasn't any extra work.) For very minimal effort and costs, we got four couples to sign up and buy the package, equalling about $100,000 in potential revenue for a promotion that cost about $150. As an added community-relations bonus, this promotion also connected with couples who were struggling. Instead of being sad or frustrated on Father's Day, we wanted to give them an outlet to help reach their goal of starting a family. (See Figure 13.1 on page 250.)

CREATE A BONUS GIFT

The founder of Digital Marketer, Ryan Deiss, has a lot more going on than this online membership organization. Ryan's holding company, Idea Incubator LP, employs more than 80 people all over the world and owns dozens of companies, both online and offline, ranging from survival blogs to industrial water filter manufacturers. One of the companies he owns is RAW, Really Amazing Women, which describes itself as "A community for women, by women. Our goal is to nurture an

FIGURE 13.1: The Fertility Center Holiday Package Offer

environment where we can be the best version of ourselves. Where we can grow, connect, engage, but most of all be free to express ourselves and learn more about embracing our world and loving this life."

In a promotion for RAW, Really Amazing Women, its sales funnel does not start with a promotion about RAW. Instead, it starts with a free gift that pulls the viewer in to a series of micro-commitments. The site www.MakeUpTutorials.com starts the customer relationship by offering one makeup brush for sale.

FIGURE 13.2: RAW Free Gift Promotion Landing Page

Once the purchasers say yes, they are then taken to another landing page where they are offered the chance to add more brushes and sign up for the makeup tutorial subscription. (See Figure 13.2 and Figure 13.3 on page 252.)

FIGURE 13.3: RAW Free Gift Promotion Nurture Page

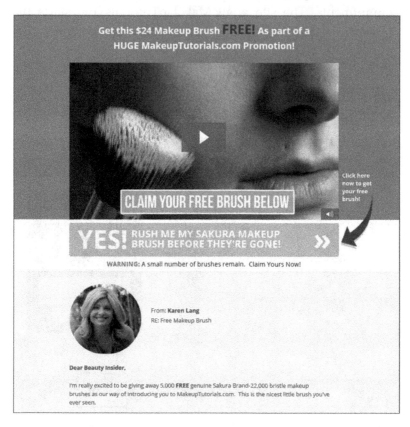

Not until step three are you asked for credit card information (see Figure 13.4 on page 253).

When you complete the purchase, you are then invited to get an entire set for free as long as you take the subscription to RAW, which is $19.95 a month. (See Figure 13.5 on page 254.)

It is building subscriptions for an online community of women that focuses on building self-esteem and self-confidence. It is leading with this, though. They are leading with makeup brushes, a much easier sell.

FIGURE 13.4: RAW Free Gift Promotion Credit Card Page for Shipping and Handling

Claim Your FREE Sakura Makeup Brush Plus Your FREE Quick How To Care For Your Brush Video

Free Sakura Makeup Brush   How To Care For Your Brush Video

+

You Get a FREE Sakura Makeup Brush (a $24.00 Value) Plus a
FREE Quick How To Care For Your Brush Video, All Absolutely 100% FREE!
All we ask is that you cover the Shipping and Handling

Your Shopping Cart   Your order is safe and secure

Quantity	Product	Price	Total	Remove
1	Sakura Brush Sakura Makeup Brush	Free	$0.00	X

Subtotal:	$0.00
Shipping:	$4.95
Total:	**$4.95**

Billing Information

Required fields are in **bold**.

BUY WITH
MasterPass

Norton
SECURED
powered by Symantec

First Name	
Last Name	
Phone	
Email	
Confirm Email	
Address	
Address 2	
City	
ZIP/Postal Code	

We have used this strategy for other clients as well, from products in front of membership to a book as the starting point in a launch. We are reaching people where they are with what they want and giving them what they actually need later on.

FIGURE 13.5: RAW Free Gift Campaign Upsell Page

Be creative when you are thinking of lead generation and that first sale. It does not need to be directly tied to what you do, but instead aligned with the needs of your target market. Remember, those that buy from you are 70% more likely to buy from you again. Your goal should be to get that first sale in place.

From Sales Funnels to "Income At Will"

by Dan Kennedy

A business that obtained a mailing list of over 100,000 well-chosen potential customers launched a major marketing campaign, with high hopes. The list was targeted to match up with the demographics of its current, avatar clients. There was significant disposable income to be had. The copy was good. And the open rate and click-through rate were high.

The campaign was a total bust.

A mystery, but not one without clues. To borrow from a Sherlock Holmes tale, it's about what was *missing*, not what was *there*. The dog that didn't bark.

The one thing not known and certain about these 100,000 was whether or not they were buyers in this product category who bought by the means through which this marketer was selling. Matched demographics do not equal matched behavior.

One of my best rules is that buyers are buyers and non-buyers are nonbuyers. Offline, with direct mail, lists available in the rental marketplace are divided into compiled and response lists. A compiled list contains people chosen by age, gender, geography, household income, and other demographic facts and statistics. A response list, which costs considerably more to rent, has that information but also only assembles people who have responded, that is, they have requested information or purchased.

An example of the difference is women, age 45 to 60, married, with household income above $100,000.00 vs. women, age 45 to 60, married, with household income above $100,000.00 who have purchased a $100 to $200 collection of anti-aging skin-care products within the last 90 days from a direct-mail piece or catalog. The first group has only potential customers eligible to buy; the latter group has buyers. It's the difference between fishing where we hope there are fish and fishing where we know there are fish.

For more about mailing lists, I recommend the book *The Direct-Mail Solution* by Craig Simpson, to which I contributed. Craig is my "go-to guy" for lists, and, beyond that, an expert freelance direct-mail project manager handling hundreds of campaigns for hundreds of clients, totaling many millions of pieces mailed each year. His clients include Beach Body, which you've seen on TV, a "brain doctor" frequently seen on PBS, groups of local financial advisors, a 23-store chain in the pet industry, and many others. You can meet Craig at www. Simpson-Direct.com.

Online you are more often building your own list, rather than renting lists others have already built. Social media plays a big role in this. That's the source of the list of 100,000 that so bitterly disappointed its owner.

So, what went wrong?

It's one thing to attract people and arouse their interest. It's another thing to extract money from them. In fact, the entire culture of social media (and a lot of other online media) is all about "free" and "cheap." It acts in conflict with a marketer's desire to convert visitors and wanderers and freebie-loving citizens into paying customers. These 100,000 were drawn from that population, then this marketer spoiled them rotten by giving them enormous amounts of free content for more than a year before attempting to move them into a sales path or funnel.

Yes, during that time, the marketer included blog links to other people's products and services (to earn affiliate commissions) and occasionally showcased some of their products and services, ever so gently. But they never once opened a door and asked the potential buyers in this population, the gold needles in the giant haystack, the ready-to-buy-now folks in the giant herd of casual window shoppers—to come on in and then to sell them something. It put a store in the mall, then kept its doors locked for a year, hoping to build fascination and desire. Too long. Too slow.

A key strategy you need to put in place is an open door (with more doors opening frequently), through which real buyers can step to separate themselves from all the rest. By doing so, they identify themselves to you as legitimate potential buyers so you can aggressively sell to them. If your media and social media approach lacks this, you are at high risk of winding up with a low-value list that's damnably difficult to monetize. In fact, the ready-to-buy-now buyers tend to be impatient about not being invited to a good sales presentation and an offer to buy now, so they wander off and are lost forever.

You also need to teach people to respond. People need to be told and shown how they are supposed to behave with you, in your world. That's why specific Lead Generation Magnet offers (See Chapter 6) are so important. They teach people to step forward, raise their hands, ask for, and say yes to something. It's a very bad idea to push all the information you can share out to everybody. It's a much better idea to offer some of the best of it only to those who say yes to a specific offer.

Much of this is contrary to most of what you see in social media or are advised to do by social media promoters who care only about bragging-rights numbers like likes, views, retweets, etc., but not about money in the bank. Don't let that bother you. The majority is wrong about everything, particularly money. And the majority is definitely wrong about this. Marketing is mostly made up of monkey seeing, monkey doing, with no real knowledge of direct marketing, split-testing, or harsh accountability. Just money spent. Don't copy *that*. So,

- Do not leave everybody together in one space, free to wander.
- Do not create spoiled-brat children by overfeeding them for free, for very long, without at least asking for some action and indication of responsiveness.
- Segment your list by areas of expressed interest and by responsiveness.

- Speed up the sales cycle by opening doors for the ready-to-buy-now buyers.
- Create well-structured sales pathways or funnels leading to a buying decision.
- Last, don't be overly afraid of repelling or alienating non-buyers. Don't be overly sensitive to criticism from non-buyers. The votes that really count belong to the buyers.

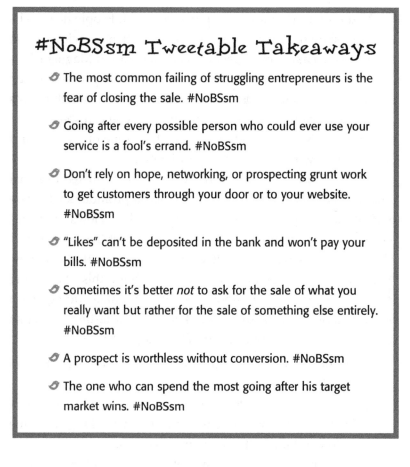

#NoBSsm Tweetable Takeaways

- The most common failing of struggling entrepreneurs is the fear of closing the sale. #NoBSsm

- Going after every possible person who could ever use your service is a fool's errand. #NoBSsm

- Don't rely on hope, networking, or prospecting grunt work to get customers through your door or to your website. #NoBSsm

- "Likes" can't be deposited in the bank and won't pay your bills. #NoBSsm

- Sometimes it's better *not* to ask for the sale of what you really want but rather for the sale of something else entirely. #NoBSsm

- A prospect is worthless without conversion. #NoBSsm

- The one who can spend the most going after his target market wins. #NoBSsm

CHAPTER 14

Transformation through
Optimization

Landing Page Optimization:
An Interview with Tim Ash

by Kim Walsh-Phillips

Social media is just a channel to acquire leads and move them toward the sale.

Pull qualified prospects out of social media as quickly as possible and onto a channel you own, such as your website or a separate landing page.

When this is your goal, you'll realize that effective social media marketing is only part of the equation.

Converting traffic into leads and sales once it hits your website is just as important.

I interviewed optimization expert Tim Ash to learn about the mistakes businesses are making with their websites and landing pages as well as strategies to increase lead and sales conversions.

Tim is the bestselling author of *Landing Page Optimization* and CEO of SiteTuners. A computer scientist and cognitive scientist by education (his Ph.D. studies were in neural networks and artificial intelligence), he has developed an expertise in user-centered design, persuasion, and understanding online behavior, and landing page testing. In the mid-1990s he became one of the early pioneers in the discipline of website conversion rate optimization.

Over the past 15 years, Tim has helped a number of major U.S. and international brands to develop successful web-based initiatives. Companies like Google, Expedia, Kodak, eHarmony, Facebook, American Express, Canon, Nestle, Symantec, Intuit, AutoDesk, and many others have benefitted from Tim's deep understanding and innovative perspective.

Tim is also the online voice of conversion optimization as the host of the "Landing Page Optimization" podcast on WebmasterRadio.fm.

Where Testing and Optimization DON'T Intersect

Kim: What are some of the biggest mistakes folks are making that they could correct to make their site more optimized?

Tim: I devote an entire chapter in my *Landing Page Optimization* book to what I call "the seven deadly sins of landing page design." They are pretty common, endemic in almost every page we see.

There is too much text on the page, usually for good reasons like SEO, but it's still too much text. There are visual distractions: an unclear call to action, too much choice. These things overwhelm people by expecting them to digest your stuff.

You have to remember that most visitors are guaranteed to be lazy with short attention spans. They are apt to act in a stupid way because they are not investing the time to understand everything.

They have the attention span of a burning match.

Kim: Companies spend all of this energy on SEO to drive traffic to their site, but if they get a lot of traffic they can't convert, it's completely wasted.

Tim: That's right. There are really three stages to online marketing. One is to interrupt people, get their attention, and get them to your site. This is traffic acquisition. The next is conversion rate optimization, or how to get them to act once they are on your site. Finally, once you have established contact (and hopefully the right to speak to them via email or some other means), it's time to increase the lifetime value of the relationship by nurturing the lead.

We basically do something that affects all traffic sources. From pay-per-click ads to when people type your URL in the browser to social media or whatever your methods are for getting them there, they still interact with the landing page or website. Those are the things we tune and improve.

Kim: For the average entrepreneurs who are trying to optimize their sites (and maybe want to get into a little bit of testing), what would be a couple of things you would recommend they start testing first?

Tim: Testing is not the same as conversion rate optimization or landing page optimization. They are not equivalent. A lot of people say, "Test! Test! Test!" and that is great, but there are limitations to testing. Maybe you have highly seasonal traffic. If you are dropping emails, you cannot really do too much testing.

A very common problem is not having enough data. People say, "I have a bazillion people visiting my site," and I ask, "How many conversions do you have, actual form fills, sales, or what have you?" Unless you have ten conversions a day, you cannot even talk about basic A/B split testing where you have the original version vs. another version you are testing.

Testing is based on statistics, and for that you need a large number of conversions. It cannot even be used in a low-volume environment. Unless you are spending a lot of money to drive traffic, yes, the leads have high value, but you do not have enough of them to figure out how to optimize your landing page.

Kim: Let's say I am getting 150 conversions a day. What is something I might want to look at first?

Tim: We always prioritize when we come up with test strategy, the combination of potentially biggest impact with the least amount of work. "Biggest impact" means how much traffic and value is running through a particular page or part of your website, or how steady that traffic is.

Or how broken is a given page or system, and how easy would it be to fix? If you are talking about a very high-volume page, you might only need a headline change, a button change, or how your call to action is presented. That is very easy. It is just some graphics or text on a page.

On the other hand, if you are saying, "I am going to change my entire registration or sign-up process," it is a big project for an unknown payoff.

However, you should not think that every test is going to be a winner. In fact, you might have bad ideas that could underperform what you have right now. But it doesn't mean you shouldn't still try.

Think of it like the DEA. They get part of their budget by selling off the assets of the drug dealers they have taken down. This thing should be self-funding. If you are making money for the company, say, "Give me 10% of the improvement to put back into testing activities." It kind of snowballs from there.

Kim: I just had a conversation with a client yesterday who said, "Well, I don't think that program can produce beautiful pages or beautiful emails." She was talking about a specific product.

We talked about how "beautiful" does not necessarily convert the best. I know I have had that same conversation with this client before. She might not love how it looks, but it is the one that has done the best for her.

How do you deal with this kind of response?

Tim: Nearly half of our brain is devoted to processing visual information in one form or another. It is very important to us. We definitely have aesthetic reactions—we love it or hate it. But like you say, the only thing that matters is what rings the cash register.

If the CEO of the company comes in and says, "I like purple polka dot buttons on the landing page," we say, "Great!"

We test more and throw purple polka dots into the mix.

"Oh, look! The green button won by 20%. That means an extra million dollars a year to you. Do you still want to go with the purple polka dot one?" This is a very different conversation.

Whenever you can, co-opt other ideas. As long as you have the data rate or the traffic, the number of conversions to data test, feel free to throw some other versions in the mix. You just need to find one better-performing version. But for political reasons sometimes you need to throw dumb ideas into the test as well. Who knows? The boss may be right and the purple polka dot one may win! In that case, you are still a happy camper.

Kim: For sure. We just ran one like this. We would have assumed the logo would have been the worst possible thing to run in a social media post, but it did the best out of every ad. You just cannot assume. Ever.

Tim: It's a new definition of *pretty*: the one that makes you the most money. That is the prettiest one.

Kim: Can you talk about progressive disclosure as a way of releasing web content?

Tim: Basically, the idea is that if you ask me to take a 30-foot standing broad jump, I'm not even going to try. If you have a form or some kind of registration path or process or checkout flow on your page that is very complicated and imposing, it is unlikely that I'm going to go through the process.

However, if you ask for just a little bit of information now and then over the course of multiple interactions with me perhaps fill in the rest of it, then I am willing to do bite-sized chunks over time.

Basically, you should not ask for a whole form fill, like "What industry are you in? How many employees does your company have? How likely are you to buy in the next three months?"

That works for your salesperson on the phone, but it is not necessarily what I want early in the process. However, if you collected my email in exchange for an educational download, and then got my phone number, and then got my mailing address, and you did that over several interactions and incentivized me to do each of those in baby steps, you are still going to get the lead. It is just going to take a little longer.

In fact, you are going to get more leads because your funnel flows smoothly instead of abruptly requiring I hand over my Social Security number and my firstborn child.

Kim: It is like trying to get someone you just met at the bar to marry you.

Tim: Buy me a drink first.

For more from Tim Ash, visit www.SiteTuners.com. For the conference, visit www.ConversionConference.com. And pick up a copy of Tim's book, *Landing Page Optimization*, on Amazon or anywhere fine books are sold.

Testing, Testing, 1, 2, 3: The Number-One Way to Prevent Wasted Marketing Dollars
by Kim Walsh-Phillips

I have no desire to throw away a single dollar of my hard-earned money. And I am sure the same is true for you.

Along the same topic of conversation I had with Tim in the last section, another reason why social media should be a tool in any sophisticated marketer's arsenal is the ability to test theories and optimize accordingly in a moment's notice. Unlike direct mail, print advertising, or other media channels, there is no need to invest significant dollars or wait 30, 60, or 90 days to see if version A, B, or C of your ad works. Tracked correctly, in a day or two you will know exactly what the results are of your different ads and can scale up or down accordingly.

I attended a conference a few years ago and sat in complete disbelief. During an awards program, no one was told why the winners had been selected or how it had anything to do with the dollars-and-sense results of the ad creation that caused them to win.

Nothing.

And this was a major ADVERTISING conference.

It did not matter one bit how much money was spent on the ad campaign vs. how much was earned. Accolades and pretty crystal statues were served up regardless of ROI.

Of course it is much easier to operate this way. Fluffy awareness-based campaigns can be based on assumptions, guesses, gut instincts, or even on the artistic, whims of a quirky creative director. They are campaigns that are "fun" to put together and stress-free as they don't have any level of accountability. But they should only be used if you are also willing to light your money on fire.

Put the match away.

Foolish companies allow their money to be spent on whims.

Great marketing that produces monetary results is based on facts, not guesses. Optimized results are developed by examining data and changing campaigns accordingly.

In comes the power of social media. In real time, you can optimize an ad campaign based on an audience's behaviors, likes, habits, and hobbies. You can instantly scale advertising spend up or down depending on the results you are getting.

Split Testing

The reality is, though, that very few businesses use even 20% of social media's power. So they are wasting their dollars time and time again in this channel. They guess instead of test. They assume instead of research.

One rule of marketing that I have found to be true time and time again is assumptions are usually wrong. When I am speaking to an audience or presenting online training, I share some of our top split tests. And 90% of the time, the audience gets it wrong.

Nine times out of ten, they are wrong.

Meaning that if ads are only created on assumptions as to what will work the best, then ads would never be optimized. Just think how much money is wasted! Just think of all the vacations at the beach with a hot sun, a cool breeze, and an ice-cold drink in your hand could have been taken with this money. Stop assuming and start testing.

On the following three pages are some split tests to challenge your wits. Guess which one you think won. The answer for Figures 14.1 and 14.2 is on page 271. The answer for Figures 14.3 and 14.4 is also on page 271. The answer for Figures 14.5 and 14.6 is on page 272.

How many did you guess correctly?

If you are like my audiences, not many.

Do you know the one thing I am 100% sure about in marketing?

That is, I don't know all of the answers (or even most of them).

In my career I am blessed to be able to do a lot of professional speaking and am often asked questions about the best ways to execute strategies. I get questions such as how often to post a new Facebook status, the best times to send out an email, or the most effective headlines to generate the biggest response. While I can offer general best practices (post at most once per day, don't send out your emails on a Monday, and make the headline about the target audience's pain), I can't offer specific strategies without one very important step—testing.

FIGURE 14.1: The Fertility Center Split Test Ad #1

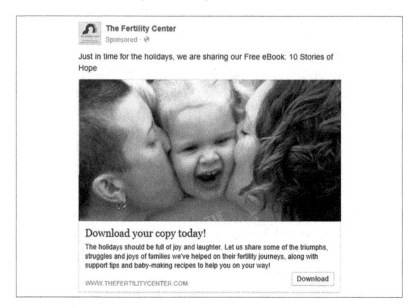

FIGURE 14.2: The Fertility Center Split Test Ad #2

FIGURE 14.3: Bath Planet Split Test Ad #1

FIGURE 14.4: Bath Planet Split Test Ad #2

FIGURE 14.5: GKIC Split Test Ad #1

FIGURE 14.6: GKIC Split Test Ad #2

FIGURE 14.7: The Fertility Center Split Test Ad Winner

FIGURE 14.8: Bath Planet Split Test Ad Winner

FIGURE 14.9: GKIC Split Test Ad Winner

Testing communications strategies to a small segment of the target audience before launching to the entire audience is a way to gather data on the most effective method of communication. Testing small is the number-one way we prevent wasting money in our clients' marketing campaigns and can show continuous improvement.

Imagine an ice cream manufacturer releasing a new flavor. It doesn't just put something together and send it directly to the stores for sales. It creates several versions, tests in-house, tests out-of-house, and then chooses the option that performs best.

Your marketing should be treated the same way—with no guesses or assumptions.

We recently split-tested email time-of-day for one of our clients and found that sending email in the evening received double the response rate vs. the same email sent in the morning. We can (and will!) use this data to optimize its future messaging.

Take the emotion out of your marketing, and execute your strategies based on measurable results from your testing.

Our motto: Test small and launch big.

When testing, keep the following social media ad-testing best practices in mind:

- *Track conversions, not clicks.* You want to optimize your overall ROI, not waste dollars on clicks. An ad that gets 100 clicks is NOT better than an ad than only gets 25, if the second ad gets more conversions.
- *Set up the target market demographics so you are always testing only one thing at a time.* If you combine too many variables in your ads, it will be difficult to optimize them well. (Was it the moms who did best or those who were recently engaged?)
- *Start with split-testing the demographic,* and then use the best performing demographic in the rest of the tests. (Do moms who like rugby do better than moms who like HGTV?)
- *For the ad image that performs the best, test changing the ad's coloring to see if it performs better.* (Does a black background perform better than blue or white? Better than red?)
- *Take the best coloring of the ad, and test different wording to see if that makes a difference.* (If we tell them to "click here" vs. "download now," does that do better?)
- *Test adding a call-to-action button vs. running without a button.* (Does adding a call to action hurt sales because your social media post now looks like an ad or does it help sales because there is a clear path the prospect can take for action?)

When you have run all of your optimization tests, it is time to move onto the landing page.

Here's a quick checklist of the items to test for:

❏ Ad images

- ❑ Headline
- ❑ Text
- ❑ Target market demographics, interests, and behaviors
- ❑ Landing page copy
- ❑ Opt-in form
- ❑ Text below the photo
- ❑ When the ad is run (time of day, day of week, week of month, month of year)
- ❑ Daily budget
- ❑ Type of bid, automated or manual
- ❑ Placement (Newsfeed, right side, mobile app, mobile and/ or desktop)

Unfortunately, social media is like any other form of marketing. If you want a continued high ROI you have to keep testing. Steven Spielberg was rejected by the University of Southern California School of Cinematic Arts multiple times. He went on to create the first summer blockbuster with *Jaws* in 1975, and has won three Academy Awards.

Do not rest on your laurels. Status quo never got anyone *Academy Award Success.* Continue to test to earn your next blockbuster actually deserving of an award.

You've Gotta Play to Win

by Kelly LeMay

Side note from Kim: *Often companies, brands, or movements have one face, person, or personality that stands out front to represent the organization as a whole. For my firm, Elite Digital Group, that is me. But in reality, there are nearly 20 people working behind the scenes to produce our client campaigns successfully. The author of this chapter, Kelly LeMay, has been with me for over ten years and is the one employee who transitioned with me from fluffy public relations firm to direct response social media agency. As much as I have been a serious student of direct response, she has been right alongside me learning, experimenting, optimizing, reporting, and improving. And in reality, she works with clients more than I do, so she maybe/probably is better at the fine details of testing than I am. After I was witness to a presentation by her about one of the apps we have done some work for, Tennis Central, I asked her to share it with you as an example for why you should NEVER assume anything about your ads.*

Yann Auzoux, a former professional tennis player, has won over 60 national and international events. He started playing tennis when he was 11 years old, which would be considered late to most pro players, but quickly accelerated to be the national champion within one year. Nowadays, Yann has a passion for teaching others the game of tennis. He has coached several professional tennis players, was the head coach at George Washington University, and taught private clients through his prestigious FifthSet Academy (http://fifthset.com/).

What was once a hugely popular sport in the '70s and '80s has steadily been on the decline. Yeah, a lot of the old-timers are still picking up the racquet and hitting the court, but there has been a significant decline in the number of younger Americans playing the sport, whether it be socially or competitively.

This is how the brainchild of Yann Auzoux was born. Being the highly motivated tennis player and entrepreneur that he is, Yann saw an opportunity in the marketplace to reach this younger demographic, a way to reach an audience who is always on-the-go, glued to their phone, and doesn't have the time to invest in the game. He developed an app that allows players to track their progress, access a library of video tutorials, find players in their neighborhood, and find available courts. Users could even engage is some friendly "smack talk" through the app. The app was called Talk to Da Back Hand. Kidding (although it has a nice ring to it). The app was named Tennis Central.

We were introduced to Yann in the summer of 2014 through our friends at the web development company who built the app and website, Sonjara. It needed a partner to help design the site and app interface. The site needed to speak to many audiences: the social player, the competitive player, and the networking player. Through imagery and a series of playful slogans like "Mixing Business and Pleasure," the site and app were launched in fall 2014.

Step 1: Image Testing

With the app launched, and the inevitable initial tech kinks worked out, we began work on our Facebook campaign to get qualified users to download the app. We knew we had a lot of testing in front of us. Even the most savvy marketers (that would be my boss, you know, the one with her name on the front of this book!) can't predict which combination of text and imagery this audience will respond to. And so we test. And we test some more. And then we do some really geeky nerdy tests.

The first test up was imagery. We started with four different images, all with precisely the same text. (See Figure 14.10 on page 277.) If you test too many variables at once, it's hard to know what the catalyst is. First up to bat:

- *Celebrity Image.* In this case it was a still shot of a training video that Yann did. I love this image for a couple of reasons: the image catches him mid-serve, which subconsciously triggers a "need to know more" flag in the viewer's brain. Also, Yann is wearing a red shirt, as he

FIGURE 14.10: Tennis Central Split Test Ads Using Four Different Images

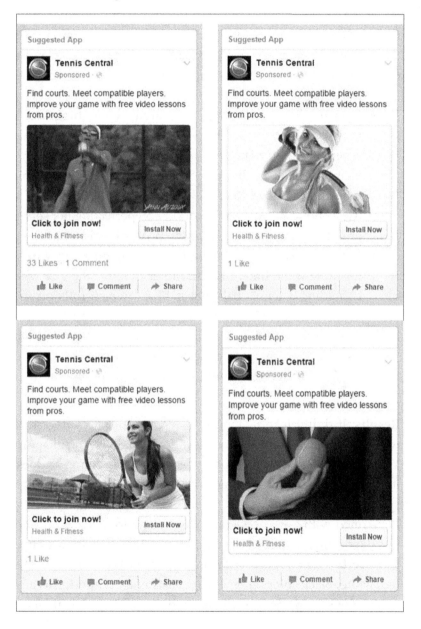

does in most of his training videos. Red shirts statistically convert at a higher rate than any other color shirt.

- *Blonde Pretty Lady.* Another image that often outperforms others is a pretty lady. And this lady just happened to be playing tennis. Bonus! This particular image speaks more to the social aspect of the app than it does to the technical or competitive side.

- *Brunette Pretty Lady.* If blondes aren't your thing, don't worry, brunettes use the Tennis Central app, too. This woman, slightly more approachable than her bosomy counterpart, is on the court and ready to play. She's a bit more universal in that she could be meeting up with a friend for a casual match, working on perfecting her serve, or networking with other young professionals.

- *Blue Ball Image.* This image had me juggling my words for quite some time. I used to refer to it as "the guy who is holding a tennis ball that is blue," which rolls off the tongue like an 18-wheeler. It wasn't until recently that I came to grips with just calling it the "blue ball guy." Yeah, I said it. This image is great because it's unexpected, and anytime we can stand out in a sea of stock photography is good.

Results: It didn't take us long to recognize that the image that was converting at the lowest cost per download was the image of Yann. (Because he's pretty much awesome at everything he does, it's only fitting that he's awesome at winning Facebook image split test competitions, too.)

Armed with this knowledge, we decided to dive deeper and test the original image vs. two additional images with a simple text overlay. (See Figure 14.11 on page 279.) We went with the red, white, black color scheme that consistently outperforms any other color scheme. Still no change in pattern. The original image

FIGURE 14.11: Tennis Central Split Test Ads with Different Images of Yann Auzoux

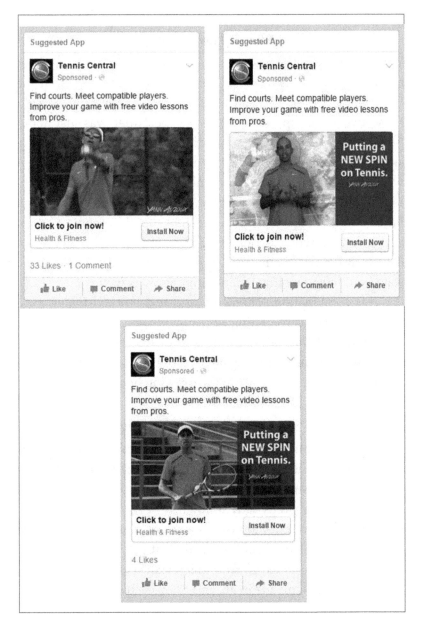

stood strong producing 40% more downloads at 38% lower cost per download.

Step 2: Text Testing

We dove deeper. The post text we had been using was somewhat all-encompassing. It covered every aspect of the app from the technical to the social aspect. What would happen if we split those two ideas up and created one post that was just about personal connection and another that was about improving skill? (See Figure 14.12 on page 281.) Well, we found that when we simplified the text, the post "Easily connect with tennis enthusiasts in your area" won the audiences' approval. Furthermore, it gave us some insights to the Tennis Central audience as a whole. Connecting to people is one of the main drivers for downloading the app. This phrase is slated to be rolled out in some offline marketing pieces as well.

This combination of imagery and text worked for us for a long time. We were getting app downloads at $2 a pop, and we'd ride that train all night long until we got kicked off. But slowly we saw the cost rising and we knew we had saturated the audience. So, we went back to the drawing board.

Step 3: More Image Testing

Going back to our original image test, the pretty lady images didn't win, but they also didn't perform so horribly that we wouldn't give them another shot. (See Figure 14.13 on page 282.) There was a new pretty lady in town, and she was wearing our favorite color . . . red. And just to make her more interesting, she was throwing a tennis ball in the air that got cut off the top of the image. Instant interest. And to boot, she came ready to play, bringing app downloads in around $1.30 each.

FIGURE 14.12: Tennis Central Split Test Ad with Three Different Texts

FIGURE 14.13: Tennis Central Split Test Converting Ad with New Image

Step 4: Audience Testing

When it comes to audience testing, there were many different avenues we could take to hit each type of player.

In our testing, the following target audiences performed the best:

- *Look-alike of FifthSet emails.* Whenever we start a new campaign, we want to start with something we know. Yann had a list of emails from his FifthSet Academy training. We knew we needed people like them, so we created a look-alike audience to find people with the same likes, behaviors, and habits.
- *Look-alike of current app users.* Once we reached 1,000 email addresses, we could create a lookalike audience of actual Tennis Central users (while this was more than

likely similar to the lookalike of the FifthSet email list, it was more accurate from a statistical standpoint).

- *People who have visited www.TennisCentral.net.* This was an obvious hot lead list (and yes, we excluded existing members). Our numbers proved this was a key list to use, and web retargeting continues to be one of the top audiences for most of our client accounts.

Engaging with Fans

Aside from Facebook ads, we wrote posts and managed daily content on the Tennis Central Facebook, Twitter, and LinkedIn pages. What I loved about these posts is that we got to play a bit as this brand is a bit conversational, super fun, and a little risqué. (See Figure 14.14 below and Figure 14.15 on page 284.)

FIGURE 14.14: Tennis Central Risqué Ad Increased Engagement

FIGURE 14.15: Fun Tennis Central Ad Encourages Audience
Engagement

Tennis Central
Published by Hootsuite [?] · February 1 · ⬤

How to freeball: just download our free app, take a screenshot, and post it to our Facebook wall. If you're one of the first 50 to do it, we'll hook you up with your own can of Tennis Central tennis balls! http://ow.ly/HYyvO ⬤

free·balling *verb*

🔊 \ frē - bȯl - liŋ\

: to win a free can of Tennis Central
tennis balls by posting a
screenshot of the app

*"Why are you taking a screenshot of your
Tennis Central app?"*

*"Because I'm **freeballing**, and you can too!"*

The Social Effect

No matter how fun posting may be, the bottom line is really all that counts. And for Tennis Central, social channels continued to be the top referral source for TennisCentral.net as well as app downloads. To me, it seems only natural. Things are a lot different than they were back in the day when tennis ruled. Now we live in a world where technology rules, but we can use that technology to connect other humans to play a game of tennis and maybe engage in some quality smack talk.

Why Doesn't a Click Turn into Business?
by Parthiv Shah

Side note from Kim: *If you have made it this far in the book, congratulations are in order. I believe you have a greater chance of implementing the strategies contained in it. And if you do, then you are going to need to do something with all of those leads you begin to bring in. If you leave it up to you or your team to manually facilitate them, then you have a great chance of losing leads and the dollars and time spent bringing them in. To effectively manage your lead flow, you need a system in place, something that can be automated and optimized. In this chapter Parthiv Shah, President of Elaunchers, www.Elaunchers.com, shares how to develop a system for social media.*

Let's say your social media has done its job. You have attracted your ideal prospects, patients, or clients to your Facebook fan page. They liked your page. Then you ran clicks to a website ad and drove these people off Facebook to your website.

What happens once they get to your website?

If you are like 97% of most businesses, nothing happens.

You spent all that money on a website. Why doesn't a click turn into business?

Does your website tell your prospects what you want them to do? Is that information displayed front and center, above the fold? Is your website too cluttered?

After studying thousands of websites and working on hundreds of websites and landing pages, I developed a formula for building a "perfect" website. I call it "Parthiv's Perfect Website Layout." Here is my philosophy. There are four types of people visiting your website:

1. Clients who visit your website for logistical reasons (login, request appointment, seek driving directions)
2. Prospects who have never heard of you before and are there for the first time
3. HOT prospects and referrals who are ready to interact with you and need a strong call to action
4. Information seekers who want to read up on you, check you out, and build trust and credibility in their own minds before they decide to engage

In this layout we cater to ALL FOUR VISITOR SEGMENTS individually. (See Figure 14.16.)

FIGURE 14.16: Website Mock Layout Caters to All Four Visitor Segments

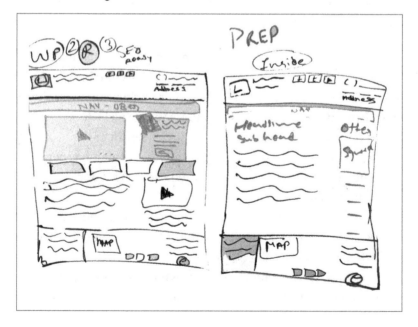

- In Parthiv's perfect website layout, there should be a video or a slide show on the left two-thirds area directly below the navigation bar and a squeeze form to the right of video/slider. This area caters to prospects who have never been to your site before. The soft squeeze will get them started in a lead nurture sequence.
- The squeeze form can be either a single offer squeeze or it can have other layouts.
- You can have multiple offer buttons in that area that would take you to offer-specific landing pages.
- OR you can have one squeeze form with an option button, "Which free report would you like to read?"
- Notice the four black boxes below the video and squeeze. These are called "HARD" Call to Action. The four HARD Call to Action buttons cater to warm through hot prospects and referrals that come to your website who already know you, who have seen your stuff before, and who are ready to make an initial commitment. We always recommend the following four HARD OFFERS:

1. Special Offers
2. Current Events
3. Testimonials
4. Tell-a-Friend

- The interior pages are offer/product specific squeeze pages with HARD calls to action like "Buy Now" or "Download a coupon/gift certificate."

The header area will be constant throughout the website. It should also be visible on the mobile-friendly responsive layout. Therefore, the header should not be ONE BIG IMAGE. It should be a collage of multiple elements including:

- Your logo
- Your tag line

- Your telephone number (as text, not as image)
- Your social media buttons
- Your customer-friendly interaction buttons like:
- Login to portal
- Request appointment
- Driving directions

Now let us look at this layout in action: Here are a couple of pictures (see Figures 14.17 below and 14.18 on page 289):

FIGURE 14.17: Campbell Wealth Management Website

FIGURE 14.18: Petrover Orthodontics Website

These sites are clean, comforting, and professional. On the right—where your eyes go first—is a squeeze form where you should offer a free report or a free three-video course when a prospect fills out your form. Now the prospect has entered your funnel, and you can start building a relationship.

Underneath that offer is a newsletter and video update.

In short, it is an easy-to-understand website with multiple clear calls to action that result in sophisticated follow-up marketing. Much better than a car dealer.

What would make it even better is if your Facebook ad led prospective clients to a specific landing page that only referenced the offer from the ad. That way the visitors would know they were on the right page, and not "mistakenly" sign up for anything else before doing what they came there to do.

If this whole process of attraction, engagement, and conversion seems familiar to you, it should. It's just like sex. (See Figure 14.19 on page 291.) I explain this concept in great detail in my book *Business Kamasutra: From Persuasion to Pleasure* (www. businesskamasutra.com).

Think about it: Relationships between businesses and their customers are very much like those built between humans.

Let's talk about sex. How does it work? Well, the first step is segmentation. You don't want to sleep with just anybody; you want to be picky.

Kim and Dan have done an excellent job in this book sharing with you how you can use social media to target your ideal client, customer, or patient.

Once you know who you are, once you know who you want to go after, then you are going to organize, orchestrate, and execute an approach.

Do you walk up to the first person you meet in a bar and ask them to marry you? Of course not. You want to approach in the right way. You are seeking *consent*. And you should not be seeking consent for mating, you should be seeking consent for *dating*. Make sure your message is using the right moves so you don't get a drink tossed in your face.

Once you approach people, what happens? Will they ignore you? Will they like you and consent to continue the conversation? Or will they get upset that you had the audacity to approach them?

If you are not meant to be together, accept the "no, thank you" and move on. The world is filled with other opportunities.

FIGURE 14.19: Audience Attraction, Engagement, and Conversion Is a Courting Process

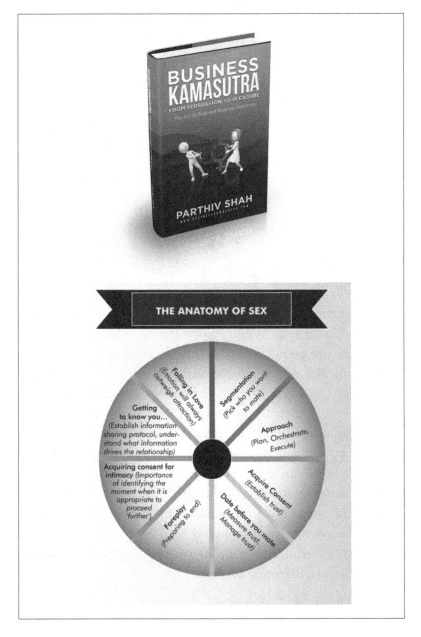

Let's say you are successful in persuading someone to raise a hand and say yes. He is interested in talking to you (or at least in getting your irresistible free offer). Now what do you do? He didn't give you consent to mate. He gave you consent to date. So *date*! (See Figure 14.20.)

FIGURE 14.20: Audience Courtship Can Be Segmented Into Routine Processes

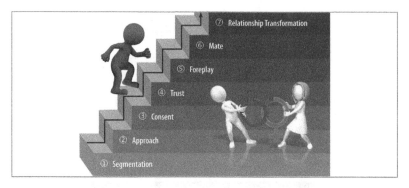

What happens during the dating and courtship period? How long should you date? While you are dating, what are you going to do? You are going to establish trust. How do you establish trust? Trust is a very mathematical thing. In my opinion, trust is 10% emotions and 90% mathematics. You can build your business in a way that you establish trust with whomever you wish to build a relationship with. If trust is controlled by data and can be mathematically measured, you can manage and maintain trust. You can elevate trust. You can improve your intimacy by increasing levels of trust.

How do we do this from a marketing perspective? First, you have to deliver what you promised.

If you offered a free report as your lead generation magnet on social media, there should be:

1. An instant PDF download of that report,

2. An opportunity to receive a hard copy via direct mail (to capture full contact information),

3. Perhaps an email that goes out right away with a link to download the report, and maybe, just maybe . . .

4. A tell-a-friend page where the prospective customer can send his friends a copy of the report as well.

We are going to talk about monetization of trust. (See Figure 14.21.) That's the mating part. Well, hopefully dating and courtship will reach to a point where you get consent for intimacy. When you get consent for intimacy, you are ready to mate. You are approaching a point where you are about to get intimate. It is a very delicate moment, what do you do?

FIGURE 14.21: The Anatomy of Trust

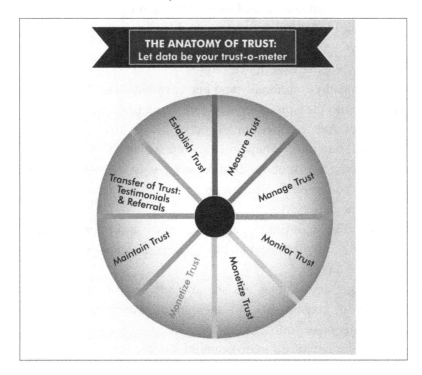

What does mating mean from a business standpoint? You are about to make your first sale.

You want to make sure the process is filled with pleasure.

What does it take to make someone happy, prepare them for mating, *and* make the experience pleasurable? When did you last experience pleasure during a business interaction? Think. Was an experience at Starbucks pleasant? Was an experience at Marriott pleasant? Was an experience at Walmart pleasant? How about at the used car dealer? Or the dentist?

What happens if the experience is *not* pleasurable to people? Well, if you are the only game in town, they will stay. But if they are doing business with you and you constantly agitate and annoy them, it's still not going to work.

They will proactively look for someone else who does what you do who can take care of them better. If they are not annoyed, realize they will still be approached by other businesses. You may lose your customers to a better looking supplier who promises a better experience.

People buy emotionally and justify rationally. If your process is filled with pleasure, they will give you a tight hug back. They will repel your competition. They will keep buying from you. They will buy more. They will generate a better relationship

Now let's talk about transforming your relationship after mating. You need to provide good value in exchange for the money they are paying you.

Spend enough time, energy, resources, and money to make someone comfortable. Establish the relationship and then capitalize on it.

If your deliverables are shallow and if you are unable to please your constituents in a meaningful way, you will not be able to monetize your relationships.

You cannot afford to do segmentation, organize, orchestrate, and execute your approach, get consent, build relationship, do the whole dating routine, make them comfortable when they are ready to mate, engage in foreplay before mating, and then mate—only to lose them after the first sale. Too much time, money, and effort are at stake if you don't build a long-term relationship with your customer.

Now it's time to have babies. The term "having babies" means asking your customers to help you build your world— asking for referrals, asking them to usher you into relationships where you can do business with someone they already know, like, and trust.

If they can usher you into new relationships, you will not have to work so hard to organize, orchestrate, and execute an approach. The dating ritual will be shorter, foreplay will be more pleasurable for you and your clients, and mating will be more meaningful. Relationship building and seeking referrals from existing customers is the end game.

Now that you see where this is all going, let's break it down into bite-sized manageable chunks.

What is your irresistible free offer? Do you have one? Does it convert well? What I mean by conversion is, if 100 people were to visit that offer, how many of them would take you up on it? How do you know if you should be happy with the number of people who take you up on that offer? Every industry is different, and every offer is different. I would be happy to give you some perspective as to how many people should be signing up for your offer if you call me at 301-760-3953 to request a free consultation.

You see? I just practiced what I preached. I made an offer to you if you are ready to take the next step with me.

In order to craft an irresistible free offer that gets a good number of ideal prospects to sign up for it, you have to think like prospects. What do they want? What pain are they feeling that led them to seek you out? What keeps them up at night? What are they hoping someone like you can do for them?

My clients at Elaunchers are small-business owners with $500K to $2.5MM in revenues. They fiercely compete against larger rivals with deeper pockets. They often feel they need 18 arms to run their businesses. They don't have enough hours in the day to get everything done, let alone learn all they want about marketing their business. They are tired of money going out the back door of their company without coming in the front door at a much faster pace. They are frustrated with how demanding their business has become. Sometimes they feel like all they did was create a job for themselves that doesn't pay enough for the level of stress they have to deal with. They lay awake at night wondering when it will ever get easier.

Does that sound like you? If so, then you will love our "Step-by-Step Profit Multiplying Marketing Automation Blueprint."

You see how that works?

When you communicate your irresistible free offer to your target market, you are looking for one of the following reactions: 1) How do you do that?; 2) How can I get one of those?; and 3) Where have you been all my life? If you get one of those reactions (or they offer to give you money on the spot to alleviate their pain), then you know you hit the nail on the head.

You want them thinking that you understand them, and wondering if you have installed a secret webcam in their office (that's a joke—forgive my Indian sense of humor).

So let's review what we have done so far:

1. Picked a target market that has a pain you can get rid of and who can afford to pay you what you want to charge to fix this pain.
2. Crafted an Irresistible Free Offer that follows Dan Kennedy's proven copywriting formula. (For more on this formula, get a copy of *The Ultimate Sales Letter* and the *Magnetic Marketing* course by Dan Kennedy.) The formula

FIGURE 14.22: Communicating the Irresistible Free Offer

is: Problem—Agitate—Solve. You want to identify their problem, make sure they are agitated by it, and then position the next step with you as the solution for their pain.

3. Ideally you would use a marketing automation system like Infusionsoft to capture their contact information, deliver the irresistible free offer, and follow up with them to take the next step with you.

4. Of course, you need to promote that offer to your target market, and in this book you've seen numerous ways to find them and get your offer in front of them.

So let's hypothesize that all this worked. Your ideal prospect clicked on the ad to like your Facebook page. Then they clicked on the ad from your fan page that took them to your website. They signed up for your offer, and you delivered it to them. Congratulations! You have just established trust. You did what you said you were going to do. Now you need to get them to take the next step in your relationship.

That next step could be:

- Opening your next email
- Clicking on a link in your next email
- Sharing your Facebook page on their news feed so their friends see it
- Filling out a Tell a Friend form on your website to spread the word about you
- Using your website to book a consultation with you
- Attending an event (either in person or online)
- Coming in to your office
- Buying something from your website
- Showing up at your store or restaurant with some type of tracking code that lets you know how they got there

You get the idea. This list is only limited by your imagination.

No matter what you have them do, you need to make sure you can track that behavior. As you can imagine, the more ways they have to interact with you, the more data that behavior will generate inside of their contact record in your customer relationship management or marketing automation software. (See Figure 14.23 on page 299.)

Let's talk about how you manage and monetize all of that data, or as I like to call it—establishing your rhythm.

Why is establishing rhythm important? Because without rhythm, you will be randomly doing things that may or may not help you get where you want to go in regards to your new relationship with your new prospect.

To establish rhythm, create an annual marketing calendar. It should have a list of proposed daily marketing activities, weekly marketing activities, monthly marketing activities, quarterly marketing activities, and annual marketing activities. The calendar my company creates also has a marketing ROI calculator and a monthly marketing expense budget.

FIGURE 14.23: The Breakdown of the Role of Data in a Relationship

So, how do you go about establishing your rhythm, and why don't you feel that you have a rhythm already established? Do you feel like you have a bunch of people living and working on an island and they just do whatever they do but there is no synchronization or harmony among them?

Unfortunately, you are not alone. Most growing businesses have this problem. Some often refer to it as "growing pains," but in reality it is a problem that can be avoided or fixed.

Here is the root cause of the problem. Most businesses start with A HUMAN. The human buys or builds the apparatus that the human is comfortable or experienced with. As a business grows, the human brings more humans, and more humans bring more apparatus that they are comfortable with. A growing business is a random collage of humans, apparatus, processes, and silos of data. Eventually, everything gets out of hand, so the first human buys a management book or hires a management consultant who comes in and tells you that everything you have ever done is WRONG and you have to start over and build a so-called "system."

The problem with that line of thinking is, it's a bit too structured, too bureaucratic, too rigid, and it slows down the pace of a GROWING business. You can't put a toddler in the military. A business needs to grow to a certain maturity before the "professional" project management and/or process management systems can kick in and actually work. Therefore, a successful, growing SMALL business should use a simplified version of process management. I call that RHYTHM.

Here's one way to build your RHYTHM without disrupting what you already have working. You first start with your MONEY line. How do you make money, and how do you spend money (who pays whom, when, how, how much, how frequently, and why)?

Once you have your stakeholders listed in this way, you are ready to draw the "data line." You can do this exercise with either "toy soldiers" or "Lego pieces." Just put something on the table that gives you a visual.

You want to write down who consumes what data at what frequency and at what velocity—before, during, and after the money exchange.

Start with money, add humans to money, figure out how humans consume data and what VARIETY of data needs to be generated by what process in what VOLUME at what VELOCITY.

Once you have your three Vs of Big Data figured out, build ONE central database that captures, warehouses, catalogs, analyzes, and displays the VOLUME and VARIETY of data at the VELOCITY that is meaningful to you and your ecosystem.

Once your central database is built, connect your current apparatus and your current humans to the new Rhythm and train them.

If your business is at $500k to $2M in revenues, you might benefit from a workflow called "Perfect Customer Lifecycle" from Infusionsoft. Please visit www.perfectcustomerlifecycle. com to request a copy. To get the most out of it, be sure to ask for the digital, fillable PDF of the book.

I just made you another irresistible free offer!

Now that you better understand how the courtship begins, I hope you'll jump into the dating pool with YOUR business and start building stronger relationships.

To find more about marketing automation, Parthiv Shah, or ELaunchers, visit www.Elaunchers.com or call 310-760-3953.

#NoBSsm Tweetable Takeaways

🖋 Aim for "biggest impact" website traffic, meaning traffic that is high quality and goes where you want it to on your site. #NoBSsm

🖋 Don't ask a new marketing lead to hand over a Social Security number and firstborn child. #NoBSsm

---

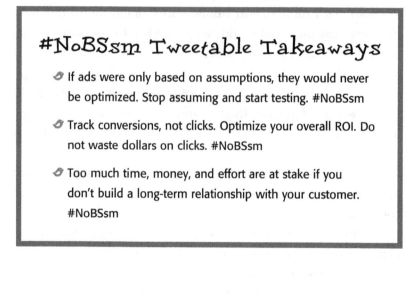

#NoBSsm Tweetable Takeaways

- If ads were only based on assumptions, they would never be optimized. Stop assuming and start testing. #NoBSsm

- Track conversions, not clicks. Optimize your overall ROI. Do not waste dollars on clicks. #NoBSsm

- Too much time, money, and effort are at stake if you don't build a long-term relationship with your customer. #NoBSsm

CHAPTER 15

The Winner's Circle

Book Winner Case Study

by Kim Walsh-Phillips

What makes up No B.S. Social Media?

Results-driven, measured, and high-ROI-producing campaigns.

As mentioned earlier in Chapter 6, we held a contest for a Small Business Social Media makeover as a pre-publication promotion for this book. Four finalists were selected to receive a social media makeover, and one was chosen as the grand prize winner to be featured in this book.

For a writeup on all of the winners, visit www.NoBSSocial MediaBook.com.

Honorable Mention: Fitness Revolution

Justin Yule and his wife Janelle own a personal training studio, Fitness Revolution, in Chanhassen, Minnesota, www.chanhassenfitnessrevolution.com. Prior to this contest, they were heavily engaged in Facebook. They posted daily and used their Facebook account to run private support groups for members.

When they decided to take the leap into using Facebook Ads, they knew how important it is to be diligent about tracking ROI. (We loved that characteristic in a finalist for this contest.)

The average monthly membership cost for Fitness Revolution group personal training program (the program they would be advertising) is $175/month for a 12-month agreement. Each new member would be worth AT LEAST $2,100—and that number would go up with back-end offers throughout the year. While the majority of Justin and Janelle's members renew at the end of the year, to track their ROI for this contest we purposely chose to focus on the more conservative one-year, rather than lifetime value. And the numbers are still extraordinary.

The first ad campaign was for a Front End Offer (FEO) of $79 for a four-week pilot class. The ads featured pictures of actual clients and contained a short quote from each. To maximize effectiveness, ads were targeted toward specific age groups and featured members in those same age groups. In addition, each of these ads went to a different landing page with the same offer, but the testimonials matched up to the ad.

These ads were all split-tested with different images, and the winning combination was fully launched in the campaign.

In addition, a change in the standard campaign increased the ROI dramatically. Within the sales video and the landing page, other start dates and session time options for the program were mentioned. This proved to be very fruitful as the MAJORITY of purchases were NOT for the initially advertised session time.

The results:

- $2,979 spent on ads
- $2,139 brought in on the FEO
- $15,719 sold in memberships
- $17,858 total revenue
- $14,879 in profit for a 500% ROI. This number will continue to increase as back-end sales and referrals are made, both of which have already started as we report this.

Any time we can put $1 into a machine and get $5 out, we're willing to play all day.

The second campaign run wasn't so fruitful—only a 316% ROI, but we'll take that, too. Because a handful of leads from that campaign are still in trial, the ROI could certainly catch up to the first campaign. Better odds than roulette.

Justin shares, "Overall, we're very excited about adding Facebook Advertising to our lead generation toolbox. Naturally, like most direct-response marketers, we won't rely solely on one strategy, but will put more focus into it moving forward."

See Figures 15.1 through 15.4 on pages 306 and 307 for samples of the ad split test winners.

Grand Prize Winner: Surface Creek Veterinary Center

Surface Creek Veterinary Center in Cedaredge, Colorado, provides routine preventive care, vaccinations, surgery, dentistry, x-rays, laser therapy, in-house lab testing, reproductive services for large and small animals, farm visits, herd health consults, and much more. Dogs, cats, small mammals, cattle, goats, sheep, llamas, and alpacas are all welcome, and it makes farm and ranch calls as needed.

Right off the bat, we knew we were going to need to focus its offerings to gain momentum in its Facebook marketing ROI.

FIGURE 15.1: Chanhassen Fitness Revolution Ad Split Test Winner

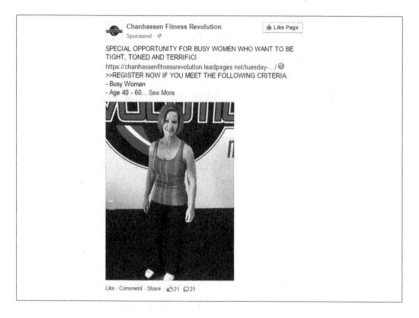

FIGURE 15.2: Chanhassen Fitness Revolution Ad Split Test Winner

FIGURE 15.3: Chanhassen Fitness Revolution Ad Split Test Winner

FIGURE 15.4: Chanhassen Fitness Revolution Ad Split Test Winner.

When we started working with Surface Creek Veterinary Center, its overall social media marketing was minimal. Its posting was sporadic with minimal engagement on its page. It did not have a proven digital sales funnel, and it was not running any ads on Facebook outside of Boosted Posts, which offer a low overall ROI.

We selected Surface Creek as our winner, and Account Manager Danielle Passaro worked with veterinarian Dr. Susie Hirsch to optimize the Surface Creek Veterinary Facebook page, create a sales funnel, and run ads via Facebook for which we could show a proven ROI.

In the Beginning

Our first step was to update the cover photo, which was a great shot of the full Surface Creek team, but was from the new office construction back in 2011. We chose a photo of Dr. Susie and Dr. Jeff holding the office cats while standing just outside of their office. (See Figures 15.5 and 15.6 on page 309 for before and after covers.)

We added text on the image that would show at-a-glance what this business is all about: Helping your pets live longer, healthier lives. The photo instantly increased page engagement as it received 95 likes, six comments, and two shares, all without spending any ad dollars. Increased engagement leads to free lead generation, so this was a great way to kick off the account.

Beyond the social response to the image, the reasons we chose an image like this were multifold. We wanted to introduce the veterinarians to their audience and put friendly faces with the business. We also wanted to clearly show what their focus is and what they can do for prospects—and establish them as experts and authorities in the market.

We also updated the profile image. Surface Creek was already using its logo, but the dimensions of the logo image

FIGURE 15.5: Surface Creek Veterinary Facebook Cover Photo—Before

FIGURE 15.6: Surface Creek Veterinary Facebook Cover Photo—After

caused Facebook to crop it and made it unreadable. A small tweak was all that was needed to fix the image, making it not only readable but also easily recognizable.

Before and after (see Figures 15.7 and 15.8 on page 310):

FIGURE 15.7: Surface Creek Veterinary Facebook Profile Image—Before

FIGURE 15.8: Surface Creek Veterinary Facebook Profile Image—After

These two tweaks created a more welcoming and focused homepage. (See Figure 15.10 on page 311 and Figure 15.11 on page 312 for before and after homepages.)

SOCIAL MEDIA POSTING

Surface Creek had previously been posting every couple of days. The content skewed too salesy as it often shared the current month's promotional offer with occasional cute

FIGURE 15.9: Using a Positive Review as a Social Media Post

Surface Creek Veterinary Center
Posted by Megan Phillips [?] · April 7 at 8:04pm · ☀

Pet Parent Review: "Surface Creek vets saved our dog Buckley! After a totally ugly deer attack involving goring injuries to his eye and side, he has fully recovered! Thanks, Surface Creek and Dr. Hirsch!!" - The Knutsons, Cedaredge, CO

FIGURE 15.10: Surface Creek Veterinary Facebook Homepage—Before

pictures of animals or a relevant news article from an outside source.

We ramped up the posting to once daily, and expanded types of content posted. The page engagement increased almost immediately. Its seven-day schedule:

Day 1. Meet the Staff (photos of the staff and a quick description or quote from them). Because there are only so

FIGURE 15.11: Surface Creek Veterinary Facebook
Homepage—After

many staff members, future schedules could shift to "Meet
the Patients" and show images of the pets who come in
along with a quick story about them. (See Figure 15.12 on
page 313.)

Day 2. Funny Pet Memes and Pictures. Because we know
people spend hours looking at these on their own, we
wanted to share some cute ones here. They effortlessly
encourage interaction and sharing. (See Figure 15.13 on
page 313.)

Day 3. Pet Health Tips. We pulled a lot of these posts
from content already available in past blogs and newsletters written by Dr. Susie and Dr. Jeff. (See Figure 15.14 on
page 314.)

Day 4. More Pet Facts. This could be anything from information on vaccinations to what type of foods to feed your
pet. (See Figure 15.15 on page 314.)

FIGURE 15.12: Day 1—Meet the Staff

FIGURE 15.13: Day 2—Funny Pet Memes and Pictures

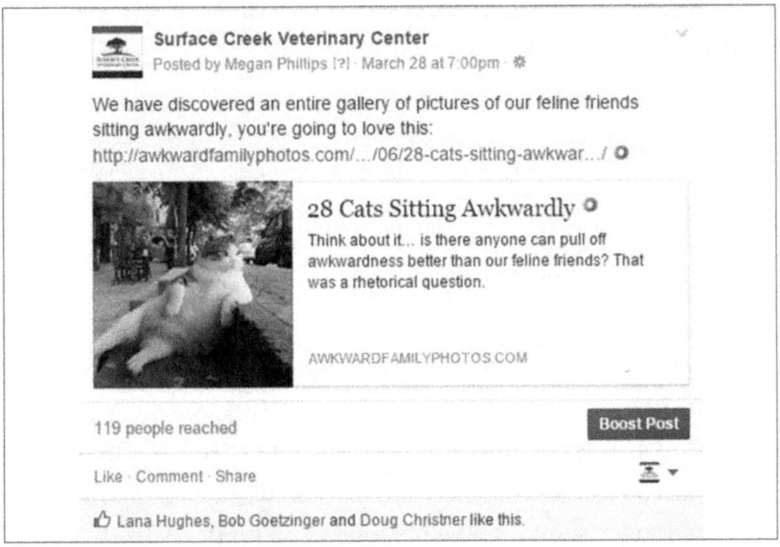

FIGURE 15.14: Day 3—Pet Health Tips

FIGURE 15.15: Day 4—More Pet Facts

Day 5. Pet Parent Reviews. This is an easy way to share testimonials and reviews from patients. New reviews can be shared as they come in and older reviews that have already been collected can also be used, thus giving them a longer shelf life. (See Figure 15.16 on page 315.)

FIGURE 15.16: Day 5—Pet Parent Reviews

FIGURE 15.17: Day 6—Inspirational Pet Quotes

Day 6. Inspirational Pet Quotes. These typically include a cute photo and quote, and often garner a lot of response. I mean, cute puppies and kittens. You can't lose. (See Figure 15.17.)

FIGURE 15.18: Day 7— More Pet Health Information

Surface Creek Veterinary Center

Posted by Megan Phillips [?] · March 26 at 7:55pm · ☀

Want to lower Fluffy's risk for infection? Learn why you should get your animal spayed/neutered by 5-6 months by clicking here: http://www.surfacecreekveterinarycenter.com/monthly-newslet... 🔗

Monthly Newsletter 🔗

Springtime is just around the corner, and you know what that means... Corned beef and cabbage! Just kidding, it actually means kittens, and puppies, too! In the spring animals are out and...

SURFACECREEKVETERINARYCENTER.COM

Day 7. More Pet Health Information. (See Figure 15.18.)

THE SALES FUNNEL

It's one thing to get people to click "like" on a photo of an adorable animal. But what about the ROI?

Surface Creek Veterinary Center does run monthly offers and shares them via newsletter to current and prospective clients, on the website homepage to all who visit, and typically via a social media post. However, we wanted to create a sales funnel to bring new patients into its offices, which would allow its team to then create a lifetime relationship with the pet owners.

Dr. Jeff also recently published a dog food recipe book called *Cooking with Buck: Healthy Recipes for Dogs*, for which he was interviewed on national TV. We figured we could use that to our advantage!

The offer we came up with was a $20 checkup plus nutritional consultation for first-time patients. The typical value of a checkup is $38, so the average annual value of a pet patient is $625, and the lifetime value is $3,000. The $18 price reduction on the initial checkup would easily be made up in the first year alone.

We carefully chose our text for the offer to help qualify prospects. We reached out to pet owners to remind them they need to have their pets checked out with our opening line: "When was the last time you took your furry friend for a checkup?"

We added a sense of urgency by offering it as a "limited time offer." The call to action is a simple "Click to Claim" to make it easy for readers to figure out what to do to get the offer. And finally, the descriptive text gave a little more detail and left an open loop by running off the page. We added some qualifiers to get readers to schedule before April 15th, which was three weeks after the start of the campaign. (See Figures 15.19 through 15.21 on pages 318 to 319.)

We integrated the landing page for this offer within the Surface Creek Veterinary Center's website. By integrating directly within its website, we could use retargeting to follow up with anyone who didn't opt-in.

On the landing page, we included the most successful image from our Facebook ads, and provided more information on the Veterinary Center as well as the offer. We mentioned "bringing in your pet" to make sure the readers would know the offer was not for a farm or ranch visit, as those are typically much more expensive.

The form was hosted by AWeber and once filled out, immediately triggers a thank-you message and enters the user

FIGURE 15.19: Add a Call to Action

FIGURE 15.20: Create a Sense of Urgency—Limited Time Offer

FIGURE 15.21: Leave an Open Loop Where Some of the Text Runs off the Edge of the Ad

into a follow-up sequence that shares pet-owner information in addition to sending an alert to the vet offices. The thank-you page is a pop-up that shares the phone number with readers who want to reach out immediately, and sets the expectation that the user will be contacted via phone as well as email.

A great reason for asking users to submit their information to you for an appointment is that they can do it at any time of day or night, not just during office hours. Many users are online in the nighttime hours, and many submissions came in for Surface Creek after hours. This allowed us to receive the request at the time that best suited them, then the receptionist could call back during office hours. We also asked for a "Best time to call" as we originally noticed that reaching out to users during the follow-up was not always successful. This way, the respondent could let the receptionist know when to call back. Additionally, by collecting user data, Surface Creek can now reach out to users via email with additional offers and information. (See Figures 15.22 below and 15.23 on page 321.)

FIGURE 15.22: Use a Landing Page and Opt-In Form to Schedule Discounted Appointment and Garner Contact Information

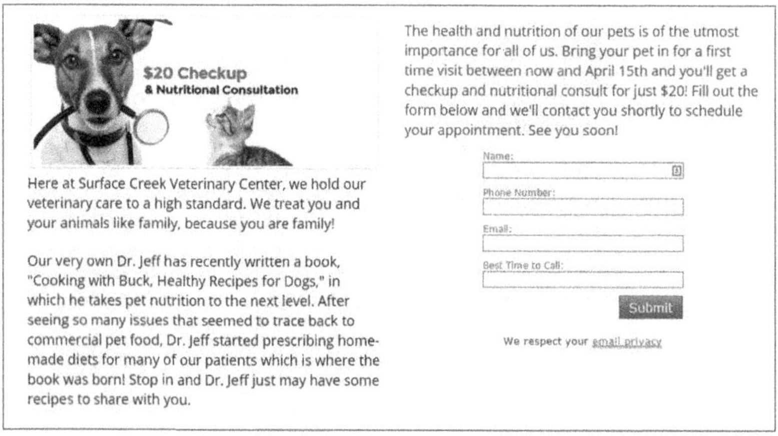

$20 Checkup & Nutritional Consultation

Here at Surface Creek Veterinary Center, we hold our veterinary care to a high standard. We treat you and your animals like family, because you are family!

Our very own Dr. Jeff has recently written a book, "Cooking with Buck, Healthy Recipes for Dogs," in which he takes pet nutrition to the next level. After seeing so many issues that seemed to trace back to commercial pet food, Dr. Jeff started prescribing home-made diets for many of our patients which is where the book was born! Stop in and Dr. Jeff just may have some recipes to share with you.

The health and nutrition of our pets is of the utmost importance for all of us. Bring your pet in for a first time visit between now and April 15th and you'll get a checkup and nutritional consult for just $20! Fill out the form below and we'll contact you shortly to schedule your appointment. See you soon!

Name:

Phone Number:

Email:

Best Time to Call:

Submit

We respect your email privacy

Once we developed a great offer and sequence, we needed to warm up the traffic we wanted to send the offer to. We typically did this by finding blog or newsletter content that was of high interest to readers. We researched which blogs were the most popular. We saw that vaccinations were a common topic, and used that to our advantage.

We pulled a few blog articles that already existed on the Surface Creek website and created another set of ads to drive traffic to those blog posts. We utilized the multiproduct ads so that we could show four different blog topics—some more relevant to dogs, others to cats—in addition to the general Surface Creek link. We incorporated a few funny and cute images to help grab Facebook users' attention, and included text that asked, "Is your pet's wellness something that is weighing on your mind?"

FIGURE 15.23: Thank-You Page

to help get readers thinking about their pets' needs. (See Figure 15.24 on page 322 and 323.)

We retargeted people who visited these blogs and extended the checkup offer to them. Those users had recently visited Surface Creek's website and will have been thinking about their pets' wellness, so the obvious next step would be to come in for a checkup. It's much easier to sell on Facebook, or anywhere for that matter, to people who have already interacted with you and your brand, than to cold traffic.

Targeting was tricky for Surface Creek because its market is a local area. We focused on the zip codes of the cities it serves, and created a look-alike of the current Surface Creek patient list. That group was the most successful for clicks to the blog and

FIGURE 15.24: Funny and Cute Pet Images to Grab Facebook Users' Attention

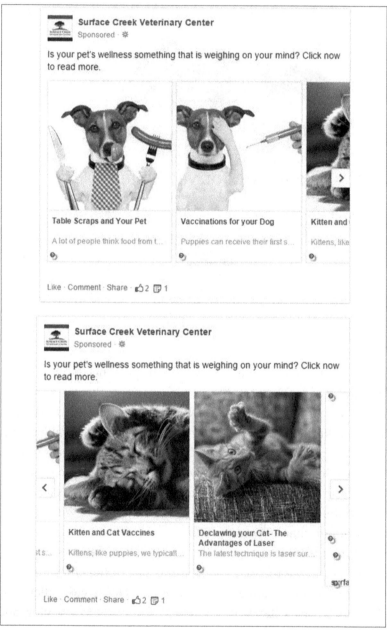

FIGURE 15.24: Funny and Cute Pet Images to Grab Facebook Users' Attention, continued

those who had visited the website previously. We also paired that with other interests and behaviors like: Purchased pet-care products, cat products, dog products, pet products; people who identified as being cat owner or dog owners; people who donated to animal welfare organizations,; people interested in the ASPCA or Humane Society, cats, dogs, kittens, puppies, pet stores like PetSmart and Petco, or dog training and obedience. Many of these audiences were small, so we needed to run a few days to test them. We found we had hit most of the people in that audience during that time, so we needed to rest them for a while before sharing ads again. Overall we found success with many of those audiences, garnering 600 clicks with an average of $0.80 per click, and some as low as $0.56 per click.

A few days after the blog campaign started, we began to run the $20 Checkup offer to the website traffic audience as well as to audiences that had been particularly successful through the blog campaign. Within three weeks we were able to get 12 new patient appointment requests.

The total spend for the campaign was $878. With 12 appointments requests and a per-patient value of $625, the total value of their new patients was $7,500, giving Surface Creek over a 900% ROI.

That's *even cuter* than baby puppies and kittens.

For all of the contest finalists and more tips on how to get a high ROI with your Facebook ads, visit www.NoBSSocialMedia Book.com.

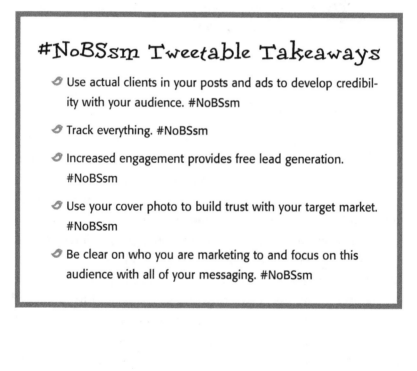

#NoBSsm Tweetable Takeaways

- Use actual clients in your posts and ads to develop credibility with your audience. #NoBSsm

- Track everything. #NoBSsm

- Increased engagement provides free lead generation. #NoBSsm

- Use your cover photo to build trust with your target market. #NoBSsm

- Be clear on who you are marketing to and focus on this audience with all of your messaging. #NoBSsm

CHAPTER 16

The Big Picture

Reaching More People

by Kim Walsh-Phillips

One of my favorite quotes is *"I learned that courage was not the absence of fear, but the triumph over it. The brave man is not he who does not feel afraid, but he who conquers that fear,"* Nelson Mandela

I recently heard a story that personifies so many entrepreneurs' journeys:

A young man's mother told him something he didn't want to hear, "You are going to have to go back to being a waiter at Red Lobster." This was not the answer he was looking for. He hated being a waiter there. The restaurant had just released its free cheddar biscuits. The tips were decreasing, but work was increasing.

His small company had already tasted success. LL Cool J had promoted him and others were asking to wear his clothes. Orders were pouring in, and now he was going to go back to being a waiter?

The reality was that they had already mortgaged his mom's house, sold everything they owned, and had nothing left. Yet the company couldn't fund the supplies and production of the orders it received. Not knowing better, it let the retailers order with terms only favorable to the retailers, including 120 days to pay for the clothing they were receiving.

So, reluctantly he went back to being a waiter. He promised his mother he would earn the $2,000 she asked for. He trusted her. After all, she had mortgaged her house for him. But he was still uneasy about spending $2,000 on one last-ditch effort.

With enough biscuits served and $2,000 earned, he gave his mom the money, and she finally revealed what she was going to do. She was going to take out a direct-response advertisement seeking funding.

He fought her at first. He thought that was the craziest idea he ever heard. Did she know how hard it was to earn that money?

But as smart moms do, she proceeded with faith and courage and placed that ad in the *The New York Times*.

It read:

"Need partner to help fund 1 million dollars in orders.
Serious inquiries only."

Most of the respondents were not legitimate businesspeople (folks with names like Rocco, Tony Two Times, and Small Guy Stan), but a few were. Ultimately, they struck a deal with Samsung Textiles, which would underwrite the manufacturing of their orders.

This entrepreneur of course is Daymond John with a current net worth of **$250 million** who founded clothing line FUBU.

Today he is on the hit show *Shark Tank*, risking his own money in deals presented on the show, and started Shark Branding as a marketing company.

Daymond John is incredibly successful. Now. But he had a long journey filled with an incredible amount of hard work to get there.

I have yet to meet a successful person for which this wasn't the case. Generally before the success came long hours, fear, doubt, sacrifices, struggles, and failures.

The journey of the entrepreneur is not easy.

I struggled for years before my company started to thrive. A long time of very little social life, lots of debt, and exhaustion. I almost gave up many times and at least once per year for the first ten years in business. I would apply for a job just dreaming about things getting better. Thankfully I never got called in for an interview. Not once.

I am just not meant to work for anyone else.

I am guessing the same might be true for you. If you have made it this far in the book, you are one of the few.

According to *The Atlantic*, The Pew Research Center found nearly a quarter of American adults had not read a single book in 2014. As in, they hadn't cracked a paperback, fired up a Kindle, or even hit play on an audiobook while in the car. The number of nonbook readers has nearly tripled since 1978.

And most that bought a book, didn't finish it.

It's not just business books, though. Even *Fifty Shades of Grey* went unfinished by 75% of those who read it.

The Wall Street Journal reports that the book's completion is calculated by the passages highlighted in the book.

Fifty Shades of Grey by E.L. James was only finished 25.9% of the way.

So if you read this book through, you are seeking better things for your business and your life. You want a change.

There are a lot of strategies contained in these pages. It can seem overwhelming and daunting, but the road to success often is.

How do you eat an elephant?

Start small. Get to know your best customers better. Seek more of them. Create great content and distribute it for free. Dabble your dollars in the paid platforms and keep an eye on your return.

Most of our clients start with a small testing marketing budget and only scale beyond a few thousand dollars a month after several months of testing—even the very big companies and firms.

I encourage you to take the first step toward your next chapter today. I'm excited to see what happens because of it. Please visit www.NoBSsmBook.com for free resources and strategies to get you started and report back on how your journey is going.

You have value that should be shared with the world.

It's time for you to find those people who need you.

The Trouble with Trending

by Dan Kennedy

I've said it before and I'll say it again, you should *never* try to be everything to everyone with your marketing.

This is how companies get themselves into trouble when they use social media. It goes something like this: Company sees trending topic, company contributes to trending topic without understanding its context in an effort to appear "relevant" or "hip." Then, there's backlash similar to what DiGiorno Pizza encountered in September 2014.

To provide some backstory, the backlash occurred when #WhyIStayed started trending on Twitter to bring to light the issue of domestic violence. This was (and still is) a serious topic of public discussion after the NFL released the video of the

Baltimore Ravens player, Ray Rice, assaulting his then-fiancée in a hotel. DiGiorno Pizza tweeted, "#WhyIStayed You had pizza."

So what was DiGiorno's reasoning behind this tweet? Did it think it was funny? Did it think Ray Rice should have gotten treatment that was more lenient? No. Its answer was so STUPID it makes me nauseous.

DiGiorno said that it "didn't know what the hashtag was about."

A tenet comes to mind that relates (if you've ever given an excuse when pulled over by a cop, you've heard this one): Ignorance of the law excuses no one.

The alarming revelation here is that this isn't the first and certainly won't be the last example of a company that misstepped in the wild, wild world of social media. As of writing this book, there are over 1.36 billion registered Facebook users, and more than 42 million Facebook pages. There is a lot to learn from companies that are getting social media right and those that, quite frankly, are failing miserably.

So, how do we separate the winners from the losers? Dollar-measured results, that's how. Everything else is just a waste of time.

Provided that you are getting a return on your investment, social media can be a valuable asset to add to your marketing plan. That being said, using social media solely is a dangerous (and NOT recommended) path to follow. All of Kim's clients have a multilayered approach to their marketing, so if Facebook bit the dust tomorrow, they would still soldier on. The value in social media is how it can complement, NOT replace, your traditional marketing activities like direct mail, email marketing, so on and so forth.

This is especially important considering that new social media networks are developed almost daily. If you are going to chase every social media network down the "Yellow Brick

Road," you might as well give your paycheck to the flying monkeys. Seriously. How much sense does it make to deliver a watered-down marketing strategy to multiple audiences, instead of hitting a home run with one social media network? I'll save you the five seconds of contemplation. None.

There were multiple social media strategies, case studies, and solutions for the everyday marketer presented in this book. Use these examples as a guide for your own journey to social media success. While you may think, "My business is different. These steps can't be applied in my situation," I'm here to tell you that you're wrong. You must, however, follow the foundational rules for a high social media ROI.

You've read many stellar examples in this book that demonstrated a high ROI from social media. Don't be fooled. These examples are the exception. And they only occur because of a strict adherence to direct response marketing with a hawk's eye on measurement.

If you decide to proceed with your social media marketing strategies, keep in mind these foundational rules at all times:

You can (and should) make yourself a celebrity through social media. Utilize social media to create your celebrity status to your target market. This is a platform you can control, and it should be leveraged for celebrity positioning. Think of the Kardashians. They practically built an empire off of what most thought would be Kim Kardashian's 15 seconds of fame. The "video-seen-round-the-world" spawned a reality show that's currently on its tenth season, multiple clothing stores, and an app that earned $43 million in the third quarter of 2014 (Glu Mobile).

However, as a business owner, you might take a less extreme approach than a sex tape. But to each their own.

Niches bring riches. There are niches all over the world, some that you may not even be aware of, that come in the form of associations, groups, interests. You name it, and someone will be willing to lay a pretty penny to work with someone they believe speaks directly to them.

Whether or not you choose to advertise on the platform, Facebook has powerful tools to help you research your list without giving Facebook a dime. At least for now. It's worth checking out before it starts charging. If you do use the platform to advertise, make sure you are not only targeting your ad but also your audience, too. Too many businesses get a segmented list to market but use the same ad for each audience.

Don't copy someone's social media ad, just because it "looks cool." I can't tell you how DUMB this strategy is, especially on social media, when you have no idea whether or not the ad is even breaking even on the investment.

Kmart had a "viral" video called "Ship My Pants" that was the talk of the web. Did it increase sales of online purchases? Kmart's store sales were down 2.2% again last year, so my guess? Once again, it forgot who its target market is.

Do not copy what others are doing just because they are doing it.

If someone tries to convince you otherwise, slap yourself in the head. Preferably with this book, so through some act of freakish osmosis, it will remind you of the rules.

Get to know your best customers better, find out their wants and needs, and fill them. Surveying your target audience is a serious exercise that you should use so you can better deliver your product or service. This can be as simple as drafting a survey with only a few questions. It's what comes back in these surveys that is really exciting.

With this data, you can identify potential improvements, referrals, and other business opportunities. These questions can also help you to develop a lead magnet offer (free report, ebook) that will answer a question that is burning in the back of your ideal prospect's mind. Base your marketing strategies on fact, not guessing.

Well, this is where I leave you. If you decide to continue on in your social media marketing efforts or begin them, do so armed.

Kim has laid out a thorough, sensible plan for you to establish your presence on social media and, more importantly to my mind, get measurable return on your investment. This is what works. Personally, I continue to be fed financially through businesses I have interests in, by the social media strategies Kim has described. I'd be the last guy on earth to suggest *not* using it for all it's worth. A lot is done on social media in my name, as if it were me. The work I do for many of my clients incorporates and integrates social media.

But, if you ever find me *personally* tweeting, you'll know the world has ended.

#NoBSsm Tweetable Takeaways

- ⤬ Create great content and distribute it for free. And dabble your dollars in the paid platforms and keep an eye on your return. #NoBSsm

- ⤬ You have value that should be shared with the world. It's time for you to find those people who need you. #NoBSsm

- ⤬ *Never* try to be everything to everyone with your marketing. #NoBSsm

- ⤬ If you ever see Dan Kennedy tweeting, know that the world has ended. #NoBSsm

About the Authors

DAN S. KENNEDY is a multimillionaire serial entrepreneur, strategic advisor, and direct marketing consultant, one of the highest compensated direct-response copywriters in the world, and the author of the *No B.S.* business book series and editor of six marketing-related newsletters. He influences more than one million business owners annually, and has a long track record of taking entrepreneurs to seven-figure incomes and multi-millionaire wealth. As a speaker, he has frequently appeared on programs with celebrity-entrepreneurs like Gene Simmons (KISS), Debbi Fields (Mrs. Fields Cookies), George Foreman, Donald Trump, Ivanka Trump, Joan Rivers, Jim McCann (1-800-Flowers), and many others, as well as top business speakers Brian Tracy, Tom Hopkins, and Zig Ziglar. All *No B.S.* series books are available at Amazon, BN.com, Barnes & Noble,

and other booksellers, with additional information at www.
NoBSBooks.com. To contact Dan directly about speaking or
consulting availability, fax 602-269-3113.

KIM WALSH-PHILLIPS, @KWalshPhillips, is the award-
winning speaker, author, strategist and CEO of Elite Digital
Group (www.EliteDigitalGroup.com), a direct-response social
media agency. She is a techie marketing geek with great shoes, a
strong faith, a hatred of awareness campaigns, and an obsession
for marketing with a sharp focus on ROI. Kim has worked with
successful direct-response marketers such as GKIC Insider's
Circle and Dan Kennedy, Rich Schefren, and Ron LeGrand, and
with big brands such as Harley-Davidson Motor Co., Sandler
Training, Chem-Dry, and Hilton Hotels to increase revenue
through direct-response marketing. Kim is also the author of
*Awareness Campaigns Are Stupid and Other Secrets to Stop Being
an Advertising Victim and Start Monetizing Your Marketing* (I&K
Publishing 2011). She is thankful to God for all of the blessings
in her life and for her "people" for their love and support every
day and especially during the making of this book, including
her husband, Ian Phillips, entrepreneurs-in-training/daughters
Bella and Katie, the team at Elite Digital Group, especially Kelly
LeMay, Danielle Passaro, Shamatee Mitchell, Mary Yeaple,
Megan Phillips, Amber Ritter, literary agent Jeff Herman, and
her main squeeze editor, Demi Stevens, for her brilliance.

SHAUN BUCK has been a serial entrepreneur for the past 14
years, owning a variety of businesses ranging from multiple
hot dog stands to a publishing company. Shaun currently owns
and operates The Newsletter Pro, based out of Boise, Idaho.
Although The Newsletter Pro has only been operating for
four years, Shaun and his 34-plus-member team have grown
the company into the nation's largest custom print newsletter

company—printing and mailing millions of newsletters annually for diverse industries spread across four countries. In addition to running The Newsletter Pro, Shaun is a loving husband and father of five boys. He had his first son at just 16 years of age, and unlike other teenage dads, it was Shaun who raised his son, a choice that both inspired and motivated him to become the successful man he is today. To connect with Shaun, visit http://www.thenewsletterpro.com.

ARI GALPER is the author of the bestseller *Unlock The Game*. He has been interviewed on major news networks such as CNN/Money and SkyNews and is a sought-after international speaker and business mentor. For free access to Ari's breakthrough audio seminar, "Sales Secrets Even the Sales Gurus Don't Know," visit www.unlockthegame.com/NoBSGuruSecrets.

KELLY LEMAY serves as Elite Digital Group's Chief Operating Officer (next step, world domination). She has a passion for boundless creativity, impressive ROI, fresh design, iced coffee, and ChapStick. When you boil it down, Kelly's job is to make sure things are happening when they are supposed to happen. Outside of the Elite Digital Group world, you can find Kelly spending time with her husband and cheering on her two kids in whatever new thing they are accomplishing.

GRAIG PRESTI is founder and CEO of Local Search for Dentists and CEO of FindMyCompany.com. Both of his companies have made the coveted *Inc.* 500/5000 Fastest Growing Companies in the country, a rare and unprecedented two years in a row. Graig has been recognized as one of the world's top industry leaders in the marketing world and has led the marketing and PR campaigns that have driven his clients' businesses to record years. Graig has been seen in *The Wall Street Journal, Newsweek,*

Inc. magazine, Inc. 500, as well as in CNN, Fox, NBC, ABC, and CBS in major markets across the nation. To connect with Graig, visit http://graigpresti.com.

PARTHIV SHAH is the president of Elaunchers.com, a locally grown and internationally known marketing automation company serving small and midsized businesses, professional services practices (dentists, orthodontists, CPAs, attorneys, etc.), and elite information marketers. Parthiv has been an implementation craftsman and data scientist practicing big data.

Index